Kids, Parents, and Power Struggles

Kids, Parents, and Power Struggles

Winning for a Lifetime

Mary Sheedy Kurcinka

HARPER

NEW YORK . LONDON . TORONTO . SYDNEY

A hardcover edition of this book was published in 2000 by HarperCollins Publishers.

HarperCollins books may be purchased for educational, business, or sales promotional use. For information please write: Special Markets Department, HarperCollins Publishers Inc., 10 East 53rd Street, New York, NY 10022.

FIRST QUILL EDITION PUBLISHED 2001.

Designed by Joseph Rutt

The Library of Congress has catalogued the hardcover edition as follows:

Kurcinka, Mary Sheedy.
Kids, parents, and power struggles / Mary Sheedy Kurcinka. — 1st ed.
    p.   cm.
Includes bibliographical references and index.
ISBN 0-06-018288-1
    1. Parent and child.   2. Child rearing.   3. Emotions in children.
4. Control (Psychology)   I. Title.
HQ755.85.K85 2000
649'.1—dc21   99-40294

ISBN 0-06-093043-8 (pbk.)

08 09 10 RRD 30 29 28 27 26 25 24 23

Dedicated to

Four of the world's greatest emotion coaches, colleagues, and friends, who have shared their knowledge and skills with me, pulled me through, and at times even carried me on this journey.

- Kim Cardwell—without your willingness to review every single word of this manuscript, your organizational skills, and your insights . . .

- Lynn Jessen—without your insights into how kids think, your practical strategies, and your desire to be entertained . . .

- Marietta Rice—without your breadth of fresh ideas and your incredible teaching skills . . .

- Jenna Ruble—without your sensitivity to feelings and your insights into the complexities of emotions . . .

this book would not exist!
Thank you

CONTENTS

ACKNOWLEDGMENTS

Writing *Kids, Parents, and Power Struggles* was at times a real struggle. This book would not have been completed without the insights, stories, questions, and support offered by many, many people. To them I wish to say thank you. In random order as always . . .

Joseph M. Kurcinka, my husband, friend, and life partner, who keeps me centered with his wit, helps me to see the vision of where I need to go, and offers endless hours of support.

Joshua and Kristina Kurcinka, my children, who have taught me a great deal about my own emotions, have helped me to hone my skills, and have been an absolute delight to parent.

Richard and Beatrice Sheedy, my parents, who have always believed in me and have been there for me.

Joseph A. and Mary E. Kurcinka, my father- and mother in-law, who raised a really neat son.

Megan Newman, my editor, who has trusted me, given me space and time to work, and offered key insights for the manuscript.

Megan's assistants, Hillary Epstein and Matthew Benjamin, who always made sure that I got the information and support I needed.

Heide Lange, my agent, who has now coordinated three great book projects for me.

Susan Weinberg, an associate publisher at HarperCollins, for her leadership and support.

LeeAnn McCarthy, who first named my workshop "Kids, Parents, and Power Struggles" way back in 1993.

Barbara Majerus, Kathy Kurz, Helen Kennedy, and Suzanne Nelson, my sisters, who call and e-mail to offer their support.

Gary Smolik, the guy with the incredible vocabulary who as a fellow writer made the writing process much more fun and vibrant.

Debbie Ross, who coordinates my classes at the Jewish Community Center.

Peggy Gilbertson, the persistent, spirited adult who insists that I also teach for Southlake Clinic and Minnetonka Community Education.

Paul Krambeer, from the Jewish Community Center, who always ensures that my classroom is organized and ready for class.

Sharon Kaniess, Monell Jakel, Molly Hartenett, Joan Bergman, and Sue Ward, the staff at St. Paul Highland ECFE, who taught with me and shared their insights.

Terry Bedard, who helps to make our home a place of rest and rejuvenation.

The staff of Paidea, who let me watch them teach and share their stories with me.

Kelly Olson, Anne Gallagher, and Peggy Rhoden Rosemount, Apple Valley ECFE staff, who teach with me and put up with extra-long "debriefing" sessions.

Judi Marshall, Linda White, Jennie Smith, and Mary Kemper, ECFE staff, who have also tested the material for me.

Vicki Cronin, colleague and friend, whose enthusiasm is invaluable.

Ann Porter, Mary Boozell, Susan Reppe, Danielle McClusky, Marcia Sosso, and Lana Hanson, ECFE and Learning Readiness office staff, who always make me feel special with their warm greetings.

Karen Peckles, coordinator of Family Services for Rosemount Apple Valley, who has always supported my work.

Tom, Lindsey, and Kellen Fish, great neighbors and friends.

Tim Payne, the computer whiz who keeps my computer going.

Sharon Wentzel, who makes my slides for me and keeps my mailing list in order.

Megan Gunnar, Ph.D., University of Minnesota, who took time out of her very busy schedule to provide me with information.

Susan Hoch, Oleanna Books, who makes sure I'm aware of the latest publications.

Belina Reisman, who has offered rich insights into emotions and asked thought-provoking questions.

Ellen Seesel, for helping to edit the temperament questionnaire.

Jean Kummerow and Elizabeth Murphy, who shared their knowledge about individual differences with me.

Dr. Martha Erickson and Laurie Kanyer, who took time out of their busy schedules to discuss the attachment theories with me.

Sheila Thomas and Linda Lane, who provided information about sensory integration disorder.

Bonnie Sevcik and Cindi Martin, school psychologists who were willing to spend time with me developing and reviewing the medical chapter.

Sue Rybak, an occupational therapist who also helped me with the medical chapter.

Dr. Marjorie Hogan, a heartwarming pediatrician who provided information for the medical chapter and reviewed it after working a very, very long on-call shift.

Dr. David Griffin, a great pediatrician who allowed me to interview him for the medical chapter.

Judy Sagen, an Eastview teacher and choral director who helped me see the "steps."

David Rice, Ph.D., and James Cameron, Ph.D., who spent hours with me reviewing the newest research on temperament.

Dr. George Shears, M.D., Nancy Christianson, Joe Pulice, Jeanette Garcia, and Robert Brooks, Ph.D., all busy professionals who were willing to talk with me and share their knowledge.

Dan Ruckavina, who provided resources for me.

Harley Hanson, who handles the details of my travel so that I can write.

Dr. Stella Chess and Alexander Thomas, who have encouraged and supported my work and been tremendous role models for me.

In memory of Joanne Ellison and Nancy Melvin, Ph.D., two very special women who have significantly influenced my life.

And, finally, to all of the parents and children who have been willing to share their stories with me, ask their honest and straightforward questions, and go below the surface to the real feelings and needs.

Thank you!

Greetings!

When I was writing my first book, I had recurring nightmares. Always I was on a mountainside or in an open field totally exposed. Each time people were throwing rocks and stones at me. One night the dream changed. On that night I was precariously perched on a narrow mountain trail. I carried my manuscript in outstretched arms. The steep incline of the path and the package I carried made it impossible for me to proceed. Stymied and exposed, I broke out in a cold sweat. It was then I heard my mother's voice. "Look," she said, "your father and I have been here ahead of you. There are steps you can walk down." She pointed them out to me, then reached up and added, "Hand me your manuscript. I can hold it for you." Gingerly I passed it to her, but I was still too frightened to take a step down. It was then I heard my husband say, "It's okay. I'm right here behind you. You can do it."

I woke from my dream with a great sigh of relief. After that night the nightmares stopped. The warmth and support I felt from my family protected and carried me. I was able to finish my book.

I thought of this dream and the deep connection I felt with my family over the next few years as I watched parents working with their kids. I saw parents who could scoop up a toddler heading for the electrical outlet, blow on their child's tummy, and turn a potential power struggle into a delight of giggles. I watched the mother of a four-year-old stop him with just an arch of her eyebrow. I listened as a ten-year-old skillfully negotiated with his parents a plan that allowed him to spend time with his friend *and* get his room clean. And I saw parents and teens who were happily living and working together instead of declaring war. I wondered, How did they do it?

In my gut I sensed a connection between these parents and kids, like the one I felt with my own family, but I didn't know what to call it or even how to describe it. It was more than love. I remember reading a newspaper column in which a woman had written, "When I was young, my mother never missed a chance to tell me how dumb, stupid, or unattractive I was. Although she told me often how much she loved me, she undermined my self-esteem with her cruel remarks." No, love alone wasn't enough. There was something more, and I was determined to discover it.

Fortunately, at that time there was a huge burst of research on emotions and emotional intelligence. When I first read Daniel Goleman's book *Emotional Intelligence*, I knew he'd found the key. Emotional intelligence describes our awareness of our own feelings and those of others. People who are emotionally intelligent are able to use their knowledge of emotions to nurture their most important relationships, and to build the connections that lead them to want to work together.

I brought the information about emotional intelligence to the parents in my groups. It was met with great relief because they, like I, were frustrated with most of the existing advice for parents that didn't deal with the emotions that fueled their children's behavior, and, even more important, didn't help them understand their own. Could this information, they wondered out loud, help them to understand how a tike no taller than an adult's kneecap could send a two-hundred-pound dad to the moon? And how an eight-year-old screaming "You can't make me" could reduce an adult to tears? Indeed it could.

What I've learned is that children who recognize and understand their emotions are able to soothe themselves more effectively and blow up less frequently. They also don't get into as much trouble because they're less impulsive and more focused. Understanding emotions allows them to get along better with others. Emotional intelligence plays a significant role in their happiness and success in life.

So I scrutinized the emotional intelligence research and tried to solve the puzzle of how to apply it to real-life family situations. The parents in my groups helped me.

In the process of our study we were jolted into reality. In order to teach our children what they were feeling and how to manage their strongest emotions, like anger, frustration, and fear, we had to be able to do it for ourselves—even in the heat of the moment. The task is not an easy one, and it does take time, but it is feasible and definitely worth the effort.

Kids, Parents, and Power Struggles brings you the information and insights parents in my groups found most helpful on their journey. I've also included their stories, fictionalized a bit to protect their privacy, but stories of real struggles, honest challenges, as well as crowning moments of success.

You can use *Kids, Parents, and Power Struggles* as your guide to go below the surface of those tugs of war to the world of emotions, a world where your heart connects with your child's and results in a relationship you will both treasure. Here you will discover how to turn those flames of misbehavior into opportunities for learning and growing with your child. Here those most perplexing and difficult moments will be less confusing, and you will find parent-tested strategies that can allow both you and your child to be successful and happy.

Being a parent is like climbing a mountain. It's an arduous task, and your work is exposed to review by the public at large. The world of emotions is just now being explored. When you choose to create that emotional bond with your child, you may feel as though you don't know the way, or your arms are too full, or the task is daunting.

You don't have to take this journey alone. You are among friends. This book can help you. It can show you the steps, lend you a hand, and point out to you others in your own life who can assist you as well. So come along. Take it at your own speed. Grab the handholds and choose the steps that feel most comfortable to you. Discover the world of emotions where the fights are fewer and further between, and parents and kids are working together because they *want* to.

PART ONE

A New Perspective on Power Struggles

ONE

Winning for a Lifetime

"Like a great mystery, power struggles are never solved until the real culprits have been identified."

—Diane, mother of two

On the *surface* power struggles look like a tug of war. Parents and kids pitted against one another. Opposing forces pulling in different directions. Two individuals at odds with each other, both determined to *win*!

The trouble is that if you win by simply outmuscling your child, you still feel lousy. There's little pleasure in victory when your child is left distressed and angry. If you lose, it's even worse. What kind of a parent can't even get a child to brush her teeth or finish her homework? Power struggles are frustrating. You don't have all day to negotiate. You just want to get out of the door! And power struggles make you angry. Aren't you supposed to be the parent in charge? Power struggles can leave you feeling scared and helpless. If it's like this now, how will you survive your child's adolescence? And power struggles can make you sad. Screaming at your kids wasn't part of your dream.

What I've learned after more than twenty years of working with families is that daily fights are not inevitable. You don't have to walk constantly on eggshells in order to avoid the blowups. You don't have to doubt yourself or feel exhausted from defending yourself. Like a diver discovering the beauty of a coral reef, going *below the surface* of a power struggle can take you to a new place, a place where parents and kids are working together and power struggles are few and far between. *Below the surface,* you'll discover that power struggles are about feelings and needs—yours and your child's.

Recognizing those emotions is the key to stopping power struggles before they ever start. Responding to those emotions builds the relationship that makes your child *want* to work with you.

Discipline isn't just about winning or losing. Every power struggle offers you the opportunity to *connect* with your child or to *disconnect.* The relationship you will have with your child when he's an adolescent lies in the words and actions you use today. Ultimately your real power is in that emotional bond.

Why Emotions?

Over the years as I've worked with families, I have found that every family experiences power struggles. I've heard parents express frustrations over kids who've looked right at them, smiled, and then done what they've just been told not to do. Kids who've vehemently declared, "You're not my boss!" Capable kids who've suddenly refused to walk upstairs alone, finish their homework, or cried "Don't leave me!" when it was time to go to bed, even though they've been going to bed on their own for months or years.

The parents have told me they've tried time-outs, reward systems, insisting that their kids "toughen up" or stop being a "baby," and even spanking, but the struggles haven't stopped. I finally realized that the struggles continued because reward systems, time-outs, demands to "not feel that way," and spankings put a "lid" on the behaviors but failed to address the real fuel source behind them. As a result it was as though someone had put the lid back on a pot of boiling water but failed to turn down the heat. The water continued to boil and inevitably the lid popped off again.

Emotions are the real fuel source behind power struggles. When you identify those emotions you can select strategies that teach your kids what they are feeling and how to express those emotions more respect-fully and suitably. The pot doesn't keep boiling over because ultimately the kids themselves learn to recognize the heat and turn it down! That was true of Kyla.

Whenever she was bored, ten-year-old Kyla would ask her mother Anne what she could do, but every suggestion made was rejected. No, she didn't want to call a friend. No, she didn't want to bake or read a book. And she was not the least bit interested in playing a game with her mother. Exasperated, her mother would ask, "Then what do you want to do?" But Kyla would only snap at her and complain about the "stupid" suggestions. Pushed to the boiling point, her mother would finally send Kyla to her room, which resulted in a screaming fit and nasty retorts like, "You're the meanest mother in the world!"

But all that changed when Anne learned that Kyla wasn't trying to frustrate her. There was a feeling and need that were fueling her behav-ior. It was a feeling that Kyla couldn't label and didn't know how to express respectfully; as a result she was irritable and disrespectful. But Anne could help Kyla to identify her emotions and choose more suit-able ways to express them. Instead of offering suggestions, she chose to ask Kyla questions such as: Do you feel like doing something inside or outside? Do you want to be with people or alone? Do you want to do something active or quiet?

By asking questions instead of offering suggestions, Anne taught Kyla how to figure out what she was feeling. When she understood her feelings, she could choose an activity that truly met her needs. *Instead of frustrating each other and disconnecting, Anne and Kyla learned to work together.*

What I've discovered as I parent my own children and work with the families in my classes, workshops, and private consultations is that understanding and working with emotions can totally change relation-ships. You become aware of what you and your child need and what's important to you. Kids who are emotionally smart are self-motivated, willing to cooperate, and able to get along with others—even their sib-lings. Instead of fighting with your child and disconnecting, working with emotions allows you to connect, creating the emotional bond that links you and fosters a relationship that's alive, dynamic, ever-changing, exciting, and even *fun*!

This style of discipline is called "emotion coaching," and the latest research on human brain development tells us that enhancing your child's emotional intelligence is more important to his success in life than is his IQ.

It may surprise you. Initially I was wary, too. Emotions, after all, have not been given much credibility. Even though I have personally witnessed power struggles being diffused or diminished as parents addressed the sadness, disappointment, frustration, fear, determination, or other emotions that fueled them, I still worried that others might find this a "fad" in parent education, a new form of pop psychology. Certainly our parents and grandparents never spent much time thinking about emotions and may even have felt that to address emotions was to coddle a child or just "stir him up." And then Daniel Goleman wrote *Emotional Intelligence* and everything changed. His work provided the tested research that matched my experience and intuition. Emotions do indeed make a great deal of difference.

The Research

The most recent research in psychobiology and neuroscience has demonstrated that children are born with billions of brain cells, probably all they'll ever need in their lifetime. However, the way in which that brain gets wired and which brain cells get used depends on you and your child's environment.

At birth a child is primarily working from his limbic system—the primitive, reactive brain. He experiences an emotion and acts. But as you help your child to understand what he's feeling, enforce limits, and teach him how he can express those feelings respectfully, he starts to build linkages to the neocortex, or thinking brain. The more plentiful the linkages, the stronger the wiring, and the easier for your child to stop impulsive behavior. Ultimately your child is able to identify what he's feeling, shift out of a reactive response, and *think* of a more appropriate one and use it!

Why Power Struggles Stop When You Teach Your Child About Emotions

When you take the time to help your child understand his emotions, label them, and learn respectful ways of expressing them, you enhance his emotional intelligence. He doesn't have to fight with you! He knows how to get along with you and everyone else in his world. The research by Peter Salovey, a Yale psychologist, shows that emotionally intelligent kids:

1. **Understand their emotions.** They are able to recognize a feeling as it happens. This is the keystone of emotional intelligence. It is this awareness that allows your child to understand himself. He isn't a victim of his emotions, blindsided by strong feelings such as frustration or jealousy. Instead he can "catch" his emotions when they are easier to manage and use those emotions as a guide to help him understand what he needs. When his brother pesters him, instead of immediately getting furious and lashing out, which only gets him into trouble, he can recognize the entire spectrum of emotions in between—like irritation, annoyance, and frustration—as they happen. Recognizing emotions when they're "little" makes it much easier to manage them and choose a more effective and suitable response.

2. **Stop themselves and manage intensity.** Emotionally intelligent kids can stop themselves. They don't spend their days rolling from one outburst to another. Instead of hitting, biting, swearing, and throwing things, they are able to enforce standards for themselves. They can recognize their rising intensity and take steps to soothe and calm themselves by doing things like taking a break, breathing deeply, or going for a run. Temper tantrums become an unusual occurrence rather than a daily event.

3. **Identify their triggers.** There is a genetic aspect to our personalities that affects whether we prefer to solve problems by talking or thinking about them. It also governs whether we like surprises or find them stressful, whether we find parties, movie theaters, or shopping

centers fun or irritating, and if we take no for an answer or keep coming back despite the obstacles in our path.

Emotionally intelligent kids possess this self-awareness, and so are able to predict their triggers, avoid or minimize them, and learn effective coping skills. The child who can't leave a friend's house without getting upset learns to understand how difficult transitions are for her and how to make a plan to ease the distress. The child who screams at a friend, "Go home, I hate you," or shoves and pushes other children learns to say, "Let's watch a video for a while" or "I'd like to do this by myself right now," recognizing that he's an individual who needs space and quiet and may be exhausted by being in a group. The child who becomes emotionally distraught over seemingly "little" things learns to say, "I just need to feel sad for a while," instead of insisting that his life is ruined. And the silent resister learns to say, "I need to think about that for a while" or "I'm not ready to talk yet," rather than covering his ears, turning away, and refusing to talk.

4. **Are able to cope with life's ups and downs.** Kids never tell us they're stressed. Instead they revert to younger behaviors such as refusing to dress themselves, whining, or waking up in the night. Four-year-olds tend to have toileting accidents and fear things in their closets, while twelve-year-olds may become lethargic or oppositional. By learning to recognize stress cues, the emotionally intelligent child is able to identify his fears and anxieties and make adjustments for them. He doesn't have to act out because he knows what he *can* do to make things better. It is this sense of personal power that helps him to be more resilient as he faces life's challenges.

5. **Recognize the emotions of others and work well with them.** Emotionally intelligent kids know the important differences between statements like "You're not my boss!" and "Can we talk about this?" They are able to assert themselves without being aggressive. They know when and how to negotiate, allowing them to work *with* others rather than *against* them.

6. **Motivate themselves.** Emotionally intelligent kids get their homework done, practice the piano, and get themselves organized—even when you're not there! Because they understand their emotions, they

know how to use their "peak" times to work, manage their frustration, get help when they need it, and prioritize their time and tasks.

7. **Maintain healthy relationships**. Daniel Goleman says, "Emotionally intelligent people are social stars." Emotionally smart kids have what it takes to get along with you and with others. As a result they're successful in love relationships and in their careers. Most important, the bond with you remains strong—even during adolescence.

The Importance of Every Day

How can your children learn these skills? These abilities can be taught to children and the opportunities to teach them arise every day. Kids learn today the skills they'll need for tomorrow. The abilities to calm oneself, to be assertive rather than aggressive, to solve problems, and to be trustworthy don't suddenly appear at age eighteen. These are skills that take time and repetition to learn. The lessons begin today as you deal with bedtime, homework, curfews, and all the other power struggles in a normal day. As you teach those lessons, you become your child's emotion coach, her self-discipline guide.

It isn't easy to think about power struggles as an opportunity to teach your child skills she'll need for a lifetime, especially on the days when it seems as though she's woken up thinking, I'm really going to drive my parents crazy today! But by going under the surface of power struggles, you can help your child identify the feelings or needs that are fueling the behavior *and* teach her suitable responses. In *Magic Trees of the Mind*, author Marian Diamond writes, "Our experiences with parents, siblings and caregivers—loving or harsh, supportive or destructive—help to establish a mental map that will guide our emotional life and in turn its influence on all of our thinking processes."

And if that's not enough, John Gottman, author of *The Heart of Parenting*, says, "Emotion coaching is like an immunization." According to the research, emotion coaching enhances your child's physical health and academic development. It protects him from youth violence, antisocial behavior, drug addiction, premature sexual activity, and adolescent suicide. Emotion coaching also lowers your child's stress level and resting heart rate, and reduces the number of colds and bouts with the flu he will experience!

Your parents didn't have this information, but you do. You can use it to help your child manage his strong feelings, build that bond with you, and get you out of those power struggles.

How It Works

Kathy is one of the thousands of parents I work with each year in classes, workshops, and personal consultations. She'd never heard of emotion coaching until she started attending my class called "Kids, Parents, and Power Struggles." Even after the initial weeks of class, the ideas still seemed foreign to her, until she put them to the test and found they worked.

It was supposed to be a fun outing to the zoo. A friend and her family had been visiting Kathy and her sons, four-year-old Nathan and two-year-old Todd. Over three days they'd visited the Children's Museum, Camp Snoopy at the Mall of America, and the Conservatory. Friday was reserved for a trip to the Minnesota Zoological Gardens. But when it came time to go, Nathan refused. "Fine," Kathy responded. "We don't have to go. I can stay home with you and the others can go." Five minutes after they left, Nathan changed his mind. He wanted to go, so off they went to meet their friends at the zoo.

Unfortunately, Nathan's contrary behavior continued at the zoo. Initially he didn't want to ride the monorail, then he did. He didn't want to visit the snow monkeys, but a few minutes later he did. Each time he said no, his mother would stop and cajole him and he'd move along. Finally exhausted by her efforts she decided they'd had enough. "We're going home," she announced unexpectedly. Turning to her friend she said, "Stay as long as you like; we'll meet you back at the house." The friend, with her kids in tow, strolled away.

Nathan's shriek in protest was death defying and ear piercing. The momentum of it dropped him to the floor. "I want to see the frogs!" he wailed.

In an attempt to quiet him, Kathy promised, "Next time we come to the zoo, we'll go straight to the frogs."

"No," Nathan wailed, his screams exponentially increasing in volume.

Sensing all eyes on her and judgment in them, she picked him up to carry him out. But it was impossible to carry a flailing four-year-old and push a toddler in a stroller. She set Nathan down on the floor again. Her own intensity now surging, she threatened to leave him and started walking away. He jumped up, lunging after her, shrieking louder. "I want to see the frogs!"

She stopped. I was just in class, she reminded herself. What did I learn? Think about the emotions! Go under the surface. What is he feeling? What does he need? Taking a deep breath, she calmed herself enough to guide Nathan confidently out of the traffic in the hallway to a more private spot where she sat down on the floor with him. He seemed to sense the difference in her touch and allowed her to hold him on her lap. "It's so sad when you don't get to do what you wanted to do. It's so frustrating when you have to leave before you are done," she soothed.

The shrieks died down, replaced by deep, slow sobs. "You really wanted to see those frogs," she continued. Nathan sniffled, nodding his head yes.

Feeling his body relax against hers, she stroked his brow and suggested, "On the way out, why don't we stop in the gift shop. We won't buy anything but we'll look at the timers you love." Brushing the tears from his cheeks, he stood up, took her hand, and walked out.

Later that night, when she put Nathan to bed, they talked about their outing. Both of them were calm now, and she knew he could hear her. This was a teachable moment. "I think you wanted to be with our friends and go to the zoo, but you were too tired. When you're tired, it's difficult to make decisions. And then I surprised you when I said it was time to leave. You were disappointed. You wanted to see the frogs." Nathan nodded and Kathy continued. "But it's not okay to shriek at the zoo. You scare the animals and hurt other people's ears. Next time you can tell me you want to go, but you are tired. Next time you can tell me you are sad, and I will listen. You don't need to scream."

"It was incredible," Kathy told me. "Initially when we were at the zoo and he started to scream, I felt sorry for *me*! That's when I got angry. But all of a sudden I could hear his sadness. It wasn't a demand. I could actually feel his disappointment and fatigue. I don't ever remember feeling so connected before. I honestly think he was relieved when I gave him words for his feelings. He doesn't like to 'lose it.' That level of intensity scares him. And I do think he listened to me when we talked at bedtime. I know he'll try—he might not be successful—he's only four—but he'll try." Her voice dropped as she finished her story. "It was so special," she whispered, thrilled by the realization that she and her son had experienced a whole new world, a world of emotions where the willingness to listen and cooperate spring from a deep sense of connection.

It is that emotional bond that keeps your child working with you. Emotion coaching doesn't imply that you always say yes. Kathy still took Nathan home. It doesn't mean you constantly negotiate. She didn't buy him anything at the gift shop. It doesn't mean that you give him free reign on his emotions. You don't. Emotions are *never* an excuse for hurtful or disrespectful behavior. It means that you will listen, trying your best to understand your child's point of view, label his emotions for him, enforce clear standards for behavior, and teach him what he *can* do to express them respectfully. As a result, your child will learn that he can trust you and be open to your guidance, leading ultimately to his own sense of self-control.

You're Not Alone

Sometimes as an emotion coach you can feel alone. Cab drivers, fellow grocery shoppers, and grandparents may look at you funny when you're explaining to a six-year-old that she's frightened or disappointed. You can wonder if you're really doing the right thing. It's important to remember that most people have never had the experience of going *below the surface* of a power struggle. They've focused on the *surface* like the fisherman in a boat who has no idea that beneath him lies the fascinating world of the coral reef.

So in case you're missing role models, or feeling lonely, the thousands of parents in my classes and workshops have agreed to share with you the trials, tribulations, and, most important, the successes of their journeys as emotion coaches. Included are strategies that have proven to be helpful in *real* life situations and supported by the most recent research. As you go along, there're a few things I'd like you to remember.

1. **Power struggles aren't just about winning or losing.** They provide rich opportunities for learning how to deal with strong emotions and solve problems together. You are not a failure when you find yourself in a tug of war. You are a parent with an opportunity to learn what's important to you and to your child.

2. **There are patterns that can help you identify your child's emotions.** If attempting to figure out what your child might be feeling seems a daunting task, know that there are patterns of behavior that can help you to identify the feelings. In this book I'll show you how you can use information about *temperament, stress, development,* and *medical issues* to identify the real culprits behind your power struggles.

3. **By changing your reaction you can change your child's.** Even in the darkest moments when you feel totally inept and out of control, you have the power to stop and change your behavior. It is possible to learn how to keep your cool even when your child is losing his.

4. **Emotions can be your guide.** Identifying your emotions allows you to recognize when your boundaries are being invaded and it's time to hold the line. Understanding emotions helps you to identify the real fuel source behind the fires of misbehavior and to teach your child a more suitable response. When you can trust your gut, your confidence grows.

5. **Your child is not "out to get you."** Every challenging behavior is fueled by a feeling or need. You can discover that feeling or need and help your child address it respectfully. Listening to your child does not mean spoiling her. Working with your child doesn't mean giving in. You are modeling the kind of respectful interaction you want your child to have with you and others. And as you do it, you change the physical structure of your child's brain.

6. **Repeating lessons is normal.** Emotion coaching involves teaching essential life skills. It can take months, even years for your child to learn the lessons well. When you get frustrated, take a break, don't

give up. Practice is necessary and normal. Celebrate your successes—the little steps—and allow your child and yourself to be
learners.

7. **You can learn about yourself as well as your child.** The exciting
thing about emotional intelligence is that it's predominantly learned
behavior. The lessons don't stop in early childhood. They continue
throughout our entire lives, and we get to reap the benefits in *all* of
our relationships—at home *and* at work.

8. **Your dream can be a reality.** You don't have to fight with your kids
every day. Your dream of harmony, peace, and mutual respect can be
a reality!

Our Journey Together

As we go along together, there will be good days and not so good ones.
My hope is that this book will be your guide and your friend—helping
you to understand yourself and your child, easing the tough times,
offering you support when you get frustrated, and encouraging you to
celebrate your successes. It is divided into three sections.

Part II, "Building the Connections," will help you to build the relationship that keeps your child working with you because he *wants* to. It
begins with a vision of where you want to go in the long run and
explores the kind of relationship you want to have with your child in
adolescence and adulthood. It also addresses the realities of how difficult it is to make that connection. So this section also includes strategies
for keeping your cool, enforcing standards for your kids, and teaching
them how to soothe and calm themselves.

Part III, "Caring: Knowing Yourself and Your Child," will help you
identify those emotions that fuel the power struggles. An understanding of temperament triggers, and how stress and medical factors impact
behavior, can help you predict your triggers and your child's. This section is chock full of practical tips to help you diffuse and manage those
triggers before they can hook you and pull you and your child into
power struggles.

Part IV, "Developing Competence: Teaching Life's Essential Skills," explains the normal stages of emotional development. Teaching your child how to motivate and to stop himself, how to be assertive rather than a little bulldozer, and how to negotiate are all essential skills that your child will need for success in life. Practical kid- and parent-tested techniques for learning these skills are included in this section.

Keep the Vision

The lessons of emotion coaching are powerful. Relationships once shadowed by anger and hostility can change to joy and cooperation. The teen years can actually be a time of reaping benefits of lessons well learned rather than a time to "bear." That's why I'd like to provide you with a vision of what can happen when you are your child's emotion coach, her guide to an understanding of emotions, her teacher of respectful responses.

Imagine for a moment you're lying in bed, just coming to consciousness. There's music playing in the distance. You realize it's your child's alarm clock going off before yours. She's fifteen now. Before the morning news rouses you, she's in the shower. Twenty minutes later you meet her in the kitchen. She's sitting at the table eating a bowl of cereal, drinking juice, reading yesterday's paper. Today's hasn't yet arrived. You ask her about her schedule for the day. She asks if you can pick her up from practice at five PM. She's got a test she needs to study for and would like to avoid the thirty-minute bus ride home if at all possible. "No problem," you reply.

At seven o'clock she's out the door, hair combed, teeth brushed, just a touch of makeup adding highlights to her eyes, homework done and in the backpack. She's vibrant, healthy, and laughing. You watch as she stops in the driveway to toss today's just-delivered paper to the door stoop, so that all you have to do is reach out to pick it up. It's her "gift" to you this morning.

You're off to work then, able to focus, elated by the morning, realizing not every morning goes quite this well, yet the good days are far outnumbering the tough ones. Your dream of connecting with your child isn't a pipe dream. There is respect, cooperation, and harmony in your home. You and your child really have found ways to work together. The tugs of war are more infrequent and the frustration level lower. There's more laughter than tears, more problems solved than fights erupting. But what really keeps you going is the realization that you are winning—and so is your child. Emotion coaching is allowing you and your child to be more caring, competent, and connected, and *together you are winning for a lifetime!*

PART TWO

Building the Connections

TWO

Emotion Coaching

The Decision to Connect

"The best antidote to U.S. teenagers' major health problems—bad habits such as drinking, smoking, promiscuity—turns out to be a close connection with caring parents."

—The Journal of the American
Medical Association

From my office window I watched the kids across the street pulling with all their might on opposite ends of a jump rope. Their heels dug trenches in the dirt and muscles strained before they collapsed in a heap of laughter. Minutes later, two of them were on the ends of the rope twirling it, while the third jumped. The words of their chant, along with their giggles, filtered through my window. In and out they went taking turns twirling, then jumping. Twenty minutes later they stopped to rest, downed glasses of lemonade, and chatted. The energy of their words rose to a challenge. "Beat you to a hundred!" one shouted as she leapt up and started jumping. The next thing I knew all three of them were swinging their own ropes. Faces grew red, lips moved, but no words escaped.

I don't know if they made it to one hundred, but I do know that I made an important realization while watching them: When we're in those tugs of war with our kids, it's much easier to see those struggles as an opportunity once we realize we have the same options the kids across the street did. *We always have control of our end of the rope!* We can decide that this is the time to hang on tight, stand firm, and insist, "In our family this is the rule!" Other times we may decide to step in and work with our child, enjoying together what we couldn't do alone. And then there are occasions when we realize it is time to let go of our end of the rope, to hand the whole thing over to our child, and say, "You're ready. Take it. You can make this decision. You can handle it on your own."

The challenge, of course, is to know when to make which decision. A vision of where you're going in the long run can help.

Begin with the End in Mind

I was dusting and halfheartedly listening to a national talk show. A renowned psychologist was discussing power struggles. His advice to the host was, "If your three-year-old wants you to sit with him at bedtime, let me just say, don't start habits you don't want to continue until graduation."

I stopped dusting and turned to the screen. I couldn't help thinking of Stephen Covey's words, "Begin with the end in mind." "How many parents wish their teenager would trust them enough to talk with them," I wondered out loud. How many parents wish their kids would see them as someone who could help them answer their questions or make decisions. Is sitting with your three-year-old a bad habit, a waste of time? Or could it be the beginning of a strong, healthy communication system with your child?

Whether or not you choose to sit with your child is your decision, but as you make it, begin with the end in mind. Hold a clear understanding of your destination—the kind of relationship you want to have with your child in the long run.

Imagine for a moment your child is graduating from high school. How do you want him to feel about himself? How do you want her to feel about you? Are the words and actions you're using today taking you in that direction? A look at your own experience may help you answer these questions. Your answer will be unique, but let me take you to one of my classes and allow you to hear what others have to say.

Meet the Group

It's the movements and sounds you notice first as the parents and children enter the family center. A jaunty pace highlighted with a big smile indicates a good week. "I've got a success story!" a parent may call as she holds open the door for her children, who squeal in delight and dash for the climber.

Quick, sharp, rushed steps, accented with heavy sighs, unzipped coats, missing mittens, and crying children, tell me it's been a tough one. My intuition is often confirmed by a curt announcement of "We need to be here!"

No matter what the tenor of the moment, the parents know that in the next two hours they'll get forty-five minutes to play with their kids without the interruptions of telephones or televisions, and the staff will clean up the mess! They'll also get a chance to separate from their kids, sit down with a hot cup of coffee, and talk with other adults who really understand the struggles they are facing. While they relax and share stories, they can even watch through the one-way mirrors while their kids continue activities with the staff.

Where Do You Want to Go?

Today on the whiteboard I have written: "Think about a significant adult in your life, someone who has helped you to understand yourself and to develop your strengths. What were his or her characteristics?"

Each parent is given an index card on which to write an answer.

Smiles begin to light faces as they remember those special individuals in their lives. Voices rise and fall, and laughter intermixes with the chatter. Suddenly I notice a furtive glance from Kate; her eyes are moving from side to side, attempting to catch what others have written on their cards.

I realize I need to say, "If you haven't had someone like this in your life, imagine that you do. What would he or she be like?" Kate looks relieved and begins to write.

Waiting until the pens have stopped moving, I ask, "Who would like to share your description?" Hands shoot into the air, eyes sparkle, each individual appears eager to share fond memories.

Jim, an outgoing father of four, volunteers to begin. "A great listener," he says. "I don't know how he did it, but my dad always made you feel like he had time for you. I remember family dinners. He always knew what we were doing and asked about classes and games. If we needed help or support, he was there. He liked to listen to public radio on the way home. He was always telling us stories, some hilarious, others challenged us to think about an issue."

Kate, who was sitting across the table from Jim, was incredulous. "My father wasn't anything like yours. Do you do that?" she wanted to know.

"I try," he admitted, "but I can't say I'm perfect." Debbie held up her card. "I've got one," she said. "She was my sophomore history teacher. What I appreciated most about her was how dependable she was. You always knew where she stood. She wasn't a pushover, but she was gentle and calm. No matter who you were, she saw the good in you, and I really think she believed we wanted to do our best."

They continued sharing descriptions and heartwarming stories. Cushioned in the glow of fond memories, the atmosphere of the room was light.

The Person You Disliked

And then I changed things. "Now tell me about an influential adult you disliked. Someone who to this day the mere thought of can make the hair on the back of your neck stand up." The mood in the room immediately shifted. Sinister laughter erupted. Peter's jaw clenched so tight the muscle jumped. But it was Jim's eyes that caught my attention. They slammed into me, blazing with anger. "Mean," he spit out. "Rotten, low-down, self-centered, two-faced." He paused. "You don't want me to finish this," he remarked, and his voice trailed off.

Peter stepped into the void. "Untrustworthy, judgmental, pessimistic, pushy, never listened, rigid, and quick-tempered," he read from his card. "High school geometry teacher," he explained, the cords in his neck continuing to pulse. "And I was dreaming of being an engineer." He shook his head and looked away.

Debbie blurted into the silence, her voice vehement, the words sharp. "Inflexible, punitive, sarcastic, critical, rough," she snapped. "He didn't have time to help, he was *too* busy." Her hands trembled as she set down her coffee cup.

The passion of their emotions crackled in the room. Bodies tightened and shuddered as they remembered. I completed a chart on the board as the words were whipped at me.

Characteristics of the Person You Liked	Characteristics of the Person You Disliked
good listener	lousy listener
patient	self-centered
funny	sarcastic
flexible	rigid
challenging	punitive
dependable	untrustworthy
gentle	rough
positive	pessimistic
encouraging	critical
calm	quick-tempered
fair	played favorites

The contrasts were stark. Each of us silently realized there were moments when we could fall on either side of the list. The awareness made us squirm.

What Happens to Us

"How did the person you liked make you feel about yourself?" I asked.

Smiles returned. "Great!" Peter confirmed

"Energized and motivated," Donna added.

"Confident, competent, and capable," Jim offered, grinning to let us know he enjoyed his alliteration.

"Worthwhile," Kate whispered.

And then I did it again. I dashed those good feelings by asking, "How did the person you disliked make you feel?"

Kate slumped in her chair. "Worthless," she replied.

Peter's eyes glinted. "Angry and rebellious."

"Incompetent, incapable, and inadequate." Jim sighed. This time the joy of his alliteration was lost in a frown. I added their answers to my chart.

How the Person You Liked Made You Feel About Yourself	How the Person You Disliked Made You Feel About Yourself
great	angry
worthwhile	worthless
competent	incompetent
capable	incapable
confident	inadequate

Pointing to the left side of the chart, I asked, "How willing would you be to work with the person you liked?"

"Anytime," Peter stated confidently. "I'd love to." The others agreed.

"And this person," I continued, pointing to the right column, "the one you disliked, how willing would you be to work with him?"

"Never," Jim retorted.

Kate huffed, "I divorced him!"

The Emotion Coach vs. the Intimidator

The people who truly made a positive difference in your life were what I now call emotional intelligence coaches. They built a relationship with you. They were able to help you understand who you were, what you were feeling, and how to respond respectfully. The base of their power and influence lay in the emotional bond they held with you. As a result you *wanted* to work with them.

The people you disliked are what I refer to as the intimidators. It's likely that they not only rejected your feelings but may have even punished you for experiencing them. Many intimidators view a child's tears as a form of manipulation and react with anger and fear. John Gottman writes in *The Heart of Parenting,* "He doesn't ask how do you feel, because he believes that focusing on uncomfortable feelings is like watering weeds. It makes them grow bigger and more noxious." The base of the intimidator's power lies in humiliation and domination. As a result you do *not* want to work with him. You want to rebel or withdraw.

It's very likely that you've experienced an intimidator in your life. In fact she may be your only parent role model. But a recent study of twelve thousand adolescents nationwide, reported in the *Journal of the American Medical Association*, states, "Parent connectedness is the single healthiest force in the lives of U.S. teenagers." Emotion coaches connect with kids.

Starting today, you can choose to stop using strategies that distance you from your children. It really isn't that difficult to be an emotion coach. You can begin simply by choosing to discipline in a manner that builds a relationship with your child and connects you rather than disconnects.

Redesigning Your Role

Research completed at the University of Minnesota by Ruth Thomas, Ph.D., and Betty Cooke, Ph.D., has found that the most effective parents, those I call emotion coaches, are:

Sensitive.   They pick up the cues of their children and sense how they are feeling. They listen and empathize.

Responsive.   They respond in ways that fit their child's cues. If the child is frightened, they comfort him. If he's intense, they calm him. But they don't excuse disrespectful behavior. Their limits are clear and enforced.

Reciprocal. There is give and take in the relationship. The parent respects the child's emotions and teaches him to consider thoughtfully the emotions of others.

Supportive and encouraging. They understand that learning to manage one's emotions takes time and effort. They support and encourage their child as he practices.

These actions enhance their children's development, foster a positive sense of self-esteem, and, most important, build healthy relationships.

The least effective parents, those I call the intimidators, are:

Insensitive. They miss the cues of their children or misinterpret them.

Unresponsive. They do not respond to their children's cues. Either they choose to ignore them or respond in ways that don't fit. What the child feels or needs doesn't matter. This parent might say something like, "I don't care if you're hot. I'm not, so leave your sweater on!"

Intrusive. Their actions are invasive. They talk too much, demand performances, invade the child's space, move too quickly, or hover over the child in a smothering way.

Dominating. They tend to overpower rather than support their children.

Dr. Thomas and Dr. Cooke found that as a result of being raised by the least effective parents, the intimidators, the children suffer. Their development is slowed, their self-esteem is damaged, and they often become angry and hostile, refusing to cooperate with adults.

Getting Kids to Stop and Start

No one sets out as a parent to be bullish, cocky, or shaming, but unwittingly our techniques can take us there, especially on the tough days. Let's take a look at the emotion coaches and intimidators in action, so it's clear what I mean. Once again we'll go back to the group for their help.

"I need an example," I said. "Who's willing to describe a situation where you had to stop your child?"

Abby volunteered. "Yesterday afternoon," she said, "I was putting the baby down for his nap upstairs. I'd given my three-year-old a choice to come with me or stay downstairs. He'd chosen to stay down, but suddenly I heard a racket. Thud, thud, thud—books were being pulled off the shelves. I could only imagine what the room looked liked. Suddenly the thuds turned to crashes, when he started hurling books across the room. Odds were the knickknacks were next."

"Think about your emotion coach," I said. "The person you'd still love to work with and be around. How would she stop this child?"

"She'd stop you," Margie said. "She might even yell stop, especially if it was unsafe, but she wouldn't bellow or shriek and when she moved in to stop him, her touch would be firm, but not hurtful."

"Yeah, she wouldn't overreact," Bob agreed. "She might even help him pick everything up, all the time talking to him about feeling angry and frustrated, but that it wasn't all right to throw books."

"She might ask what he was doing or why," Kate offered.

I listed each of their answers, then asked, "How would the intimidator stop this child?" Tom's chuckle was deep in his throat. "I can tell you, there wouldn't be any discussion. The guy would just grab and jerk," he said. "Maybe even pinch him."

"If it was my mother, she would scream and then smack him," Cindy offered.

"The person I'm thinking of would call him names, like stupid little jerk," Betsy replied.

Peter hooted, "He'd be in his room for the next half hour, without any questions asked."

Here's a chart showing the different responses. Feel free to add your own.

Emotion Coach	Intimidator
touched gently	jerked
was firm but didn't overreact	screamed
gave the look	pinched
helped him pick up	hit
redirected him	criticized him
took a break with him	called him names
showed him how to stop	wouldn't talk to him
used a firm but gentle voice	threatened
asked questions	punished

Kate reviewed the list carefully. "What's the difference between a firm touch and a grab?" she asked. "I mean, really, when the kid's pulling books off the shelf, you're not going to gently pat him on the head."

I picked up the chair sitting next to me and pretended it was about to fall over on Abby. Placing one hand on each side of it, I grabbed it firmly as I righted it. My motion was swift and confident, not angry. I was relieved when I caught it. "That's an emotion coach," I replied. "Here's the intimidator." Once more I tipped the chair, but this time I lunged for it, grabbed it with one hand, jerked it upright, and angrily pushed it aside. My face twisted to a snarl as I set it back. "That's the intimidator," I replied. The force of the movements, the tone of the voice, the body language were subtly different, but the impact was stark.

"I think I get it," Kate said, "Move instead of pounce; take ahold of instead of jerk; be gentle rather than rough."

I nodded. "Many of the differences are about voice tone and force of the motion. But those subtle differences can make the difference between connecting and disconnecting."

"Hmmm," Kate responded and then turned to Abby. "So what did you do?"

"I was afraid he'd pull something down on himself," Abby responded. "So I went downstairs. I stopped him by taking hold of his hand and then I told him, 'I think you're frustrated, but you can't throw books.' He started to cry. I just held him until he stopped, and then I had him help me pick up the books. I realize now he's too little to be given the choice of staying downstairs. Instead I've created a 'baby-care basket' for him. When I'm taking care of the baby, he can play with the things in the basket. When I'm done, he's done, so he doesn't get bored with the toys. So far it's working."

Listening to Abby, I couldn't help pointing out all the emotion coaching she'd done. "An emotion coach is sensitive to cues," I said. "Abby realized the situation wasn't safe for her son, so she stepped in, set a limit, calmed him down, helped him pick up the books so he learned about being responsible, and planned for success next time. Wow!" I exclaimed. Abby grinned.

"Who has an example of trying to get their child to start something?" I continued. It was Peggy who raised her hand this time. "Last night we had guests for dinner," she explained. "I asked my eight-year-old son Aubry to set the table. He refused, declaring it wasn't fair. His sister had set a table for four people the night before and now he was supposed to do it for eight."

"How would the emotion coach get Aubry started?" I asked.

"She'd work with him," Tom replied.

Tonya agreed. "Yes, and she'd probably offer sympathy, setting a table for eight rather than four is harder work."

"She might make it special, pulling out pretty napkins, or candles, or even letting him make name cards so that he could choose where he wanted to sit."

And then I asked them, "How would the intimidator get him started? Again, the voices were tight. "Do it now!" Peter bellowed.

"Threats," Debbie added. "Either do it or you won't watch TV for a month!"

Bob agreed, "And lots of yelling. She'd be on his case to hurry up, too." Once again I made a chart of their responses.

The emotion coach	The intimidator
works with	Do it now!
sympathizes	threatens
makes it special or a game	screams
talks with and explains	rushes

Peggy listened attentively and then sighed. "I tried those things," she said, "but he was so upset he couldn't even hear me. I finally just had to send him out to take a break, and set the table myself because the guests were arriving in five minutes. After dinner he was fine and helped with dishes without complaining, but I'm not sure I did the right thing."

Peggy was an emotion coach. She recognized the intensity was too high and the time too short to bring it down before the guests arrived. She did what she needed to do. But she won't want to stop there. As an emotion coach, she'll go back and talk with her son, thanking him for helping with the dishes, but also letting him know that when he's frustrated or tired, "fits" are not acceptable. Next time she expects that he will say something like, "This doesn't seem fair," or "I'm very tired, may I please have a different job?" Then together they will figure out a solution that will feel right for both of them.

The Choice Is Yours

As you review the lists, I suspect you'll realize that the methods employed by the emotion coach *and* those used by the intimidator can stop or start a child, but the question is, At what cost? Which strategies foster that emotional bond and keep your child working with you? Which strategies help the child learn to understand his feelings and develop coping skills?

No one is a perfect emotion coach. Building healthy, strong relationships with your children is a process. You have to give yourself permission to be a learner, to practice and try again. All of us have a bit more or less of the intimidator in us. But we can choose to be more of an emotion coach for our children. As you respond to your child you can choose to be firm without being intimidating. You can be a teacher without being an interrogator. You can be assertive without being aggressive. When you decide to respond respectfully and gently, you can stop your child and still keep him working with you—even when he's fourteen.

Think about the last twenty-four hours. How did you stop your child? Did you wash his mouth out with soap when he spit or called you names, or did you clearly let him know that this behavior was unacceptable and at the *same* time teach him what he was feeling and what he could say or do instead? How did you get your child to start something? Are you happy with the words and actions you used? Are they helping you to build the kind of relationship you want with your child in the long run?

Making the Decision

Kate groaned, "How am I supposed to think about all this stuff in the middle of the night, when my daughter's screaming and I'm exhausted?"

"Let me tell you about a phone call I received last fall," I said.

It was late, and I was sitting quietly reading when my telephone rang. I chose to let the machine answer it. The voice was familiar and frantic. A child's screams echoed in the background. "We have an issue," the voice said. "We're kind of fried. We don't know where to turn and how to deal with—well, a sleeping problem or lack-of-sleep problem. If you get this message, would you call us . . ." I snatched up the receiver.

It seems two-year-old Annie was adamantly refusing to go to bed. When her parents tried to leave her, she screamed in terror, "Don't leave me! Don't leave me." If they walked out the bedroom door, she followed them, heartbroken sobs choking her.

"What should we do?" the dad asked. "We don't want to start a bad habit, but we also hate to hear her scream. She seems terrified."

It's true that late at night it seems impossible to think about what your child might be feeling or needing. How can this possibly be an opportunity to connect with and teach your child? She won't listen. You want to scream!

But you always have the choice to choose strategies that connect you with your child or disconnect you.

"Grab a piece of paper," I directed the group. "Write down on the left side of your paper all of the strategies that you've heard people describe or recommend for dealing with late-night meltdowns. Include them all, the ones you like and the ones you hate. Snatch at those deep memories of the worst nights—the times when you haven't slept for days, are scared stiff, and the baby has just vomited on your sweatshirt and the only way to take it off is over your head. Stick them all down right here. And then on the right side of your paper, ask yourself: Does this strategy connect me with my child, empathize with his feelings, and build a relationship with him? Or does it disconnect us, negating or even punishing him for his emotions?

Your list may look like this:

Potential Strategies	Result
lock the door and walk out	disconnect
stay with him and pat his back	connect
put a gate on the door	disconnect
spank him	disconnect
take him for a ride in the car	connect
put him in bed with you	connect
ignore him	disconnect
rock him	connect

The fact is that all of these responses may *stop* the behavior at least temporarily, but the question is, How? Do they do it in a way that builds connections with your child, or disconnects you?

The Decision to Connect

"So what did the parents do?" Peter wanted to know.

Fortunately for Annie, her parents didn't just react. They thought through their response, and as we talked, they realized that usually Annie went to bed easily. Screaming was not typical behavior for her. Indeed something was wrong. And so we talked about what had been happening in their lives. It was then I learned that Annie's mom was pregnant and was just two weeks from her due date. It had been a very difficult pregnancy, and Mom had been put on complete bed rest for the entire summer. She could get up, go to the bathroom, shower, and lie on the couch. That was it. Annie was scared. An active kid, suddenly she was pretty grounded. She'd spent most of her summer sitting in the rocker next to the couch or with friends and neighbors. Now the baby was due, and in order to prepare her, they'd let her know that soon Mommy and Daddy would be leaving in the middle of the night to get the baby out of Mommy's tummy. Their friend Janet would be coming to stay with her.

As soon as they heard themselves tell me this, they realized Annie really was scared. They gave Annie the support she needed by sitting with her and patting her until she went to sleep. This ritual lasted for the next two months, until after the baby was born. When things calmed down again, Annie's parents gradually shortened the patting time and returned to the old bedtime routine of a simple story, prayer, and kiss. Annie accepted it. And six months later when I ran into them at the grocery store, Annie proudly announced to me, "I go to bed all by myself!"

These parents were emotion coaches. They identified what Annie was feeling and needing, and they selected strategies that validated those feelings. They weren't pushovers. When they knew that Annie's stress levels had returned to a more comfortable level, and were confident that she no longer was feeling fearful, they "held the line" and returned to the old routine. It's true it took time and patience on their part, but their daughter learned a very important lesson. Now she knows that she can trust Mom and Dad to help her when she is frightened. It's a lesson she will remember even when she's sixteen and needs to talk to an adult about the things her peers are doing that make her uncomfortable.

Remember Your Own Emotion Coach

You can teach yourself to be a more effective emotion coach by building off of your own memories. Think about your favorite adult, *your* emotion coach. What's one step you can take to be more like him or her?

If you're like Kate and never had an emotion coach in your life, you may not even be sure where to start. If that's true, listen to the parents around you, and look for individuals who are sensitive and supportive of their children. Take classes to educate yourself. If that seems daunting, there's a Chinese proverb that may be helpful to you. It says, "The journey of a thousand miles begins with a single step." You can start with just one step today.

Start with the Little Steps

In class the parents shared their goals. Peg decided she'd take the time to rub her daughter's back in the morning before she got up. Peter vowed to try to listen more. Debbie decided to try to plan ahead more. Jim was going to stop rushing his son. Lisa wanted to remember that her kids had reasons for their behavior and weren't just out to get her.

Each individual set up little steps, actions they could take to help them build that positive relationship with their child. Their progress reports a week later were exciting. Peg's morning hassles with her daughter had almost disappeared. Bedtime had gone better for Jim, who, instead of scooping his son off the floor and immediately trying to put him to bed, started fifteen minutes earlier than usual and carried his son around the house saying good night to the dog, the plants, and the teddy bears. When it was actually time to put him in bed, he didn't fight it so much. Debbie had eased into the change to daylight savings time by predicting that the night they moved their clocks ahead the kids would need more help getting settled. They did. But she'd planned to spend time with each one, and, as a result, the evening had gone smoothly and she'd never lost her cool.

Whether it was listening more, thinking ahead, informing the children, or spending more time with them, all of the little actions paid off. Kids felt important and heard; cooperation became a reality.

Building a healthy relationship with your child begins with the choices you make each day.

- When you take the time to listen to your child, instead of brushing her off, you are building connections.
- When you respond in a manner that validates her feelings instead of invalidating them, you are teaching her to be caring.
- When you help her to choose appropriate actions, you are helping her to be more competent.

If you find you can be that emotion coach for about five minutes, and then start slipping into the role of the intimidator, don't give up! Read on, and I'll show you how to increase the odds of keeping your cool, even when the kids are losing theirs.

Coaching Tips

- Connect instead of disconnect.
- Assist instead of taking over.
- Listen rather than lecture.
- Stop firmly rather than grabbing or jerking.
- Help instead of abandon.
- Explain instead of force.
- State rather than shriek.
- Smile more, frown less.
- Think about your relationship in the long run.
- Start with a single step.

THREE

Bringing Down the Intensity

You're the Role Model

> *"Never let Mommy brush your hair when she's mad at Daddy."*
>
> —Family Circle

At Putnam Elementary in Minneapolis, the staff were concerned about the number of suspensions for defiant behavior and decided to take action. They were not going to tolerate more disruption but instead wanted to train the students and themselves to handle confrontations more effectively. They realized they had to begin with themselves.

One teacher pledged to control her voice when she got angry. Another vowed to listen carefully to every child who came up to her in the morning. A clerk decided to try to change physical posturing that could be intimidating to the children. A third-grade teacher promised to try to keep her voice low and calm when she was challenged by a child. These simple goals, along with a lot of hard work, cut the number of suspensions from three hundred two years previously to seventy-two!

Learning to express strong emotions, like anger and frustration, respectfully and selectively is learned behavior. You don't have to be a victim of your emotions. You can choose your response. You don't have to react. And as you make those choices, your children are watching and listening. You are their role model, teaching them with your words and actions what adults do when faced with a rush of powerful emotions.

Understanding the Physiology of Anger

Wrestling with our own anger means taking on Mother Nature. Anger isn't just about free-floating emotions. It's physiological. Our bodies are actually finely tuned "reaction machines." When confronted with threatening or frustrating situations, stress hormones surge through our body, triggering the brain to be ready for "fight or flight."

If you pay close attention, you can actually feel the stress hormones collecting in your body. The reaction is cumulative. Wake up in the morning thinking about all the things you have to do, and the stress hormones start to flow. Your teeth and hands clench. Neck muscles squeeze your spine. Shoulders tighten. Arms ache. Your body is on alert. The gates are open. When your child refuses to get out of bed, more stress hormones march into your bloodstream. You can feel the tension rising, and you urge her to hurry. It's when she asks you to help her find her notebook that you lose it. Suddenly, seemingly without warning, her simple request turns you into a shrieking shrew. The stress hormones have built to volcanic proportions. You blow.

Sometimes it doesn't take three or four cumulative events to transform you into a human volcano. If you're surprised or threatened, a rush of stress hormones can send you over the top with one *swoosh!* Caught off-guard, you can easily find your response on autopilot. You stop thinking and just act. Afterward you feel repentant. You know that on any other day her request wouldn't have fazed you. You're not even sure what happened or how.

You've been emotionally hijacked. Your stress hormones have created what's called "neural static." You can't think straight, much less see this situation as an opportunity to connect with your child and teach her how to work with you. Instead you react instinctively and reflexively. The intimidator takes over.

Recognizing the Instinctual Responses

Learning to recognize when you're "reacting" rather than thinking is the first step toward choosing a different response. There are four common instinctual reactions. Think about which ones are most typical for you and your child. What do you do when you get upset and you're not thinking?

Striking Back

When you feel threatened, you might find yourself attacking right back. You want to smack someone or something! Even when you're able to quell the urge to physically strike out, you may let loose with words that escalate into full-fledged name calling or a shouting match.

Giving In

The opposite of striking back is giving in. Exhaustion drives you. You cannot bear to deal with another angry outburst, so you give in or let your child off the hook. The trouble with giving in is that later you feel as if you've been had. Your child just keeps pushing, asking for more as he tries to find out where the limit is. Resentment grows until ultimately you have taken more than you can bear. That's when you find yourself moving from giving in to striking back.

Shutting Down

Sometimes when that rush of adrenaline hits, you literally shut down. Flooded with emotion, it's as though you were a deer caught in the glare of headlights, unable to respond or perform. You can't think. You feel helpless. Your greatest fear is that there is nothing you can do to make things better.

Breaking Off

The fourth instinctual reaction is to throw up your hands and emotionally break off your relationship with your child. You might say, "I just can't deal with you!" "I don't want to be with you!" or "Maybe you should find a different parent or family!" It could be hours or days of silence. No matter whether the breakoff is verbal or silent, to your child the message is clear: I don't like you. I don't want anything to do with you. I can't think of anything about you I ever liked. I wish to sever this relationship.

These instinctual reactions tear apart relationships. They bring up a host of hurt feelings, leaving you feeling lousy and your child feeling angry and resentful. The emotional costs are great. Rather than finding a way to work together, you're pushed apart. Fortunately you can learn to stop reacting and instead to respond deliberately, with careful and full consideration of the situation.

We can decide even in those difficult moments to choose responses that connect us with our kids instead of disconnect us. These responses allow us to step back, collect our wits, and see the situation more objectively and sensitively. Our goal isn't to suppress, muffle, stuff, deny, or bury our feelings, but to express them more selectively. As we do it we are teaching our kids how to express *their* strong emotions respectfully and how to manage *their* intensity.

There are four basic ingredients to managing those strong feelings:

1. Changing the frame
2. Setting standards
3. Monitoring your feelings
4. Learning effective strategies

1. Changing the Frame

When my son was thirteen, he got a new mountain bike with a black racing helmet and gloves. It was the most magnificent bike I had ever ridden: The gears flipped with a quick twist of the thumb, precisely snapping into place; the suspension system smoothed the "bumps" out of the ride. One night, my daughter had a soccer game at the high school. I told my husband I wanted to ride the bike over to the game and that I'd meet him there. I didn't notice that my son dashed out the front door before I'd even finished my sentence. When I got into the garage, he had the bike in hand and refused to give it to me. I admit I tried to grab it from his grasp. It didn't work. By then he had a good thirty pounds and three inches on me. Flustered, I declared, "Joshua, in our family we share." He didn't budge. Nasty thoughts flashed through my mind. I'd raised a selfish kid! He was spoiled and self-centered. Then guilt struck with thoughts like, I'm a lousy mother—a failure. I stomped back toward the house. "Are you going to get Dad?" Joshua asked. I didn't want to admit it, but I *was*!

My husband had heard the entire exchange. "Don't look at me," he said. "I'm not getting involved." I huffed.

"What would you tell a parent in the same situation?" my husband asked. I paused long enough to grumble, "That there's a reason, go and find out what it is." I marched back out to the garage. "Joshua," I demanded. "Why won't you let me ride your bike?"

"Because, Mom," he answered. "What thirteen-year-old guy wants his mother riding over to school on his bike, with his helmet and gloves? It would be so embarrassing."

A bubble of awareness trickled to the surface of my brain. I hadn't thought of that! A sigh escaped from me. I wasn't raising a selfish kid. I wasn't dealing with a major character flaw. He did have a reason. One I could actually empathize with. This awareness changed everything, including the tone of my voice and the posture of my body. I stepped back and simply asked, "How could we make this work?" We came up with a solution. I did ride the bike. I just used my own helmet and gloves and promised not to lay the bike down on its derailleur. Reframing the situation diffused my anger. It allowed me to reconnect with my son, end a power struggle, and begin problem solving.

Changing the frame works because every message or behavior is subject to our interpretation of it. If we assume our child is out to get us, or is a bad kid with severe character flaws, our intensity spirals. We can't think clearly. We stop listening and lose the opportunity to understand his point of view. If, instead, we *change the frame* and see that his behavior is an attempt to do the right thing (but he doesn't know how), or that he has a reason for his actions (he isn't just trying to irritate us), then our intensity will diminish. We're willing to give him the benefit of the doubt and try to resolve the conflict. We become partners rather than adversaries.

In class when I told this story, Jeff shook his head and started chuckling. "You should have been with us last Saturday night," he said. "We went to a party at a friend's home. About eight o'clock it was discovered that a four-year-old had gotten locked in the bathroom. The child's mom and dad ended up in a big fight. The mom was furious that the dad let the kid go to the bathroom by himself. My five-year-old son listened and watched the entire encounter. Finally, he whispered to my wife, 'I locked the door.'

"My wife was horrified. 'That's the meanest thing I've ever heard,' she shouted at him. 'We're leaving!' With that she grabbed him and our coats and demanded that we go. As we got into the car, I said to him, 'Mark, why did you lock the door?' Tears trickled down his cheeks. 'I thought I was helping him, Dad. I didn't know he couldn't unlock the door.'

"My wife groaned as her face flushed red. She'd assumed he'd done it maliciously, but instead he was trying to give the kid a little privacy!"

So the next time your child acts up or refuses to cooperate, tell yourself that there's a reason. Your child isn't intentionally out to drive you wild, be bad, or act lazy. There's a feeling or need that's fueling this behavior that he doesn't know how to express more appropriately. Changing the frame will make it much easier to keep your cool.

2. Setting Standards

If you're going to choose another response, you have to know your target. Like a thermostat set at seventy-eight degrees, you have to know what you're shooting for, what your goal is. What words and actions are you going to stop yourself from saying or doing even when the stress hormones are pounding through your head? Clarifying your standards is the key to managing strong emotions. If you don't have standards, or are confused about them, you can't choose a different response, anything goes.

My standards may be very different from yours, but that doesn't matter. What is important is that you examine your standards, clarify them, and make sure they're standards you want to be true for both you and your child today and forever.

In class I pass out index cards to record our answers to the following questions:

1. In what ways did the adults in your life express anger that you would like to avoid?
2. In what ways have you seen other people express anger that you would like to avoid?

We then toss the completed cards in the middle of the table for anonymity.

Clarifying Standards Helps You Keep Your Cool

It's David, energetic and vocal, who begins reading the index cards. "Shut up or I'll give you something to cry about." Others groan. "That was a favorite of my dad's," he adds. "My ex-husband, too," Nancy comments before she flips over the card she's pulled. "Threats," she reads. "Whenever I hear myself start to threaten my kids, I hear the exact words and tone my mother used. It isn't something I want to repeat." "Shaming," Pat offered. "Our family's been big on shaming. "I've got that one, too," Lisa acknowledged, "along with badgering."

"Let's talk about hitting and spanking," I said. "Do you want your child to hit you when she's angry?" I asked.

"Of course not," they all said.

"Are you willing to set no hitting as a standard for yourself?" Bodies shifted in chairs. I didn't wait for an answer. "What about swearing? Do you want your fourteen-year-old to call you a vulgar name?" I asked. Heads shook vehemently. "Are you willing to stop swearing when you're angry?" I continued.

It was Helen, a tiny, petite woman, who squirmed in her chair and remarked, "This is getting really tough." "Yeah," Joel agreed. "I mean, of course I've got standards for my kids' behavior, but I never thought about standards for myself."

The reality is, kids don't just learn from what we say or tell them to do. Our *example* is much more powerful. You can't get a five-year-old to stop swearing if that's what the adults around him are doing. You set the standards with your behavior. So if you swear or hit when you're angry, kids learn that's what adults do when they're upset. As they grow they'll test out those behaviors to demonstrate how grown up they are.

In class we often get into heated discussions about swearing. Many parents admit they swear when they're angry. They don't care if their kids do, too. Initially I was hesitant to say that I didn't think it was a good idea. I thought I might be placing my values on others. But then I discovered the research that found swearing easily escalates into emotional and physical abuse. Swearing also masks feelings and prevents us from developing the vocabulary to communicate emotions clearly. The opportunity to connect and communicate on a deep, personal level is lost in a barrage of vulgar language. So if swearing is a common practice in your family, take a look at it. Do you and your children recognize the emotions you're experiencing? Are you able to name them, or are swear words used to mask them? Does swearing escalate to more violence in your home? When you speak respectfully to your children even when you're angry—they learn you can be angry and still *think* about the words you are choosing to use.

Reaching to draw a card, Barb, an energetic and vocal member of the group, suddenly paused and asked, "Is it ever okay to yell? In my family if you tell us not to yell, we'll have nothing to say."

Barb's question was a *very* good one. "It isn't as though you'll never yell," I explained. "In fact, you'll want to be passionate about your standards. This is where you hold the line. But you'll want to save the screams for the *really* important things so your kids will listen. If you're yelling all of the time, your kids become parent-deaf. You want your shout to mean something to them. If it's saved for the big things, they'll know you are very serious."

There's also a big difference between a loud, wordless *humph* of frustration or a single statement like "Cut it out," and a harsh name-calling, shaming, "'you-stupid-little-jerk" shriek. That's the kind of screaming that disconnects us from our kids.

Examining our standards does not mean establishing sainthood. We're not expecting that we'll never yell or threaten our kids again, but it means we'll try harder to stop the responses that tear apart our relationship.

Sorting out the Mixed Messages

Clarifying and feeling confident about your standards can be challenging, because we sometimes get mixed messages about what our standards should be. "What are those conflicting messages you get?" I asked my group one day.

Kathy interjected, "My mother-in-law says if I'd just give him a good swat, he'd behave. Sometimes I can't help wondering if she's right. I was spanked, and for me it's a real natural response. It's awfully hard to try and change."

Nancy frowned as she listened. "I don't want to threaten and hit, but how do I justify it when last week I heard my ex-husband say to my son, 'Shut up or I'll give you something to cry about' and it worked!"

It's true that fear and intimidation will temporarily stop behaviors. But the question always becomes, At what cost? Do these strategies lead to a healthy relationship with your child? Do they enhance your child's emotional intelligence, or do they damage the relationship, limit your child's development, hurt self-esteem, and ultimately lead to anger and hostility?

The conflicting messages from others can be very powerful, making you feel uncertain about your responses and unable to make decisions. That's why you have to look at the standards and clearly decide what behaviors you want to stop.

Make a promise to yourself. Even better, write this down and post it on your refrigerator: "Next time I'm angry, I promise myself that I will *not* . . ." You fill in the blank. If you've decided you won't strike your child, call her names, or threaten to leave her no matter how angry you are, your decision will help you to stop yourself even in the worst moments. You'll no longer be that coconspirator in a tantrum. You'll be the adult choosing a more deliberate response and modeling for your child how to keep your cool.

3. Monitoring Your Feelings

Staying on a diet is much easier if no one sets a plate of freshly baked chocolate chip cookies in front of you. But once those cookies are right there at your fingertips, the smell and sight of them can be too tempting. Despite your best efforts and determination not to eat sweets, you succumb.

Standards define our goals. They help us to know what we're shooting for, but like a dieter, it's much easier to reach our goals if we don't test ourselves too severely. The earlier we can identify an emotion, the easier it is to manage it and choose a more deliberate response. The key is to learn how to monitor your emotions.

On the day I helped my son complete his college applications, and I ended up yelling at him. This activity was supposed to be a mother–son bonding experience. Instead I ended up bellowing at him. One of my standards is that I don't want to yell at my kids, but on that evening I let loose. Why? A failure to monitor my feelings put me right over the edge.

After two days of leading workshops for several hundred people, I'd gotten up at three-thirty that morning to drive from my hotel to the airport and fly twelve hundred miles home to Minneapolis. Arriving at lunchtime, I spent the afternoon raking leaves in our backyard—no easy task since it's filled with towering oak trees.

My son was hiking the Superior Trail, three hours north of us along Lake Superior. He was supposed to be home at four P.M. so we could finish his college applications, which were due into his school counselor's office the next day. At four P.M. he called from Duluth. His ride hadn't arrived on time, and they were just leaving. At seven he arrived home, hungry, dirty, and eager to tell us about his trip. By the time he finished eating, showering, doing homework, and placing a quick call to his girlfriend, it was ten-thirty P.M. I was sitting at the dining room table waiting for him when he walked past me to the family room, picked up a golf club his sister had left there, and started putting. That's when I yelled!

What happened? I ignored my fatigue—focusing instead on the deadline. I didn't say anything about my growing frustration. Nor did I unscramble the jumble of emotions whirling inside of me, including sadness that he would be leaving home. What I really wanted to yell was, "I can't believe we are already here. How can you be leaving so soon?" And my excitement, "Wow, we really are here, and I'm proud of you!" And maybe there was even a twinge of envy as I looked at all of the possibilities that were open to him and wished that I could be in his shoes. I didn't monitor my feelings. I didn't say a word—until I screamed.

Later I found out my son wasn't stalling just to get me or to be disrespectful, he was scared about filling out those applications. He, too, knew they meant he was leaving. We both failed to monitor our feelings and reacted instinctively. I struck out. He shut down.

What Are You Feeling?

When you awake in the morning and feel a sense of discomfort, think about what emotions you are experiencing. Are you exhausted? Do you dread going to your job? Are the payments on the couch that you just put on lay-a-way pushing you beyond your budget? Are you feeling guilty, wanting to spend more time with your child?

When you find yourself shrieking at your child over the bowl of cereal he's not eating or the pair of shorts she's refusing to wear, stop and ask yourself, What am I really feeling? What emotions have been boiling inside of me *before* we started fighting over this little tiny thing? Is my anger really about cereal or something else?

It's important to know that anger is often a second emotion. Before it, you've usually experienced a "first feeling," such as frustration, disappointment, fear, or sadness. Look past your anger and ask yourself, What was my first feeling? What's really fueling my reaction?

If monitoring feelings is new to you, simply try to catch yourself and pause for fifteen seconds throughout the day. Start by noting the most common feelings. Are you hungry? When do you feel fatigued? What makes you happy? What frightens you? Do noises irritate you? As you become more comfortable with these feelings, it will be easier to perceive the more subtle ones. Then, for example, the next time you're sitting on the beach and your child again dashes for the water even though he can't swim, instead of telling yourself, If he does that again I'm going to scream, recognize *your* emotion: I am exhausted. I'm getting frustrated. I'm not having fun anymore. It's time to go home. When you recognize your emotion, you can choose your response. You always have that choice.

Know Your Stress Cues

According to Lawrence Shapiro in *How to Raise a Child with a High EQ*, 55 percent of emotions are communicated nonverbally and 38 percent through voice tone. That leaves only 7 percent communicated through actual words! Often it's much easier to monitor your actions than it is to name your feelings.

During dinner one night, my daughter turned to me and asked, "What's wrong, Mom?" I was startled by her question. I hadn't said anything.

"Why do you ask?" I questioned.

"Because you just let out your 'something's wrong' sigh," she replied. Kris was right. I had had an upsetting day, but I wasn't even aware of my feelings. The sigh had simply come out of me. Her observation made me stop, reflect on my day, and check my feelings.

Think about your body cues. What do you do when the stress hormones are surging through your body? Here's what other parents have said.

- I slam doors.
- I become impatient.
- I start sounding like a drill sergeant.
- I start screaming at the kids.
- I don't smile.

- I won't talk on the phone.
- I rush.
- I forget things.
- I lock into my deadline or schedule and refuse to alter it even though everyone is falling apart.

Think about your "stress behaviors." Become aware of them so that the next time you realize you are gritting your teeth, clenching the steering wheel of your car, screaming at the kids, or feeling a headache building, you'll know that it's time to stop, think, and take preventive measures. This is especially important before you join your family for the evening or your kids come home from school or you start the bedtime routine. If your stress level is high when you begin, you'll blow up over anything. Know, too, that your stress can agitate other members of your family. Monitoring your emotions and taking steps to manage those feelings *before* you blow helps the others to keep their cool, too.

Recognize When You're Most Vulnerable

I often ask the parents in my classes what days of the week or times of the day they are most vulnerable. They always have an immediate answer. For many it's Monday mornings that are a real "test" for meeting their standards. Others name a specific night when multiple commitments keep them on the run and emotions running high. When you identify these high stress times, you can plan for them, slow down, and manage your feelings more effectively. For example, you might decide not to schedule meetings on Monday mornings until ten A.M. so you won't feel rushed. Or you might order in pizza or get the Crock-Pot going so that dinner is ready when you come home on that "crazy" night. If an unexpected change in plans—like the school nurse calling to tell you your child needs to be seen by a doctor—typically upsets you, teach yourself to recognize that you are more vulnerable to blowups when you're surprised.

Thinking about your "vulnerable spots" also helps you to "change your frame." Your kids pick up your stress. If you know this is a vulnerable time for your whole family, it's easier to pause, take the deep breath, and then give the hug, listen more carefully, or tie the shoe one more time—the right way—instead of screaming.

In many families strong feelings are often ignored or squelched. If life experiences have made your feelings unreachable to you, working with a competent counselor can be a great benefit. *Your ability to recognize your own feelings is at the heart of teaching your child how to manage hers.*

4. Learning Effective Strategies

If you're not going to shriek or hit, what *can* you do when that surge of emotions strikes? The *most* effective strategy you can use is a simple pause! Taking one second to breathe deeply or count to ten gives your brain time to shift from "fight or flight" into the neocortex, or thinking brain. When you stop, even for a moment, you can start thinking again and choose a more suitable response. That's it—a pause!

Tim used this strategy to turn what could have been a disconnect into a connect for him and his son. "I've got a home office," he told me. "My two-year-old likes to come in and sit on my lap, but last time he started to kick my papers. Normally I'd grab him, drag him out of there, toss him in his room, and let him scream. This time I paused. How do I want to respond? I thought. What do I want to teach him? Instead of yelling at him and tossing him out, I firmly took hold of his feet and told him, 'You may not kick my papers.' And then I said, 'You can choose to stay here and color, or you can get down.' He stopped and grinned. "It worked! I think because I was so calm and clear he listened. He ended up playing in the office for the next forty-five minutes, and then we took a cookie break."

Next time you get caught in the heat of the moment, *pause.* It may amaze you how effective such a simple strategy can be!

Take a Break

If you've gone too far without catching your emotions, a pause may not be enough for you to regain your composure. You may need to step away for a few minutes. Instead of stomping away or shouting, "I'm not talking to you," calmly say, "I need a minute. I'll be back." It's the reassurance that you'll be back, you're staying connected, you're simply taking a break to calm yourself, that makes stepping away very different from the instinctive reaction of breaking off. If at this point you don't dare open your mouth, you can talk later and explain to your child that when you get so upset all you can do is step away, but you will come back. It's a promise. If your child is very young, make sure he's in a safe place when you step away. Older kids can begin to understand that you just need a few minutes.

When you take your break, be sure to do something that distracts you from the issue long enough for you to calm down. Avoid stewing or building your case while you're away. Ruminating only increases your intensity. If you can, go for a walk. Remember your brain is saying "fight or flight." Walking gives you a suitable outlet. If your kids are little, put them in the stroller and go outside. If it's too cold or it's raining, walk up and down your hallway or around the table. Allow yourself to move. If all else fails, fill the sink with warm soapy water and start washing dishes! It'll actually soothe you.

When Your Child Won't Let You Step Away

Stepping away can be challenging if your child is too young to be left alone, or if she tends to follow you.

Tom was a very involved, patient dad who found himself at his wits' end after a rainy, nasty day with his two-year-old son, Jacob. Tom knew he was ready to blow up. So he said to Jacob, in a firm, controlled voice. "Daddy needs a break. You sit here on the couch and read a book for a few minutes and Daddy is going to sit in the chair next to the couch and read his paper." Big-eyed, the toddler crawled up onto the couch and started "reading." Dad did the same. After about five minutes, Jacob said to his dad, "How about if we cuddle now?" Much more relaxed, Tom was ready to hold his son.

If your child is older and will not let you step away, you might have to get help. Sandy adopted her daughter, Katrina, when she was two years old. Bedtime was a horrendous struggle every night. Sandy knew that Katrina had suffered neglect and possibly abuse. Being left alone was extremely threatening to this child, and the battles were fierce.

There were times Sandy knew she needed to walk away for a minute, but when she did, her daughter followed and hit her. If Sandy walked into her own bedroom and shut the door, Katrina pounded on it and screamed. Finally, Sandy decided to try another tactic. She told Katrina that she would always come back, but that she needed to take a break when she got too angry. If Katrina couldn't or wouldn't let her take one, the neighbor would come and help them. The neighbor had agreed that if Sandy called she would come over and stay with Katrina while Sandy walked outside.

The next time Katrina started having a tantrum, Sandy found herself seething. She tried to walk away. Katrina followed, hitting her. Sandy turned to Katrina and asked, "Can you let me take a break or do I need to call the neighbor?" Katrina hit her again. Sandy called the neighbor, who sprinted over and stayed with Katrina, calming her, while Sandy took the other kids and walked outside for ten minutes.

This happened three times. Each time Sandy would ask, "Can you let me take a break in the house, or do I need to call the neighbor?" Finally, the fourth time, Katrina allowed her mother to take her break. She sat outside the bedroom door, but she didn't pound and she didn't scream. After five minutes Sandy came out again and they were able to get ready for bed.

Sometimes children who have experienced a significant loss or separation such as divorce, a major move, death, or foster care find a parent stepping away terrifying. They feel abandoned and try everything to keep the parent with them. If this is your child, it's important to understand her vulnerability, to explain that you are not abandoning her. You will come back. You are simply calming down. It may be necessary to find someone who can support your child while you cool off.

Ask for Help

A sympathetic hug, a friend willing to listen to your woes, can be one of the most effective ways to defuse anger. If you've had a horrible, no-good, rotten day, and the kids are picking up on your stress, ask your partner for a hug. If you are single parenting, call a friend, neighbor, or your local help line. Find someone who can support you. When you're exhausted, employing a tag team is definitely the way to go.

Kathy cleared her throat. "I can't do that," she stated matter-of-factly. "If I ask for help, I feel like I'm a failure or like I'm giving in."

Brenda turned to Kathy, "My husband travels all week, so I'm alone with the kids a lot. There are nights when getting all three of them to bed seems impossible. My daughter especially can be very demanding of me. What I finally realized is that no matter how much I do or how much attention I give her, I can't 'fix' it for her. She misses her dad. I can be sympathetic and support her, but I can't keep her from feeling lonely or scared. When I realized that, it was a great relief to me because the 'trigger' for me was the feeling that I should be able to do this. I should be able to give her everything she needs, but I couldn't. It wasn't possible. When I accepted that and allowed myself to say I can't parent five days a week, twenty-four hours a day all by myself, and instead asked for help, everything started to get better."

Our value of self-sufficiency and independence can get us into trouble when it comes to raising kids. If you look cross culturally at other countries, you'll find a child's life is filled with aunts and uncles who may or may not actually be related to them, but who are adults who love them and support one another. We don't have to do it alone. Asking for help is not a sign of weakness; learning to recognize our limits is a very important skill to teach our children.

Make a Plan

The key to all of these strategies is talking about them with the other members of your family. The middle of a blowup is not a teachable time, but later, when everyone is calm, you can go back and say, "Next time let's agree that we can say, 'I need a break or a hug.' Create "magic words," phrases that you can use in the heat of the moment to remind everyone to pause, like "Break time!" "Let's count to ten." "Let's stop, then start again." Or, "Everybody, breathe deeeeeeply!"

In class I always ask parents to write down their plan for managing their strong feelings. When we have a plan, we make better decisions, are more attentive, listen better, and even ask more questions! In other words we monitor more closely, and as a result we're more effective.

Select a goal for the next month. Say to yourself, "When it comes to managing my strong feelings my goal is to . . ." Write your goal down. It's important that your goal is for the month, and not specifically for each day. You have to allow yourself to practice, and if you expect that you'll do it every day and then fail, it's more likely that you'll quit. If your goal is for the month, you can pick yourself up and try again.

Here are some goals other parents have selected.

- I'm going to learn more about managing my stress.
- I'm going to monitor how frequently I yell.
- I'm going to try to count to ten.
- I'm going to pause and monitor my feelings before I walk in the door at night.
- I'm going to stop to ask for a hug.

Savor your moments of success, your tiny steps of progress. Learning to respond thoughtfully even when you're angry is tough. It's easier if you remember that kids have a reason for their behavior and they're not just "out to get you." Discovering what those feelings are begins with managing your own strong emotions. No words or punishments will ever teach your children how to manage their feelings as effectively as your example.

Coaching Tips

- Recognize when you're reacting.
- Change the frame: Your child isn't "out to get you." Look for the reason.
- Clarify your standards. Know what you're *not* going to do.
- Monitor your feelings. Catch yourself before you're ready to blow.
- Remember, a mere pause can help you keep your cool.
- Make a plan for managing your strong feelings.

FOUR

Enforcing Your Standards and Staying Connected

"I had this fantasy that my child and I would walk hand in hand across the park. Little did I know that when he got mad he would spit on me. . . ."

—*A parent*

When my daughter was fifteen, she informed my husband and me that she and her friends were renting a hotel party room instead of going to the homecoming dance. Our response was immediate. Kurcinka kids did *not* rent hotel rooms. Acknowledging that we understood she wanted to be with her friends, we offered to host a party at our home, where it could be supervised. She didn't like our response. Grousing in disappointment, she walked out of the room and called her cousin Christine, ten years her senior. "My parents are being so old-fashioned," I heard her complain, and then she proceeded to explain that we wouldn't let her rent the hotel room. Christine replied, "Your parents are right. You're an athlete; you don't want to put yourself in a vulnerable position." If I'd paid my niece to be our "backup" she couldn't have done a better job. Her response was all we needed. My daughter knew her case was shot. She got up, put on her running shoes, and took off for a three-mile run. Over the next three days she ultimately decided that she'd rather go out of town that weekend than host a party. So together we planned a family trip to northern Minnesota.

When I shared this story in class, I didn't expect the stunned silence that fell. "Why didn't she start screaming or swearing at you?" Diane asked incredulously. And it was Peter who said, "I can't believe she didn't stomp off or refuse to talk with you."

What I realized is that over the years, my daughter had learned our family's standards—not perfectly, mind you; she is human—but pretty darned well. Those standards had helped her to keep her cool and continue to work with us.

But it's often difficult to imagine how you can teach your child those skills when his screams drown out your words or his blows are bruising your arm. How do you soothe and calm him when he's kicking and flailing at you? What do you do when he swears at you? In the heat of the moment you have to help your child to stop reacting and instead to learn to choose a more respectful and suitable way to express his strong feelings. You are his teacher, his emotion coach. The task can seem overwhelming unless you break the skills down into small steps that can be accomplished more easily.

The Steps

I can show you those steps, but as I do, I want you to know that teaching your child to recognize what she is feeling, stop impulsive reactions, and choose more respectful and suitable responses is like putting together a variety show. The pieces have to be learned separately before they're put together, and even then they have to be practiced over and over. Let me tell you about Judy Sagen so you can understand what I mean.

Judy Sagen's official title is choir director, but I see her as an emotion coach for other people's kids. Every year she pulls together a crowd-pleasing, foot-stomping variety show with students from my local high school. This is no small feat. More than two hundred kids are involved. Some of them have had years of voice and dance lessons, but many others have never trained or performed before. They're all amateurs. Yet year after year they produce a show that meets professional standards.

I asked her once what her secret was. "The show is all broken down into tiny steps," she explained. "First we learn the notes. Sometimes I bring in a recording so they can hear the song. Then I teach them style. I demonstrate the difference between a quick, sharp staccato and a slow, smooth legato. We talk about those differences, and I demonstrate the impact of each."

Notes and style are practiced until the words are memorized. It's only when the song has become second nature that the choreography begins. "You can't think about words when you're dancing," Judy says. "It has to come naturally."

So for a while they forget about the vocals and focus on the footwork. Then they go back, polish up the vocals, and put the two together. But they're not done yet. Now it's time for stage performance strategies. Using mirrors and videotapes, they review facial expressions, including when to smile and how to convey their message with their entire head and body.

It's only after these skills have been practiced over and over again that the orchestra joins them. But believe it or not, they're still not finished! They still have to add the costumes, and finally practice the curtain call. "If that's sloppy, you haven't taken the last step," Judy explains.

Luckily your "variety show" is much simpler than Judy's. You're not working with two hundred kids. You're working just with your own, and the steps are actually less complex. I'll show you those steps, but bear with me since, like the variety show, each step takes time, as does assembling the final production. First we'll work on enforcing your standards. After that I'll show you how to identify your child's emotions and help him monitor how intense he's feeling. Then I'll describe how to teach your child what actions he *can* take when he's feeling frustrated, angry, irritated, jealous, disappointed, and all those other strong emotions. Ultimately, we will put all of the pieces together and you and your child will be star performers when it comes to managing those strong emotions.

Standards Are a Beginning

Standards form your foundation. They are your guidelines for what is acceptable and what is not acceptable behavior. Standards don't change whether you're two or sixty-two. They are the rules of conduct that you will keep coming back to in order to help your child make healthy choices about how to express strong feelings. Your goal as you enforce your standards is to communicate clearly to your child, "This is not acceptable behavior. You need to make a different choice." When you understand that at this point your goal is simply to communicate your standards, it's easier to keep your cool when your child doesn't immediately stop. His failure to comply doesn't mean you've failed. You're just not finished yet. Right now you're simply working on the "first notes," an essential piece of the whole.

Enforcing Your Standards

Think about the last time your child erupted. What did he say or do? Did he rip up his paper when he made a mistake? Were you dodging your two-year-old's kicks when you tried to change her pants? Did your son hit you or call you names when you asked him to pick up his room? Did your daughter bite the baby? Was a family gathering disrupted by a shrieking toddler or a preadolescent calling you the b word?

Instead of moving into the role of the intimidator, stop to think about the standards you set for yourself. What actions or words did your child express that you've deemed unacceptable for yourself?

When your child is reacting to his strong emotions, the importance of *your* standards is reinforced. When you have clarified your own standards and know which behaviors you will not accept, it's much easier to step in and firmly say, "*Stop!* In this family, no matter how angry we are, we do *not* hit!" Or, "You can tell me you're angry, but you may *not* swear at me. I don't swear at you, and you can't swear at me." Your effectiveness increases exponentially when your words match your actions. This is why it's so important that you not stop him from hitting by slapping his hand. If you don't hit when you're upset, your child not only hears you say, "Hitting is not acceptable," he also *sees* that adults don't express their anger by hitting. Before the teen years your child *wants* to be like you. Your clear standards help her to stop reacting and instead choose a different response.

Consistency Is a Must

Standards need to be upheld no matter what, which means they need to be consistently enforced. Roy Baumeister, author of *Losing Control*, explains, "When kids are punished severely when their parents are in a bad mood, but get away with mayhem when parents are in a good mood, we create a model for kids out of control."

Kids can't make the standards their own if we are inconsistent. When your standards are enforced according to how you feel rather than what your child has done, you confuse him. He can't predict your reaction. He never knows whether you're going to step in calmly and hold the line, blow up, or let him off the hook. Since he doesn't know what to expect, he goes on constant alert, which raises his intensity, making him vulnerable to tantrums. As a result, he feels helpless and ends up angry and frustrated because he has no idea where the line is or what the standards are.

Check yourself. If you're letting your kids push and shove one another when you're busy or engrossed in something else, but you stop them when you have the energy or the focus to do it, you are not enforcing clear standards. If you're telling your child not to shove, but then roughly grab her, you are confusing your child. If you don't want your child to hit when he's angry, you have to take his hand and stop him no matter if it's just a little hit, or he didn't really mean it, or he was upset or tired. Don't ignore the behavior, stop it. When your standards are enforced *every* time, you make it much easier for your child to make the standards her own. If you are single parenting and Dad's rules are different from Mom's rules, you can tell your child there are Daddy's rules and there are Mommy's rules. When you are with me, you follow my rules. Then be consistent about your rules.

Dealing with the Guilt

When you enforce your standards, your child is never going to say thank you. Instead, he may be stunned. This is especially true if you're the caregiver who hasn't been saying no and suddenly you start saying stop! His initial reaction may be to scream louder.

You hate to see your child sad and upset, and it can be embarrassing to carry a screaming child out of the shopping center. Your gut may twist with guilt while doubt fills your mind. How could you be doing the right thing when you get such a negative reaction? It's important to realize that you are asking your child to stop his actions and consider other people. While the message may be painful to receive, it's a very important one and essential to his future relationships.

If you avoid enforcing standards, your child will become an unbearable tyrant. He won't learn that he can manage his emotions whether he's at home or in public. Without standards he is a victim of Mother Nature telling him to "fight or flee." His strong feelings control and overwhelm him. While it may not be easy to enforce your standards, one of the most important messages you can give your child is, "I'm not afraid of your strong feelings. I will help you stop."

Match Your Words with Actions

When it comes to enforcing standards, Beth Cutting, a St. Paul family educator, likes to tell the story of the picnic and the mosquito. She says, "When you're having a picnic in Minnesota, it's inevitable that a mosquito will try to bite you. You swat at it. It comes back. You swat at it again. It comes back again. It isn't until you get up and go after that mosquito that you can stop it from biting you."

If you only use words to enforce your standards, it's like swatting at that mosquito. It won't work. You're wasting your energy. Lynn Jessen,

Director of Paidea Chill Development Center, says, "Words are the standards. Actions are the enforcement."

If you want your child to make your standards her own, you have to
add actions to those words. Not harsh rough actions like spanking or
jerking, but gentle firm actions that clearly express, If you can't stop
yourself, I will stop you.

Developmentally, toddlers are at the stage of learning what they can
do and how things work, which is why they put things in their mouths,
dump toys and food on the floor, climb on counters, and get into cupboards. Their brains are screaming, Find out what happens; see what
you can do! That's why a two-year-old will look right at you, smile, and
then do what you just asked him not to do. Words alone will *never* stop
a two-year-old. Usually by age four, however, when your child is more
verbal and knows from experience that you always follow through, he
will be able to stop himself when you say, "Stop." If your child has a language delay, it will take him longer to be able to stop with words alone.

Shouting Isn't Action

Tom thoughtfully listened as I talked about the importance of matching
words and actions. "In our family we don't act," he said. "We just yell
louder." Tom's experience isn't unusual. Many times when our kids
don't respond to our words, we become frustrated. Our intensity goes
up, and we end up yelling louder, hoping that the power of our voice
will somehow stop them. We might even believe they don't hear us
until we yell. But in reality shouting simply brings up the intensity,
which hinders problem solving. The next time your child does something that needs to be stopped, say "Stop" and at the very same time
move. If you aren't willing to get up to go after your child to help him
stop, he's probably not going to stop on his own.

Review Your Standards

Emotion coaches don't surprise kids with their standards. Before you
enter a situation, talk with your child about the feelings he might expe-

rience and the standards you have for expressing those feelings. If you're going into the grocery store, you could say something like, "The lights are bright and the aisles are crowded. You might feel irritated or grumpy. If you do, you can tell me and we'll find a quiet corner to take a little break, but it is not acceptable to whine or throw a tantrum."

You are not "feeding" your child ideas when you help him to predict emotions he might experience. You are building his vocabulary so that he can talk to you instead of acting out, and you are teaching him your standards. You help him to honor those standards when you teach him what he *can* do or say.

Teach Your Child What He Can Do

What scared Abe's parents the most were the temper tantrums. He could be a great kid and he often was. His mom could take him to the office with her, and people would remark about his charm and good behavior. But put Abe on a baseball field, and a different kid emerged. This one threw down his helmet and swore when he struck out. Stomping and shouting were all part of the display. His parents had told him clearly that this behavior was not acceptable. They'd taken away privileges when he acted this way, and yet the outbursts continued. Why, they wanted to know? What were they doing wrong?

Abe's parents were enforcing their standards, a very important step, but standards alone are not enough to help a child learn to choose a more suitable response. We can't expect our kids just to squelch their emotions. We have to teach them what they *can* say or do when that intensity starts to surge through their bodies. Next time Abe is going to a game, his parents might say, "During the baseball game, you might feel frustrated or disappointed. If you do feel that way, you can take a deep breath or step around the bench to give yourself a little space, but it is not acceptable to throw down your bat or helmet."

Like driving a manual transmission, if you only put on the brakes, the engine will sputter and die. In order to keep things running smoothly, you must simultaneously push in the clutch and downshift. When it comes to kids, "downshifting" means naming the feeling you think they might be experiencing and teaching them what they can do or say—what their choices are.

When Your Child Hits You

If your child is hitting you, before you take hold of your child, *get ahold of yourself*. Then catch his hand and firmly but gently hold it. Remind yourself, This is an overload. My child is not out to get me. She is feeling overwhelmed by the emotions that are flowing through her system. This is not my failure. Then clearly and emphatically state, "You may not hit. No matter how angry you are, you may not hit." This is not the time to say, "Please don't hit," or "Stop, okay?"

Rather than trying to figure out what punishment to mete out, name the emotion you think your child might be experiencing. At this point it is a guess, but the further you move along in this book, the more likely you'll be able to identify that "real fuel source." Then teach your child what he *can* do in this situation. For example, you can say, "I know Jeff pushed you. It hurt, but you may *not* hit him back. You can say to Jeff, 'Stop, I don't like that!' or 'Stop, that hurts.' Then you can come and get me, and I will help you."

When Your Child Throws Things

If your child is throwing things, remove them from his hand. Then try to name the emotion. You might say, "I think you were disappointed and irritated when I said it was time to come in." Or, "It was frustrating when I said no, but you may not throw things when you're angry." Firmly let him know he may not break things or hurt others when he's angry.

When You're in the Car

It was time to go home, but three-year-old Jacob didn't want to get in his car seat. "You have a choice," his mother said. "You can either get in yourself, or I will put you in." "It's too hot," Jacob protested. So his mother put a towel in the seat. "It's too tight," he complained. So she adjusted the straps. But he still wouldn't budge. Finally she picked him up and put him in the seat. The other people in the car, including his mother, aunt, and grandmother, were held captive for the next forty-five minutes as he screamed the entire way home.

Jacob needs to hear from his mother that screaming, kicking, and flailing in a car are a danger to all. In order to clearly enforce her standard, Jacob's mom may have to step out of the car or tell him the car cannot start until he stops screaming. If they're already on the road, she may have to pull off, stop the car, and clearly state the standard, "It's not safe for me to drive when you're screaming. I will start driving again when you're quiet."

Try to name the feeling, "Leaving your friend's house makes you sad," or "Car seats are uncomfortable." Then offer him words or actions he can use. "You can say, I didn't want to leave." Or, "You can ask for someone to sit by you, but you may not scream and kick the back of my seat."

You may be thinking, Stopping is just what the child wants; or, I commute every day, I can't keep pulling off the road. But when you clearly enforce your standards, you won't have to repeatedly stop. Your words and actions will have communicated that this is not acceptable behavior. And because you have also taught your child what he's feeling and what he can do, he won't need to scream. He'll have other choices.

If screaming in the car is a constant issue for you, you'll need to dig deeper. There's a feeling or need your child is experiencing that makes riding in the car very uncomfortable to him. Perhaps he suffers from motion sickness. Maybe the sights flashing by give him a headache; perhaps the sounds of the radio and traffic hurt his ears. Do your best to soothe him, remembering that he's not trying to give you a migraine. Then take preventive actions. A headset may drown out the sounds. Medication that helps prevent motion sickness might be necessary for long car rides.

When You're in Public

Standards remain consistent no matter what the circumstances. But how you enforce those standards changes according to you, your child, other people, and the situation. When you're in public, you may have to adjust your technique while still enforcing the standards.

It was her beauty that struck me first. Tall and slender, she was casually dressed in black Levi's and a royal blue short-sleeved sweater. Her natural white-blonde hair was pulled into a loose French braid, and black pearl earrings finished the look.

Two little boys with hair and eyes to match hers followed her into the pew in front of me. Each boy clutched a Ziploc bag filled with crayons, markers, paper, and stickers. Within minutes of their arrival the younger one, probably about three, began loudly complaining. She bent down to him and, in a voice loud enough for me to hear her, firmly stated, "Shh, in church we are quiet." She helped him to open his bag and attempted to find something of interest for him, but once again his complaints reverberated through the sanctuary. Without any hesitation, she confidently scooped him up and started out of the pew. "No, Mommy!" he yelled and raised his hand as though to hit her. She reached for his hand and held it in hers. Walking to the back of the church, she stepped behind the glass wall. There I saw her bend down, talk to him, and rub his back. Five minutes later they both slid back into the pew. This time the little guy opened his bag and started to play. He continued to do so throughout the hour-long service. Each time he asked a question, his mother bent down and in a soft voice answered him. When he needed to be held or patted, she did so; there were no more shrieks or complaints.

This mom was in a very public situation with her two young boys. Her standard was clear: no shrieking in church where others' time for reflection and prayer would be interrupted. Initially she used words to enforce the limit. They didn't work. Then she calmly removed her son from the situation, letting him know that if he didn't meet the standard, she would take him out, and she did.

But what if she'd gotten to the back of the church and he didn't settle down, or she returned to the pew and he let loose again? Emotion coaches know something very important. They understand that their child is not intentionally trying to embarrass them or manipulate them. Emotion coaches know that the tears are just the "flames." The real fuel source at the moment is hidden. Maybe he was tired. Maybe he hadn't had any exercise that day and couldn't bear to remain quiet for an hour. He might have been hungry. Perhaps he was only two and the expectation of remaining quiet was more than he could handle at a stage when he was just learning the joy of words.

If this mom had to leave with him in order to enforce her standard, you might be thinking, Isn't he getting what he wants? At that moment he's getting what he *needs,* and actually, so is his mother. She is teaching him that shrieking is not acceptable behavior and that if he cannot stop himself she will stop him by removing him from the situation. Every child wants to be part of the "clan." Letting him know that he has a choice to meet certain standards or be removed is usually a strong motivation to change his behavior. But sometimes a child just can't do it. He's gone over the edge. Then it's your job to recognize this is not a teachable moment. Get him out of the situation and choose to try again another time.

Practice with Your Child

Making standards one's own takes practice. When your child has failed to meet your standard and has instead hit another child who tried to take his toy, practice with him what you want him to do. You have to wait until he's calm, but even if it's the next day, don't be afraid to role play with your child. Pretend you're the other child, and let your child practice by saying, "I'm not ready to share," or "I'm not finished with my turn yet." Rather than getting into another power struggle during your practice session, give him a choice. He can say the words himself, or he can listen while you say them. Either way, stress that next time you expect him to use those words instead of hitting.

Consequences Do Have a Place

At this point you're thinking, I've taught my child what he's feeling and what he's supposed to be doing. He knows he may not hit. He has to ask for a turn. He knows he may not throw the truck, but he can go outside and throw a ball. If he still isn't working with you, then it's time to talk about consequences. Consequences are not a matter of "You've done this; now I'm going to do this to you." Consequences reinforce what you are trying to teach. Alfie Kohn, in *Punished by Rewards,* writes, "If you're angry, odds are you're not establishing consequences, you're lashing out. Consequences are done in a matter-of-fact, nonpunitive, nonangry tone of voice. The purpose is to teach or to problem solve." When your consequences are laid out ahead of time, your child will be aware of them and know that he is making a choice.

Sue used this information when six-year-old Matthew didn't want to turn off the computer to go to school. "I know it's difficult for him to stop," she said, "so I warned him that in ten minutes he would have to turn off the computer. Then I told him when he had five minutes and asked him to find a place to stop. I also told him when he had one minute left. But when it was actually time to turn it off, he screamed and tried to hit me. I attempted to pick him up, but he hung on to the chair and refused to budge.

"Eventually I forcibly picked him up and took him to school. He screamed the entire way. I knew at that moment I was too angry and not thinking well, so I waited. When he came home, his intensity was down and so was mine, so I said to him, 'What happened today when I told you to turn off the computer is not okay. When I forewarn you and give you time to shut down, it's not all right for you to scream, or hit me, or hold on to the chair. If you do that next time, you won't be able to use the computer again for the rest of the day and the next day. Do you understand?'" she asked him. He shook his head yes.

Sue clearly communicated to her son that honoring standards is expected in their family and that there are consequences for choosing to ignore them. The consequence "fit" the situation, because using a computer is a privilege. If you aren't responsible, you lose that privilege. It also reinforced the importance of working together and being responsible.

The next day Matthew wanted to play on the computer again. "I let him," Sue said, "but before he started, I asked him, 'When it's time to turn it off are you going to hit?' 'No,' he answered. 'Are you going to scream?' 'No,' he agreed. 'Are you going to hold on to the chair?' 'No,' he replied, shaking his head."

But when it actually came time to turn off the computer, he started to scream. "Matthew," Sue stated in her most firm voice, "are you choosing to use the computer again or not?" He looked at her, shut off the machine, and got off the chair.

Effective consequences reinforce what you're trying to teach. If a child treats other children roughly, he loses the privilege to have a friend over for the day. If he shrieks in the store, he loses the opportunity to go. If he hits instead of using words, he loses the toy he was trying to protect.

Consequences are planned, laid out, and discussed. They are not thrown out in the heat of the moment. If you don't have a consequence for a particular situation, you can stop your child, deal with the situation, and still come back later to say, "What happened today is not acceptable. Next time this will be the consequence of that behavior." Older kids can help you devise the consequences. You can ask them, "What do you think should be the consequence for someone who hits others when they're angry?" Together you can come up with a recommendation that you both can accept. The most important factor is that there are no surprises. Your child knows he is making a choice.

When You Make a Mistake

Ben looked at me sheepishly. "Does the emotion coach admit he's made a mistake?" he asked honestly. He proceeded to explain that the night before he told his son, Tim, to clean up his room. Tim didn't comply. "I was exhausted, and the intimidator took over. Before I knew it, I was shouting, 'Fine, then you're not going to Ted's birthday party tomorrow!' Now I'm stuck. Ted's really going to be sad. My sister, Ted's mom, is going to be furious at me, and Tim is feeling awful. I'm sure he thinks I'm the meanest dad in the world. What do I do? I know I need to be consistent but . . ."

Emotion coaches are honest. They're trustworthy. That's how they teach kids to be trustworthy. They're willing to acknowledge their mistakes. When you get caught in the heat of the moment, forgive yourself. Use it as an opportunity to teach your child that sometimes it's important to admit mistakes and start again.

I clarified to Ben that he can go back to his son and explain that last night he was angry. He threw out a threat that wasn't really fair. But he will also want to clarify that what Tim did was not acceptable either. Instead of missing the birthday party, which would hurt lots of other people and not really teach Tim about being responsible, he would be expected to clean and vacuum his room before going to the party. And then they would need to plan together how to prevent the problem from occurring again. Does Tim need more forewarning of what jobs are expected of him? How can Tim tell his dad if he can't do his job? And what will be the consequences in the future if jobs are not completed?

It Takes Your Full Attention

The hard part of enforcing standards is that it takes your full attention. In order to be successful, you have to stop doing what you are doing. Sometimes you have to leave a situation you didn't want to leave. But in order to help your child calm himself and learn that a particular standard will be met, you have to give it 100 percent of your focus and attention. When kids know that no matter how upset they are, these behaviors will not be tolerated, they have an anchor, a firm foundation to stand on and hold on to as they face the onslaught of strong emotions.

Get a Backup

Maria slunk in her chair. "I'm listening to all of this and feeling so ineffective," she remarked. "Yesterday I told my daughter not to throw her ball in the family room. She looked right at me and kept tossing it. The twelve-year-old baby-sitter was standing there. She watched her and said, 'Natalie, you heard your mother, take the ball to the basement and bounce it there.' Natalie stopped dead in her tracks, turned around, and went downstairs. A twelve-year-old sitter was more effective than me!"

There's a Dennis the Menace cartoon where Dennis is speaking to Joey and says, "It's easy to know right from wrong, Joey. Wrong is when everybody yells!" My suspicion is that the twelve-year-old was effective because she was second. Research has shown that if one adult says what the standard is, kids may or may not get it. But if two people say what the standard is, even weeks later, the kids still know the standard and follow it. So if you want to increase your effectiveness, get a backup. Unfortunately, this is often easier said then done. Frequently, even when we are parenting with a partner, instead of backing each other up, we end up fighting, accusing each other of being too tough, or a complete pushover! When two authority figures disagree about standards, kids become confused. They don't know what they are supposed to do or not do, and as a result they stop listening to us.

"That's exactly what happened to us," Karen replied. "We were driving in the car. Micah was sitting behind me. He started kicking my seat. I told him to stop, but he didn't. I told him again, louder this time. He continued kicking. Then my husband blew up. 'You're too easy on him,' he yelled at me. 'Why don't you whack him or take away TV for the next month? You're such a pushover.' We ended up in a huge fight over my being too easy and his being too tough."

"Yeah, what do you do?" Sara wanted to know. "My husband and I have different ideas of what's acceptable and what's not. He says I'm too soft, that I let them be disrespectful. I think he's too harsh, that he doesn't listen to them."

The room erupted as parents exclaimed, "My husband's never home."

"I'm a single parent!" Getting a backup was a hot issue.

Working Together Isn't an Accident

Let me reaffirm: You can effectively enforce standards without a backup, especially if you follow your words with actions. However, having a backup will make your life much easier. If you are a single parent, consider working with your child's caregiver, teacher, a friend, a neighbor or a relative—someone whom you can check in with to help you figure out how to handle a situation and, when the situation warrants it, is able to back you up. It's even better if it's someone your child trusts enough to call herself. When my daughter was upset that I would not let her rent a hotel room, my niece was my backup. She was the one who told my daughter, "Your mother is right." If you are parenting with a partner, take advantage of the opportunity this provides you. If one partner is frequently traveling or out of the home, you, too, need to look for another adult who will say to your child, "I agree with your parent; that's the rule."

Bring Down the Intensity

The heat of the moment is not discussion time. John Gottman, author of *The Heart of Parenting*, has found in his research that when things get intense, the situation will diffuse much more quickly if one partner keeps his or her cool. When you get caught in a disagreement with your partner, pause, take a deep breath, get through the situation the best you can, and then agree to talk later when everyone is calm.

Create a Plan

Two people will never parent in exactly the same fashion, but couples can come to terms. When you find yourself in a situation where you have disagreed, ask, What were you trying to teach your child? What standard did you want to enforce? These questions can help you understand your partner's point of view and then find ways to work together.

Ben and Sabrina were in a big battle. During the past three weeks, their eighteen-month-old son, Payton, had been pulling books off the shelf. Ben was stopping him. Sabrina wasn't. As a result he just kept doing it. The standards weren't clear.

In every situation there is an *event*—an unacceptable behavior. We see that behavior and make an *interpretation*. According to our interpretation, we then decide on our *action*.

I asked Ben how he interpreted his son's pulling books off the shelf.

"To me," he said, "it's disrespectful. Books aren't toys to be tossed around. He could tear them and destroy them. I want this behavior to stop."

Sabrina looked surprised as she listened to Ben. "When Payton takes the books off the shelf, I think, 'Oh, he's being a toddler. Toddlers take things off shelves. He's curious and he's going to make a mess anyway; so what if it's the books. As a result I don't stop him.'"

When they shared their interpretation of the events, Sabrina realized that Ben wasn't just being mean. He had a valid reason for his response. With that awareness she was willing to support him and stop the dumping of the books. Their united front resulted in a clear message to Payton, and the behavior stopped.

When You Want to Change Your Standards

Sometimes as you begin to enforce your standards, you realize you haven't been the kind of role model you'd like to have been. You have a nine-year-old whose screams, stomps, and demands remind you of your own. Today is a new day. If your child is under four, you can tell him that in your family no one is going to hit or pinch, etc., anymore, no matter how angry he or she is. If your children are older, call a family meeting. Let them know that as a family you've all been doing things that you now realize are hurting one another, and that beginning today you want to make different choices. Together decide what behaviors you're going to change. Agree that everyone—adults and children—will do their best to honor the new standards.

Once you've made your decisions, allow yourselves time to practice. Learning to choose more suitable responses takes years of hard work. Both you and your child will experience backslides, but once you start your journey, you'll never slide back all the way to your starting point. That's because the research demonstrates that your actions along with your words will have actually changed your child's brain, building the links between the reactive brain and the thinking brain. Through repetition, those links become stronger, and gradually you and your child will find it easier to control your initial impulses and choose a different, more suitable response.

Standards are an essential step in learning how to stop impulsive behavior. But like the songs in the variety show, you won't want them to stand alone. You can help your child to honor those standards by teaching him to recognize his emotions while those emotions are little, and to take steps to soothe and calm himself before he's David taking on Goliath.

Coaching Tips

- Clarify your standards and teach them to your child.
- Step in and help your child stop if he cannot stop himself.
- Match your words with actions.
- Remember that shouting isn't action.
- Get someone to back you up.
- Remove your child, if necessary.
- Feel comfortable admitting your mistakes.
- Honor the standards yourself.
- Enforce the standards for all children.
- Teach your child what he *can* say, like, "I'm not ready to share," or "I'd like a turn," or "That doesn't seem fair."
- Remember that you can discipline without disconnecting.

FIVE

Stopping the Tantrums

Teaching Kids How to Soothe and Calm Themselves

"In my brain I imagine that I have cards that help me sort out my thoughts, but when I get angry it's as though the cards are all scattered and I can't find the one I need."

—*Jason, age seven*

Eight-year-old Zachery and four-year-old Ben were sitting at opposite ends of a rectangular dining room table playing "soccer." Actually their ball was a small leather triangle, and instead of kicking it they were flicking it with their fingers from one end of the table to the other. A point was earned if, with one flick, the triangle slid across the table onto the place mat on the opposite end. Bodies relaxed, voices gleeful, initially both boys were having fun. But over time Ben tired. Coordinating his "flick" was tough for a four-year-old and his "ball" started to slide off the side of the table short of the goal. He sat straighter in his chair as his body tensed and his voice rose louder and sharper as he lamented his misses. "Are you getting frustrated?" I asked him. He turned to me, startled by my question, but didn't answer. "Do you want to stop?" I continued. "No," he declared firmly. "Would you like to take a break?" I asked. He stopped and looked at me once more, but still declined my offer. That's when I said to him, "When I see you sitting up straighter in your chair and I hear your voice getting louder, it makes me think you're feeling frustrated. When people are frustrated, it helps if they take a break and then go back to their game. Do you think you'd feel better if you took a break?"

This time he sighed in relief, said, "Okay," and jumped down from his chair.

"How did you do that?" his mother gasped. "Ben's the kid who always blows up!"

Teaching kids how to recognize their emotions and to take actions to soothe and calm themselves *before* they are overpowered by those emotions is the key to stopping temper tantrums. Learning how to soothe and calm oneself is an essential life skill. Acquiring it can take years of practice. And even though we're still working on it as adults, the lessons begin in childhood, which means that when you have children, you're their teacher.

Be Your Child's Ally

Sadie had had a tough day. The new puppy had eaten her favorite hat; her father had made her wear a sweater she detested; and she'd gotten into a fight with her best friend. When her teacher told the entire class that they must all be brain-dead, she was pushed to her limit and was teetering on the edge, ready to explode. She wanted to scream. Emotions boiled inside of her, making her feel crazy, but she held it together until she got home. There she burst through the door, slammed it behind her, and threw her knapsack on the floor. What happens next depends on the adults in Sadie's life.

Imagine for a moment you're Sadie. Think about the intimidators in your life. What would they have said or done in this situation that would have pushed you right over the edge into the depths of uncontrolled emotion? When I asked this question in class, the responses were immediate.

Jessica's voice was tight. "I would have been locked in my room and not allowed to come out until I was ready to be nice or apologize. But I'd end up breaking things in my room. The intensity of my emotions always frightened me, but I never knew what to do with them."

"It's no big deal!" Joanne retorted. "My mother would always say that, and it made me furious!"

"My dad would have gotten right in my face," Peter added. "I can't stand someone crowding me when I'm angry."

"My aunt would have turned up the radio and ignored me. Or she would have said, 'I'm not talking to you if that's how you walk in this door,'" Marie offered.

And it was Tom who said, "I would have been threatened. 'Slam that door again, and you've lost TV for a month!'"

Kathy mused, "My mom wouldn't have said anything mean, but she'd try to hug me and at that point any touch or extra noise would just push me over the edge."

With each response the tension in the room built. Neck muscles tightened. Fists clenched. It was as though we were watching someone splash kerosene on a fire, the flames bursting in front of us. We could actually feel the burning sensation of the words and actions.

And then I pulled out a bag of soft, white, fluffy cotton balls. I passed one around to each person, letting them hold it and touch it to their cheek. "Imagine once again that you're Sadie," I said. "But this time I want you to think of the emotion coaches in your life, the people who responded to you with words and actions that were like cotton balls. How did they soothe you and help you to diffuse the force of the emotions? What did they say or do that made you sigh with relief?"

Peter smiled, "My mom would tell my dad to back off and give me a little space and quiet. He'd storm out, but she'd stay there. She wouldn't say a word, she wouldn't touch me, but she was there."

"A hug," Kathy added. "I loved it when my mom just held me."

"My mom would say, 'Tough day?' And then she'd just listen, letting me sort out what I was feeling," Barb responded. "She didn't even yell at me when I stormed and fussed. She didn't let me get away with swearing, but I could rant."

And it was Kim who said, "My dad could always make me laugh or distract me just long enough for me to cool down. He didn't discount me, he just let me collect myself."

The words were soothing, comforting, like the sensation of the cotton balls against our cheeks. Neck muscles relaxed, fists unfurled.

Teaching children how to soothe and calm themselves begins with us. We have to be the first to monitor the emotions, to recognize the frustration, disappointment, fear, or sadness before it escalates to fury. It's our job, while the emotions are easier to manage, to step in and teach our kids suitable responses. And as we do it we can choose words and actions that either soothe and diffuse the emotions, like the cotton balls, making it easier for our child to manage them, or we can add our intensity to theirs and say or do things that fuel those emotions. The choice is ours.

Monitoring Emotions

If you watch and listen carefully, your child is constantly demonstrating his emotions. Think about the last few days. What did your child do or say that you now realize indicated his intensity was rising?

Whether it's a whine, an inability to shift from one thing to another, a refusal to listen or come to dinner, tears that spring up over seemingly insignificant issues, forgotten homework, fights with siblings, or the slamming of doors, think about the behaviors you've seen or heard your child express *before* the full volcano erupted.

Imprint the cues in your brain; train yourself to recognize them so that the next time your child starts to whine, you will understand that your child is experiencing a strong emotion. There's a feeling or need he doesn't know how to express. Rather than saying, "I'm not going to listen to you anymore," step into that emotion with words and activities that teach her how to soothe and calm herself.

Initially, as you learn to recognize the cues, you may wonder if your child is manipulating you, especially if she throws up or complains of a stomach ache. There's a wonderful book called *Why Zebras Don't Get Ulcers, a Guide to Stress, Stress-Related Diseases and Coping* by Robert Sapolsky. In it, the author explains that when your body is on alert, ready for fight or flight, it "empties" out so that you can run faster! He encourages us to watch a National Geographic film to see what the zebras do when the lions start to chase them. They let loose, emptying their bodies so that they can flee faster. Your child's "gut" reaction is to empty his system when an emotional hijacking occurs. This isn't manipulation, it's Mother Nature giving him the energy to cope.

Does Your Child Need to Escalate to Be Heard?

Most of us have not been taught how to monitor our feelings or those of others. As a result it's very easy to miss them until they are blasting you in the face.

That's what happened to Bridget. Her voice was frantic when I answered my phone. "My son destroyed his room last night. I need help!" she cried. I listened, letting the intensity of her emotions diminish. I then asked her to tell me what happened *before* her son dumped his drawers and emptied his closet.

"It started right after school," she explained. "He came storming in off the bus. Within seconds of his arrival he complained about the snack I had prepared, shoved his sister, and even yelled at the dog. When I asked him what was wrong, he started to cry and said the older boys had bullied him on the playground. We talked about it for a while and he seemed to be better, but then I needed to prepare supper. I told him to get his homework started. He complained that he couldn't do it and demanded that I help him. I couldn't, I had dinner to make for the kids and my husband was out of town that night. After dinner I tried to get him to practice his violin, but again he refused and wanted me to be with him. I've got other kids and things to do, I can't just be there with him. Anyway, he's the oldest. He finally got through the practice and came to me where I was working in the kitchen. 'Can I sleep with my brother?' he asked. I knew if I let him they'd probably start fighting, so I said no. Then he wanted to call his dad, but our phone bill was so high last month, I told him he'd be home tomorrow and he'd just have to wait. Finally he wanted to sleep in my room. Again I said no. That's when he went to his room and tore it up." She paused, sucked in a breath, and then in almost a whisper said, "He tried, didn't he?"

Sometimes life's demands make catching the emotions when they're manageable very challenging.

Research shows that when an infant begins to cry, the cries evoke empathy in most adults; but if the cries are unheeded, they become angry and harsh, which results in an angry response.

Think about your child. If she tells you she's sad, do you hear her, or does she need to wail? If she's tired, do her droopy eyelids or lack of energy catch your attention, or does she have to fall into a heap on the floor before you respond? Can your son let you know he needs space by backing away slightly, or does he need to run around the room or out the door for you to get it? When your child demands your help, do you recognize his need to be nurtured? Do you notice your child biting her nails when she's anxious, or does she have to scream, "You can't make me go!" before you realize she's scared?

The more you know about your child's day and life, the easier it is to pick up the more subtle cues. If your child is in child care or school during the day, try to talk with the teacher or your child to find out what's happened during the day. Be observant: note his body language, tone of voice, his eyes. All of these things tell you a lot. Most important, make sure your child doesn't have to escalate in order to be heard. If your child is consistently melting down into a tantrum, it may be that you're stepping in too late. Try to catch that shift in the shoulders, the tone in the cry or voice, the need for attention, while the emotion is less intense.

Be Aware of the Stress Cycle

If you are stressed, odds are your child is, too. In a tight, controlled voice, Susan told me, "My son has been awake for thirty minutes and has already been in time-out three times. I don't want to hit him, and I don't want to start screaming, but *something* has got to give here!"

If your child wakes up ready to erupt, it means the stress hormones are surging through his body and the quantity is so great that the residue remains in his system even during sleep.

I asked Susan what stresses her family had been experiencing lately. She proceeded to tell me of a recent cross-country move, a new job for her husband with more travel than he'd ever experienced before, new schools for the kids, and a feeling of isolation having just arrived in Minnesota in the middle of January.

"How high is your intensity right now?" I asked her. "I'm over the top most of the day," she replied. "I'm barely hanging on."

When your stress levels are very high, your responses become inconsistent and unpredictable. What normally wouldn't bother you turns you into a shrieking shrew or a bellowing bull. Your child can't predict your response. As a matter of survival, he goes on alert. Be ready for fight or flight at any moment, his brain tells him, and the stress hormones flow through his body. Stress also creates neural static, so while you normally might be able to read your child's cues and help him monitor his emotions, you miss them or don't pick them up until they're smacking you in the face.

There are two simple strategies that can make monitoring your child's emotions easier.

Getting Down on Eye Level

LeeAnne's mom was dropping her off for preschool. Tears welled in her eyes and then she began to protest. "Don't leave me!" she cried, grabbing on to her mother's leg. Her mom bent down and crouched eye to eye with LeeAnn. "I think you're scared," she said. "But Georgette, your teacher, is here; she'll take care of you. Look, she's getting out the paint. You love to paint." LeeAnne sniffed. Looking at Georgette, she gave her mom's leg one more squeeze and walked into the room. Getting down to eye level forces you to stop and take note of the emotions welling in your child. By looking in his eyes you can see to his heart and clearly communicate, "I'm listening!" It tells your child this emotion is important. "I'm trying to understand. We can figure out what to do."

Allow Enough Time

Power struggles frequently erupt in the morning when we're trying to get out of the house. In our rush, we stop monitoring emotions and let things escalate. But if you allow more time, you can recognize when wanting help getting dressed isn't about trying to make you late. It's about needing to connect with you before you separate. You'll also realize that dawdling may reflect a need to play just a bit before the hectic schedule of the day begins. When you aren't rushed, you have the time to make these mini-hassles opportunities to teach your child. When he gets frustrated trying to tie his shoe or finish his lunch, you can stop and explain, "Learning to tie is difficult. Sometimes when you're practicing you get frustrated. When that happens you can take a deep breath and try again, or take a break and come back to it."

Monitoring emotions is essential to managing them. As you catch them, teach your child to stop and notice them as well. Ultimately he has to take over monitoring his own emotions. You can ask him questions like these: What is your body feeling like inside right now? Can you feel fireworks inside of you? Does your body feel like a balloon ready to burst? Give him a concrete image he can use to communicate the level of his intensity. Then he will be ready to learn what he can do to soothe and calm himself before he bursts.

Strategies That Soothe and Calm

Stress hormones triggered by emotions like disappointment and anger shoot through the bloodstream. In order to choose a more appropriate response, it's essential that kids learn what they can do to calm themselves. Initially, I'll describe for you strategies that work for most kids. If you're not certain what might help your child, read on and I'll explain how to let your child actually show you what he needs.

Physical Activity

Physical exercise, especially repetitive motions like walking, running, rocking, swinging, or bouncing, produces in the body chemicals that actually soothe and calm. When your child is working on a worksheet and you realize he's starting to get irritated, you can tell him, "When I see you starting to erase, or gritting your teeth, it makes me think you're getting irritated. What helps people to feel better when they're irritated is to stop, take a break, or do something physical." Then invite him to go for a twenty-minute bike ride, run up and down the hallway, play a fast-paced game of basketball, or take a walk. Physical exercise will soothe him and help him to stop reacting. If he doesn't want to move but you *know* he's an active kid who *needs* exercise, take him by the hand and walk with him. Afterward talk about how much better his body feels.

Sometimes a child will rock and bang his head when he is upset. If this is true of your child, I suspect he's trying to soothe himself with a repetitive physical motion. Due to safety concerns, you'll want to stop this method. But do replace it with a more suitable physical activity, like jumping rope or swinging, since your child needs motion to comfort himself.

Space

When emotions are running high, some people need space to calm themselves. If your child is upset and pulls away from you, but is not hitting at you, simply step back. Tell him you'll stay near him, but don't touch him. If he doesn't want you near, step farther away and offer to check back. If he hits at you, restrict his hand and then let go again. Recognize that when you move into his space, you actually increase his intensity. You can teach him to say respectfully, "I'm getting upset, I need space."

Adam was two and a future med-tech type. He was drawing blood samples with his teeth from any piece of anatomy that came near him: fingers, toes, arms, cheeks. It didn't matter, Adam bit. His child-care provider realized Adam bit when he got frustrated or needed space.

His teachers would tell Adam to stop, then teach him to touch gently by first touching his victim's arm softly with his hand and then gently touching his own body. Most important, they taught him, "Adam, you can say, 'I need space.' You may not bite."

They worked with Adam for several weeks, reminding him over and over to ask for space. Finally, one day they heard Elizabeth scream. Rushing to her side, Elizabeth told the teacher, 'Adam hit me!' The teacher was actually relieved—it was progress that he'd hit, not bitten. She asked Adam, "Are you ready to be gentle with Elizabeth, or do you need space?" He looked at her intensely, deep blue eyes gleaming. Snatching up his blanket, he declared in his little two-year-old voice, "I need space," and he waddled off. He pulled his blanket to a quiet space and proceeded to suck his thumb and play with trucks.

Ten minutes later his teacher asked him if he was ready to be gentle with Elizabeth. He nodded, walked over to Elizabeth, stroked her arm gently, and kissed her cheek. Elizabeth slugged him!

Teaching kids is a process that takes time and patience, but they can and do learn. Even at two Adam did ultimately stop biting and instead learned to say, "I need space," when his intensity rose.

If, in order to give your child space, you have to forcibly keep her in her room, this technique is not a helpful one for her. Remember, you're trying to teach her strategies she can use to soothe herself whether she's a toddler or an adult. Your child may be one who needs to go for a run when she's upset, or slide into a tub of soothing warm water. When you realize she's starting to lose it, pull her out of the situation, but rather than sending her to her room, help her choose a soothing, calming activity that works better for her.

Deep Breathing

There's a reason women learn deep breathing in childbirth classes. It changes the carbon dioxide levels in the body and soothes and calms. Even young children can learn the benefits of deep breathing. When your child is experiencing a strong emotion, name it, then tell him he can help himself feel better by breathing deeply. Place your child's hand on his belly button and teach him to pull his breaths from there. You can also purchase a bottle of bubbles, the kind with a wand. As your child blows, help him to notice that he has to breathe from his belly to blow the best bubbles. Even toddlers can learn to take a deep breath and cool themselves down. Older kids can use this strategy before taking an exam, going up to bat, or when they're ready to punch an irritating little sister.

Distractions

Five-year-old Brent was mad. He'd been sent to the director's office after disrupting his classroom. Initially, he simply crawled under the table and sat there, but he was only getting angrier. "This isn't working," the director told him. "Come and play Construx; that always helps you." He did and was soon feeling better. At that point she asked him, "Why didn't sitting under the table help you, but doing Construx did?" "Because when I do Construx," he explained, "I can't think about what made me so angry." Offering your child an activity that engages him completely and distracts him from his aggravation can be a very effective way to bring down intensity. It needs to be something that truly engages him so that he's not ruminating, telling himself, When I get out of here, I'm going to . . . If he has time to ruminate, it's likely that his intensity will simply rise.

Sensory Activities

Opening a window, going outside, taking a warm bath, listening to music, playing with modeling clay or Play-Doh, painting, washing dishes, playing an instrument, all are sensory activities that can soothe and calm a jumpy body. When your child starts to whine, point out to her that she's feeling distressed. Encourage her to ask for a back rub, get out the Play-Doh, take a bath, play the piano, or do something else that feeds her senses. Sensory activities calm us when we need it the most. In case you're feeling skeptical, next time you're talking on the phone and your child starts to fuss or even cry, pull a chair up to the kitchen sink and let her play in warm water while you talk. You'll be amazed!

Is This "Spoiling"?

"Excuse me," Peter declared, "but I'm finding it just a bit difficult to swallow this advice. You're telling me that when my child starts stomping and storming, I'm supposed to give him the hug he wants, or take him out for a walk, or draw a nice hot bath for him. Isn't this just giving him what he wants? Aren't I spoiling him?"

Bringing down the intensity is merely the *first* step in effective emotion coaching. Your child cannot hear you, nor can he process information, when his brain is flooded with neural static. This is not a teachable moment. His "thinking brain" is out of gear. You have to calm him down before you can work with him. Once everyone is calm, the teaching begins. It is essential that you go back and talk with your child about what he was feeling, what behaviors are unacceptable, and what you expect him to do or say the next time he experiences those emotions. You're not spoiling him when you give him that hug because you're not stopping there. You're merely opening the lines of communication so that he can hear you.

When You Don't Know What Soothes and Calms Your Child

David and Beth caught me after class. "We really don't know what soothes our child," they said. "Nothing seems to work." I agreed to visit them at their home to see if I could help. When I arrived, three-year-old Seth shouted, "Hi, Mary Kurcinka," then ran into the playroom and started to bounce on his favorite horse. Up and down he went, his head a bobbing target. I sat on the floor near his horse, asking a few questions that he cheerfully answered. I offered to show him how to make volcanoes, my way of teaching kids how to monitor their feelings. He jumped off his horse and dashed for the dining room table with me. Together we talked about emotions. I asked him to tell me something that made him happy, sad, angry, and frustrated. Each time he answered we added a dash of vinegar to the "volcano," a wineglass set on a tray. When the glass was nearly full, we tossed in a teaspoon full of soda and watched the volcano erupt. He had fun, and I had the opportunity to test his emotion vocabulary and discover whether or not he recognized the experiencing of a "volcano" inside of him. I even pulled out my cotton balls to see if he knew what soothed and calmed him.

It was all a bit much for him, and the next thing I knew he was running downstairs to the unfinished basement. There he proceeded to do flips on a mattress. Then he grabbed a bat and started hitting it against a plastic climber.

Watching him, I said to his parents, "Wow, he really knows what soothes and calms him."

"What do you mean?" they asked incredulously.

I explained that when I arrived, Seth's intensity shot up. "He immediately jumped on his horse." I said. "That's repetitive, physical motion. Then we made the volcanoes. The interaction was a bit too much for him, and his intensity went up further. He needed more space. So he ran down to the basement. There he did a few somersaults for a physical outlet, and then he started repeatedly hitting the climber with the bat. That's repetitive motion."

"That's an interesting perspective," David remarked. "I'm not sure the relatives would share it with you. He does the same thing at family gatherings. They think he's just being wild."

Create a Plan

"I can understand." I laughed. "But let's talk about what he needs. If you know that repetitive physical motion soothes him, what can he respectfully do at Grandma's?

"There is a big rocker," Beth immediately replied. "I could rock him."

"We probably could take his horse," David added. "It doesn't take up that much room."

"How could you give him space?" I asked.

"I guess we could plan to take him outside when he starts revving up," David suggested. I agreed.

"Any other physical outlets?" I asked.

"I've noticed," Beth said, "that if he's had time to run and ride his trike before we go over, he's better."

"That's probably why," I agreed. "He's walking in with a few cotton balls already in his system."

"Anything else that works that you could take with you?" I asked.

Beth picked up a stuffed duck sitting on the table. "He loves his duck, and I could take some Play-Doh. He'll play with that for a long time."

Think about your child. What does she do when she's upset? If you have an eleven-year-old who bolts from the room and refuses to talk to you, she's letting you know she needs space. You can teach her to say respectfully, "I'm very angry right now and need a break." Then let her go, knowing you'll deal with this issue later when everyone is calm. If you have a high-energy child who rolls into a frenzy of activity or starts picking on the people around her when her intensity rises, teach her to get on her Rollerblades or go for a run when she feels that volcano building inside of her. Even better, teach your older child to plan daily exercise including weight lifting, aerobics, etc., into her routine as a preventive measure. Exercise raises the level of serotonins in the body. Serotonins are nature's natural soothing agents. They serve as a cushion for later when irritations mount throughout the day, making it much easier to manage strong feelings.

Whether your child is two or fifteen, you can help him plan soothing, calming activities so that he can be successful. Think about the most challenging situation for your child, whether it's attending a family gathering, an outing, or an athletic event; getting dressed in the morning; being dropped off at day care; taking or preparing for a test; coming home from school or a birthday party. Together, create a plan of what he *can* do. Include preventive measures, activities he can do *before* a stressful situation, as well as things he can do when he starts to feel that volcano rumbling in his body.

When the Anger Turns to Rage

Annette listened carefully to the suggestions. "We've been working on this," she said, "but my granddaughter still loses it and when she does she feels so terrible afterward. She'll say, 'Grandma, I don't know what happened. I just couldn't stop myself. I hate myself!'"

If you have been working with your child, consistently enforcing your standards, monitoring emotions, and teaching him strategies of what he can do and he's still struggling to be successful, it's time to call a professional, someone who can help you identify the real fuel source behind your child's rage. While it's true that all kids get angry and experience meltdowns, if the bad days are consistently outnumbering the good ones, and your child rolls from one tantrum to the next with an intensity and fury that leave both of you hurt and frightened, it's time to get help.

A competent professional can help you and your child. Don't delay. The older your child, the more challenging it is to teach him more appropriate responses. It's never too late, but it does take more time, effort, and practice.

Savor Your Successes

Paul was elated when he walked into class the following week. "Go ahead, ask for successes," he challenged me. I laughed and waved my hand to give him the floor.

"Last Friday my wife went out with her friends," he began. "That left me home with Nicole, our two-year-old. I was beat. I'd been up since three o'clock in the morning. I planned that we'd have supper and then afterward we'd watch Barney because I knew she'd like it and it would put her to sleep.

"About five o'clock she starts whining. 'I want to watch Barney, Barney, Barney, Barney.' Normally I would have said, 'You say that one more time, and you won't watch Barney at all.' But I kept thinking, Connect, don't fuel it. I didn't want to say, 'Yes, watch it,' because if she watched it at five she'd fall asleep for fifteen minutes and then she'd be up until eleven. There was no way I'd last until then. So I told her we were going to watch Barney after we ate.

"'Barney, Barney, Barney,' she wailed.

"I thought of the list of things that soothe and calm. Distraction came to mind. I'd bought a tub of popcorn for us to eat while we watched the video, so I showed it to her and said, 'When we watch Barney later, we'll eat popcorn.'"

The other parents of two-year-olds groaned, knowing what came next.

Paul grinned sheepishly. "I know, I know," he said. "It was worth a shot, but of course when she saw the popcorn, she wanted to eat it *now*! I thought about the list again. What else could I do?" he continued.

At this point, I interjected, "That's great. You tried one thing; it didn't work, so you went on to something else. That's what we have to do—monitor and adjust."

He nodded and a big grin spread across his face. "Play-Doh!" he declared. "She loves Play-Doh, and we have twelve cans of it. Do you know how long it takes a two-year-old to carry twelve cans of Play-Doh from the shelf to the table? Long enough for me to make dinner," he replied, answering his own question.

"So she played with the Play-Doh, which calmed her down, and then we ate, which distracted her. While we were eating I told her that after dinner we'd go outside for a walk. She loves to be outside, so that was no problem. Then while we were walking, I told her that we'd go in, put on her pajamas, pop the popcorn, and watch Barney. She cooperated completely, and I had her in bed and sound asleep thirty minutes *before* her normal bedtime." His chest puffed up, and his grin spread from ear to ear.

Brita laughed with Paul. "You had it easy," she teased him. "You only had to focus on Nicole. I have three kids, and my husband's usually out of town, but I had a good night, too!" He gave her a thumbs-up, and she continued, "I've got laundry and stuff to do, too, but I thought about catching the feelings while they're small, so when the kids started moaning and groaning, I stopped everything and focused on them. I sent the eight-year-old in for a bubble bath, gave the three-year-old Play-Doh, and helped the nine-year-old with his math. Everybody calmed down, including me. Then they just started to play on their own. I made dinner, got the laundry folded, and paid the bills!"

Why were Paul and Brita successful? They stopped and focused on their kids, recognizing the opportunity to teach an essential life skill. They monitored those feelings and caught them while they were still manageable. And then they helped their children to understand those emotions and choose activities that helped them keep their cool. Through their words and actions, Paul and Brita stayed connected with their kids.

When you teach your child to monitor his emotions and give him strategies he can use to soothe and calm himself, you enhance his emotional intelligence. You empower him, allowing him to feel more in control. He doesn't have to be a victim of his strong emotions. Of course, not every day will be perfect, but gradually the good days really will start to outnumber the bad ones. Your child will learn to keep his cool when you're his ally. And it's much easier to be his ally when you can see the world from his point of view.

Coaching Tips

- Be your child's ally.
- Pick up your child's "cues" while the emotions are easier to manage.
- Teach your child what soothes and calms him.
- Plan daily exercise for your child.
- Know when to take a break.
- Make a plan.
- Know when you need to seek help.

SIX

Empathy

What Really Keeps Kids Working with You

"Empathy not only matters, it is the foundation of effective parenting."

—*John Gottman*

I was standing in line at an arts and crafts festival waiting to purchase some fresh lemonade. The sun was hot, reflecting off the asphalt, and the air heavy with humidity. Perspiration beaded on my forehead, and my T-shirt clung to my back. Gnats, drawn by my hair spray, buzzed around my head and tried to crawl in my ears. Ahead of me in line a little boy about four wailed as his mother held him. I could understand his feelings. The day was sweltering, and there really wasn't all that much for kids to do. The festival was more for adults than kids, except, that is, for one colorful toy booth filled with bright, bold wooden trucks and trains. Unfortunately, they were a bit pricey, so I wasn't surprised when I realized the little boy had wanted one, but his mother had said no. Now the tears streamed down his face.

As we stood in line, his wails made the heat and our thirst even less easy to bear. But I was still surprised when I overheard the woman in line behind me mutter, "A good smack on the butt would fix that kid!"

I was troubled by the woman's words. Later, I asked my friend Marietta, "Why would someone want to hit a child for feeling sad?"

"Because, Mary," my friend replied, "she didn't hear his sadness."

The Importance of Sensitive Responses

In order to be open to your guidance your child has to be able to *trust* that you will hear his feelings such as sadness, disappointment, frustration, hunger, fear, and fatigue and respond in a warm predictable way that is in tune with his signals. A sense of trust is the foundation of all healthy relationships. If your child cannot trust you, he cannot allow you to have power over him.

Dr. Martha Farrel Erickson, Director of the Minnesota Children, Youth and Family Consortium, says, "There are two key messages a child needs to receive in order to develop a sense of trust:

1. I can count on my caregiver to respond sensitively to my needs.
2. I am worthy of attention."

All children, not just infants, need to hear these messages repeatedly in order to build healthy relationships.

Trust implies a firm belief and confidence in the honesty, integrity, reliability, and justice of another person. A synonym for trust is faith. Faith is unquestioning belief, as in, Children usually have faith in their parents. Faith is loyalty and allegiance. Your child must be able to believe in you, trust in you, and have faith in you in order to be willing to work with you.

Responding Empathetically

In order to respond sensitively to your child and build that sense of trust between you, you have to be able to consider the world from his point of view. Being able to project yourself into your child's emotions in order to understand him better is called empathy, and empathy is at the root of effective parenting.

But sometimes it's tough to be a sensitive, empathetic caregiver when your child's sadness, frustration, or fear is all mixed up with sweeping accusations, hitting, screeching, and refusals to cooperate. That's what happened to Julie.

Tuesdays were always tough. It was the one and only morning that Julie taught a piano lesson before school. She wasn't even sure how she'd gotten into giving lessons, but she had. It was a way to add to their monthly income and still be home with her kids. The family needed the extra cash, but today it hardly seemed worth it. She was rushing. Heat crawled up her neck, flushing her face. She blew her bangs off her forehead and tried to think of what she needed to do before she started the piano lesson.

It was then she remembered she'd promised to help her seven-year-old, Hannah, with her math problems. There had been two soccer games the night before, and her husband had been out of town. By the time they got to homework Hannah was too tired to do it, so Julie had sent her to bed.

So there she was trying to put on a dash of makeup and help Hannah at the same time, when she heard six-year-old Todd start down the hall. She stuck her head out the door and hurriedly demanded, "Get dressed. We're running late." Entering her room, he screamed, "No, I won't. You can't make me!" Then he lunged for his sister, nearly knocking her down and pulling her paper from her grasp. Julie screamed, "What are you doing?" as Todd crumpled into a sobbing heap on the floor.

If you were Julie, what would be your first reaction? What would you think? What would you be feeling?

When I asked these questions in class, Kathy chuckled and asked, "Has she been to class or not?"

"Let's imagine she hasn't been to class," I replied. "Or she has been and it's a really bad day and she can't remember a thing she has learned."

Lisa chewed on her lip, nodding. "One of 'those' days," she said, emphasizing "those" as she immediately identified with Julie. "If it was me," she continued, "I'd be ticked off. All she did was ask him to get dressed and he started throwing a fit. He was being a little jerk."

Tom agreed, "A blatant case of defiance."

"An uncooperative brat who's deliberately trying to disrupt the morning and irritate his mother," Kathy added.

"On a bad day," Tara replied, "I'd think he was being sassy and obstinate and that he didn't understand my needs at all."

Their interpretations of the event were honest and straightforward. On the surface this power struggle did look like a blatant case of insubordination. And when it looks that way, it's easy to get caught thinking about what warning or consequence you should mete out. The key is to stop yourself and pause long enough to look below the surface to your child's feelings and needs. Or, as Stephen Covey writes in *Seven Habits of Highly Successful People*, "Seek first to understand and then to be understood."

If Your Child's Behaviors Were Words

Let's go back and look at Todd's actions. He shrieked, lunged at his sister, crumpled to the floor, and sobbed. If his behaviors were words, what do you think he would be trying to tell you?

In class we brainstormed all the possibilities we could think of. He might be sad, disappointed, angry, in need of attention, or jealous. We couldn't know for sure. We'd have to start with our best guess. The point here is that when you look at your child's behaviors as messages rather than as efforts to "get you," it's easier to pause, stay calm, and choose a more sensitive response.

A Child's Point of View

Fortunately in this scenario, Todd was old enough to tell us about his point of view. Let me go through the scenario again, this time as it's presented from a child's perspective.

Six-year-old Todd awoke. He missed his dad terribly. Until the new job his dad never traveled, but now he did. It was his dad who used to get him up and help him get dressed for school, and now he often had to do it by himself. The soccer game last night was fun, but his knees hurt where he'd fallen and he was so tired. He knew he was supposed to be getting up to get dressed, but he just couldn't do it. Maybe this morning his mother would help him. He headed toward her room.

The intensity of his disappointment slapped him like an open hand when his mother leaned out and directed him to hurry and get dressed. And when he saw that his sister was already there taking her attention, he couldn't seem to stop himself. He lunged and grabbed for her paper as the blood rushed to his hands and then he went down shrieking.

Todd was overwhelmed by his emotions. On the surface he struck out and shouted words of defiance, but beneath the surface Todd was surprised and deeply disappointed. He missed his dad terribly. He needed his mom's attention and help. He didn't know that this was a morning piano lesson day. He didn't know what to do with his powerful emotions, and as a result his instincts took over and he reacted.

It's true, we do have to enforce our standards and stop Todd from hurting his sister. We can also expect cooperation, but in order to get there we have to remember that every difficult situation involves at least two people, each with individual feelings, needs, and plans. Attempting to view each situation not only from your own perspective but your child's as well lays the foundation for a sense of trust. Your child knows that you will listen and try your best to understand his point of view, and he will be more willing to work with you because of that knowledge.

Consider Your Child

Think about a difficult situation you've recently experienced with your child. What were you feeling? Now put yourself in your child's shoes. What do you think she was feeling?

In class, Jenna told us about her experience. "I was rushing, trying to get three kids out the door. The oldest was trying to tell me something, but I never stopped to really listen. He got very upset and refused to move. When he first started to throw a fit, I felt panic. I needed to get out that door! But somehow I understood he was really frustrated that I wasn't listening. Normally I would have just yelled at him, but I paused and then I bent down to his level and listened while he told me again. This time I actually stopped doing everything else so I heard him. I hugged him and two minutes later we went out the door. When I dropped him off, he was smiling and we both had a great day. If I hadn't stopped and connected, he still would have been upset when I picked him up."

It was Jenna's empathetic response that won her cooperation in this situation. She was able to think not only about her own feelings and needs but her child's as well. Can you put yourself in your child's shoes? Can you imagine your child's behavior as words and try your best to understand what he's trying to say?

Listening to the Cues

Listening to those behaviors, your child's "cues," isn't always easy. Imagine for a moment that you are trying to get yourself and your child out the door. You're running late. Your child runs out to the car. Suddenly he stumbles, landing on the driveway. His pants are torn, his knee is bleeding. What do you say or do?

In class, the responses sounded like this.

"How stressed am I?" Kathy wants to know. The others laughed and then added their own responses. "I'd get a cold cloth," Brenda offers.

"Yeah, I'd wash it out and give him a hug," Barb adds.

"Get a Band-Aid," Tom replies. "And if it really is hurting, I'd probably carry him back to the car."

"I'd ask what happened," Peter added.

Now imagine that you're trying to get out the door and you're late. This time your child drops in the doorway screaming, "I don't want to go! I want to stay home with you!" How do you respond?

"Get in the car!" Peter pretends to bellow.

Kathy, her voice hard, adds, "The easy way or the hard way."

And Tom admits, "I'd probably threaten to leave him and start the car."

It's often easier to put ourselves in our child's shoes when there's a physical problem rather than an emotional one. But the reality is emotional wounds need those Band-Aids as much as the bloody ones.

Think about your child. How does she tell you she's tired or hungry? What does your son do when he's jealous or frustrated? Can you "feel" his or her emotion?

When Worries and "Advice" Get in the Way

Sadie slid down in her chair, tucking her head low into her shoulders. She glanced away when I turned to look at her. "This doesn't feel comfortable to you?" I asked. Shaking her head, she replied, "If I give my son a hug when he's refusing to go out the door, my mother would have a fit. She'd say I was just spoiling him and that he was manipulating me."

Sadie isn't alone. When we stop to listen to our kids, especially in public places, worries about what others might be thinking about us or our child can fuel our anger and limit our ability to "hear" our kids and respond empathetically.

So on the board I wrote: The worries and advice that make me stop listening to my child.

Peter was the first to answer. "In our house, I was never allowed to express my feelings. My father's attitude was that kids were to be seen and not heard. What I felt didn't matter. So when my kids want to know what I'm making for dinner or what I'm doing, I find myself telling them they don't need to know. Then sending them away."

"When I respond to my son, I can actually hear my father's voice saying, 'Give him an inch and he'll take a mile,'" Ben responded. "My gut twists. I want to listen to my son, but I worry that I'm asking for it if I do."

Kate let out a breath. "Last year," she began, "Tom started feeling sick in the morning. Then he refused to go to school. I couldn't figure out what was going on. Then I found out his teacher had called him a liar. I know he didn't lie because other kids told me he hadn't. The woman really was mean and nasty. I talked to the principal. He warned me that I was making too much of it. That Tom was manipulating me, and I was turning him into a 'mama's boy.' I spent a week of sleepless nights worrying about it, but after another morning of listening to Tom's sobs I moved him to a different school. The morning fights ended and he began to excel in school. Later, I learned they fired the teacher at his old school. Thank goodness I listened to Tom."

"Don't start a bad habit," Sherry interjected. "After we moved, our four-year-old daughter wanted to come into our bed in the middle of the night and sleep with us. I knew the sounds in the house were different. I woke up, too, but I was afraid that if I let her come into our bed for a few nights, I'd spend the next two years trying to get her out."

"I hear advice all the time with the baby," Karen offered, and began listing out the most common comments she'd heard. "Let him cry. You just spoil him if you jump every time. Get him on a schedule. Is that kid nursing again? You're holding him too much. I can smell him over here he's getting so spoiled."

As they talked I listed all of their comments on the board:

Kids are to be seen and not heard.	You're spoiling him.
Give an inch, he'll take a mile.	Don't start a bad habit.
You're turning him into a mama's boy.	Let him cry.
Get him on a schedule.	You're holding him too much.
You're giving in.	Who's in control here?
At his age he should . . .	Don't you have him . . . yet?
You're teaching him that if he cries he'll get what he wants.	Are you letting him eat again? It hasn't been three hours.
You coddle her too much.	Don't let him leave the table until he's eaten everything on his plate.
Just ignore him.	He's only a kid. He doesn't know what's good for him.

I read the list out loud. "How do these remarks make you feel?"

"I doubt myself," Sherry replied. "I pull back and get defensive,"

Peter added. Karen shook her head in agreement and said, "It makes me wishy-washy. If I'm feeling rested and confident, I do what I feel is best, but if I'm feeling worn out and a failure, I shut down. I think I drive my son crazy."

Evaluate the Advice You Receive

The reality is that our child-rearing lore is full of advice that discourages us from connecting with our kids. That's why it's important to take a look at this advice and do a little detective work. Where did this advice come from? Why was it offered in the first place? Is it really something that you want to continue to use as your guide?

For example, power struggles over food are common occurrences. I've found it fascinating to ask grandparents and great-grandparents why they've offered specific pieces of advice about food and eating habits. Inevitably they tell me tales of growing up during the Depression or suffering the deprivations of war. Many grew up in large families where food was not always plentiful. The advice to clean their plates fit the era and the situation. But today childhood obesity is one of the leading health concerns for children. And food proportions served in restaurants have increased dramatically as our society has focused more on *big*. Fifteen years ago you couldn't even buy a thirty-two-ounce glass of soft drink, much less try to drink one. It isn't that this advice was wrong for its times, it just doesn't fit today.

The theories of rewards and punishments have also strongly influenced advice for parents. Daniel Goleman, in his book *Emotional Intelligence*, tells us that B. F. Skinner, a major player in the development of the behaviorist theory, as it is known, couldn't figure out how to measure emotions, so he said they didn't influence behavior. Today the research on emotional intelligence demonstrates emotions significantly impact our actions.

Additionally the attachment research conducted during the last thirty years has clearly demonstrated that children who are consistently listened to and responded to are actually less demanding and easier to care for than those who are dismissed or ignored. That's why if you pick up a baby when he cries, he'll ultimately cry less. And if you respond to his needs, he'll ultimately be more willing to wait for you, because he trusts you.

William Sears, M.D., assistant professor of pediatrics at the University of Southern California, found in his research that kids whose needs have been sensitively and empathetically responded to:

- were more likely to want to please the adults in their lives.
- were more cooperative.
- had more self-control.
- were less stressed.

These research findings were not available to our parents or grand-parents. So look carefully at the advice you are receiving. Find out where it's coming from. Has it been handed down in your family without anyone thinking about the emotional costs? You can decide which messages to keep, revise, or eliminate.

It's also important to trust your gut. *You* know your child better than anyone else. Sometimes that puts you in an "odd man out" situation. Others are telling you that you're coddling your child, but deep in your gut you know you are meeting the needs of your child. Trust yourself, and your child will be able to trust you.

What's Your Gut Reaction to Emotions?

Tara sighed. "All right," she said. "I'm okay when my child feels sad or disappointed. I don't have any problem comforting him. But when it comes to anger, I can't handle it."

Think about the emotions your child has experienced this week. Write them down. Read through the list carefully. It's in our families that we learn how to express emotions and how to respond to them. So imagine you are a child once again. When you experienced each of these emotions, how did the adults in your life respond?

In class we brainstormed a quick list. And then we listed the adults' reactions. Here's what the list looked like.

Emotion	The Intimidator Responses That Disconnect	The Emotion Coach Responses That Connect
Worry	Don't be a baby. Just ignore it. There's nothing to be scared of—worried about. Be a big boy. It's just a . . . Get real.	I'm here for you. How can I help you? What do you need in order to feel safe?
Excitement	Settle down. Cut it out.	You're excited. Your body is full of energy. Let's go run outside.
Anger	Don't be naughty. You shouldn't be angry. You're wrong. Don't talk back to me. Anger met with anger. Doles out punishments. Ignores or teases.	That makes you angry. I won't let you hurt your brother, but you can tell him you don't like that. I'm listening. I'm trying to understand. Say it this way.
Curiosity	Don't break it. That's not for kids. Don't touch it, it's mine. That's enough. Get out of there!	You like to find out how things work. I can help you try. This is how you can look at it and keep it safe.
Sadness	Get over it. What's the matter with you? Don't be so sensitive. Stop feeling sorry for yourself. You should be grateful.	I'm sorry. I know that was important to you. It's okay to feel disappointed. Would you like a hug?

Jealousy	Life isn't fair.	It's hard to have to share.
	Cut it out.	Sometimes being a big
	Go to your room.	sister is frustrating.
	Don't treat your brother	You can ask for my
	that way.	attention and I will
		give it to you.
Frustration	Stop making a fuss.	This is hard work.
	Just do it.	You can take a break.
	Settle down.	Would you like help?
	If you'd just do it,	
	you'd be done.	
	Here, I'll do it!	
	It's your own fault.	

As you review the list you might realize that it's easy for you to be an emotion coach when your child is frustrated or worried. It's when he's angry or sad that it's tough for you because in your family these emotions were ignored or considered unacceptable. That's what happened to Megan.

"When Jake is upset, I'll tell him, 'I'm so sorry. I know you're sad.' But he's so persistent. He just keeps crying. Then I want to yell, 'That's enough!' Reviewing the list, I realize that's what my parents said to me when I was sad. No wonder it's so hard for me to deal with him if he doesn't stop. I don't know what to do next. I don't have any role models."

Look at the messages you received from your family about emotions. When you were afraid, did you receive comfort and support? Or did your parent become angry and walk away? How are you responding to your child's fears today?

Old messages can stop us from responding sensitively to our child. Our goal is to hear our child's emotions and respond in a way that matches it. Empathy opens your child to your guidance.

So take a look. When your child starts to cry, is your first reaction to comfort him? Or are his tears a trigger, setting off fears that he's out to get you or trying to control you? When your child is sad, can you hear that sadness and meet his need for comfort, or do you hear only a demand to fix it? Emotion coaches recognize emotions as opportunities for connecting and for teaching.

What About Me?

You might be feeling exhausted right now, thinking, What about me? Can't I expect that my child will respect the fact I'm tired? I work all day, or I go to school. I'm a single parent, or I've got other kids and my partner travels. What about my needs?

If you are feeling resentment as you respond to your child's emotions, and if it feels as though you are expending too much energy, stop and monitor your own feelings. Do you need to take steps for reducing your stress? Do you need to try to find support for yourself? If your child is young, you are the giver. You can't expect a two-year-old to meet your needs. You have to be the adult and seek support from other adults. Sherry found this to be true for herself.

"When my daughter was disappointed, I did listen and soothe, but then I ran out of gas. I couldn't do it anymore. When my husband came home, I simply said, 'She's yours,' and walked away."

Knowing when to ask for help is important. When you need a break, accept it and seek support. Both you and your child will stand a much better chance of getting what you need.

If your child is older, you can begin to expect the relationship to be more reciprocal. Your child can learn to be empathetic, too, and you can help her by listening to her feelings and needs and then working with her to address yours as well. Brita found a solution that worked for both her and her daughter.

Brita is a single parent with two children, a seven-year-old daughter and a five-month-old son. On a night when she was terribly exhausted, her daughter Lindsey refused to go to bed, pleading, "Sit with me. Rub my back. Stay with me, I'm scared." Brita did sit with her for a few minutes and allowed her to keep all the lights on, but then she needed to attend to the baby. She couldn't stay. And she was physically exhausted.

"I know you want to be near Mommy right now," she told her daughter. "And I know you are feeling scared. But I cannot stay. What else would make you feel safe and comfortable?"

"Can I sleep in your bed?" Lindsey asked. Her mother agreed, saying, "Yes, until I come to bed. Then I will carry you into your own bed, and you'll need to sleep there." Lindsey agreed to the arrangement and crawled into her mother's bed. She felt safe and secure there. The smell of her mother's perfume and shampoo on the sheets comforted her, and she snuggled deep down into them, falling asleep quickly. As a result, her mother got the break she desperately needed so that when it was time to move Lindsey she had the energy it took to carry Lindsey to her own room, rub her back a few minutes, and let her fall back to sleep.

It doesn't always work this well. The younger or more stressed your child, the less she will be able to be reciprocal. There are times when, as the parent, you have to be the adult, pause, take a deep breath, and comfort your child.

If you struggle to "hear your child's sadness," you may not have received the nurturing you needed as a child. If the demands make you angry, consider how your attempts to get attention were met or not met. Talking with a competent counselor may help you to understand your own emotions so that you can meet your child's needs and build that connection.

Savor the Successes

Empathy begins with being able to put yourself in your child's shoes and to understand that his actions are like words. He's showing you how he feels. He doesn't know how to tell you—yet. Your empathetic response allows him to feel comfortable working with you and to be open to your guidance as you teach him more respectful and suitable actions and words he can use. But sometimes responding empathetically isn't easy.

Kate had taken her son Brad to preschool. It was Monday morning after a hectic weekend with little sleep. Brad was tired. Going to school was a new experience that required a great deal of energy from him.

Kate wasn't sure he had the stamina to get him through the morning, but she thought for the sake of consistency it was important to give it a try. Walking down the hallway to school, they ran into a neighbor who greeted Brad. Brad's response was to hide behind his mother's leg. He refused to speak. When the neighbor asked him, "Aren't you going to say hello?" he pulled back farther. Initially Kate was embarrassed, but then she realized that Brad was feeling overwhelmed. She let him stay behind her leg, said a few things to the neighbor, and moved toward the classroom. At the door Brad balked, declaring, "I don't want to go to school," before he burst into tears. The teacher reached out to take his hand and lead him in, but Brad bolted, running down the hallway, then stopping two doors down still screaming. "Just leave," the teacher advised his mother. "We'll handle it. He's just being stubborn."

Kate felt very uncomfortable with the teacher's advice. She realized his actions did look like defiance on the surface, but beneath the surface he was tired, apprehensive, and stressed out.

"I think I need to stay a few minutes," she responded, mustering all of her guts to do it. The teacher huffed under her breath before turning back to the room, firmly convinced that Kate was coddling Brad and that he'd be just fine if she'd leave.

"I might have left," Kate told me, "but he was crying so hard I couldn't believe that leaving him would work. He was really upset. He wasn't just being stubborn. He needed me, and everything in my heart was telling me to stay."

So she did. She talked quietly to Brad, letting him know that she understood it was hard to go to school today because he was tired. When the wails began to ease, she invited him to come and draw a picture with her. He did and ten minutes later when she kissed him good-bye, he was contentedly playing.

Kate listened to Brad's cues and despite the teacher's advice she responded empathetically. Brad was telling her with his words and his actions he was very upset. She listened and as a result was able to help him to be successful. Later, she could talk with him, helping him to understand his emotions and teaching him more respectful and suitable ways for handling a situation like this the *next* time he felt that way.

From his mom's example, Brad learned the importance of being empathetic and trustworthy. It's a lesson that will be even more important when he reaches adolescence.

Stepping into the shoes of another person and experiencing the world from his point of view is often difficult. Knowing there are "threads" you can follow through the complex weave of emotions can make that task much easier.

Coaching Tips

- Put yourself in your child's shoes.
- Listen carefully.
- Get down on your child's level and look into his eyes.
- Pick up your child's "emotional cues."
- Let your child know he is worthy of your attention.
- Check old "messages" that stop you from listening to your child.
- Respond empathetically and sensitively.
- Enjoy your new point of view!

PART THREE

Caring: Knowing Yourself and Your Child

SEVEN

What Fuels Power Struggles

Identifying the Real Feelings and Needs

"She really isn't out to get me!"

—A father

Every morning I feed the wild turkeys and birds that come to my backyard. The pileated woodpecker greets me with his chuckle, and I can always count on a whistle from the cardinal. Blue jays dive-bomb the squirrels as they fight for the corn. The connection with nature is a morning ritual I treasure, but there's one aggravation—I have a great difficulty opening the bag of birdseed!

When I first started feeding the birds, I'd buy a forty-pound bag of feed. The top was sewn shut, and opening it was a major task. Sometimes I'd cut the stitches on the back side one after the other, but it took forever. Other times, if I was lucky, I'd pick one stitch and a row would unravel in my hand. My frustration ended the day I finally discovered that there's a thread that runs through the row of stitching. If you grab that thread, the entire row will unravel and you can simply lift the top off the bag and reach inside for the seed.

When it comes to figuring out what your child is feeling, it can seem like you're facing that row of stitches. It's frustrating and irritating. Where are you supposed to start? There are so many possibilities. How can you begin to uncover the real feelings and needs that lie below the surface? The task can seem overwhelming.

What I've learned over the years is that, like my bag of birdseed, power struggles have threads that weave through them. By grabbing those threads you can get inside the power struggles and unravel the mysteries of the emotions that fuel them. These threads run throughout power struggles, sometimes alone and other times in combination. When you recognize them and understand them, they can provide for you an opening to the emotions you and your child may be experiencing. Identifying those feelings helps you select the strategies that can prevent those power struggles. Fortunately, there are just four major "threads" you need to remember. They are:

- Temperament/type—Your child's first and most natural reaction to the world around her.
- Stress—The environmental factors in your child's life that may be causing distress.
- Medical factors—Physiological issues that may impact your child's behavior
- Normal development—Developmental tasks your child is working on.

Let me show you how I used these four threads to help Ben's mother understand his feelings and solve a very challenging power struggle.

Searching for the Real Feelings and Needs

Ben was five and urinating on the carpet. "Nothing is working!" his mother exclaimed in dismay to me one day. "He's been toilet trained for two and half years. This is *not* an accident. It's deliberate. I've tried making him clean it up. I've told him to stop doing it. I've taken away privileges and sent him to time-out, but it's continuing. Soon our carpet will be ruined! How can we stop him?"

I needed more information before I could respond, and I started asking questions. "When does he urinate on the floor?" "If I'm busy, he'll go in the other room and let loose," his mother responded. "Are you a persistent person?" I asked, wanting to know about her *temperament* as well as Ben's. She smiled slightly and affirmed that both she and Ben were very persistent people who didn't give up when they had a goal to accomplish. This was important for me to know.

I absorbed this information and moved in a different direction. "Have you had him examined by a doctor? Could there be a medical reason for this behavior?"

She shook her head. "No, there's not a *medical* reason. I've had him checked."

My mind raced. "When did the wetting begin?" "Right after he entered kindergarten this fall," she answered. "But he doesn't do it at school, only at home." Starting school can be a very *stressful* experience for kids. I filed this information in my brain.

Finally, I inquired, "Is Ben your biological or adoptive son?" "He's adopted," she answered, looking at me inquisitively. "He came to us as a newborn but still had a very hard time. The first year of his life I had to carry him constantly. He had terrible colic, soothing him was nearly impossible."

Her response provided insights about his *development,* and I replied, "I think your son is asking, 'Am I worthy of attention?' A key stage of development for all kids is knowing I am worthy of attention and I can count on my caregiver to respond sensitively to me. During infancy, Ben's colic left him in pain. Despite your very best efforts, you couldn't always comfort him. As a result, he may now have to work a little harder to feel secure. Add the stress of starting school, and you've got a child urinating on the floor. Ben's a very persistent kid. He's going to get the attention he needs, and wetting is a very effective strategy. It requires that you stop what you're doing and notice him. Obviously it is not a socially acceptable strategy, so you'll need to help him understand what he's feeling and teach him a more suitable response."

"And how am I supposed to do that?" she questioned.

"Go home," I advised her, "and tell Ben, 'I think you're trying to tell me you need attention when you urinate on the floor. You are always worthy of my attention. You don't have to urinate on the floor to get it. Next time you want my attention, come to me and say, "Mom, I need attention," and I will give it to you.' "

I also suggested that since he was only five years old and that both of them were very persistent people who hated to stop what they were doing, they may need to make a cardboard heart or some other concrete reminder that clearly communicated "I need attention." This symbol would cue both of them that it was time to stop and connect.

Ben's mother was more than a bit skeptical about my advice, but at this point she was open to trying anything. That's why she was incredulous when it worked and the wetting stopped. Sure there were a few accidents—like the time she was gone and Ben needed her attention. Then we had to teach him how to call her on her cell phone, or write her a note, but over the next two months the wetting stopped, replaced by the words "I need attention" and warm hugs.

The Threads in Power Struggles

I'm not a psychic. I can't read kids' minds, and you don't need to be able to either. You, too, can learn to use the four major "threads" as your guides to the feelings and needs that fuel the power struggles. Let me define for you more clearly what each of these "threads" looks like.

1. Temperament and Type: What's Your Child's Typical Style?

The latest research demonstrates that children are born with a preferred style, called "their temperament." There are seven temperament traits that I'll explore with you. They describe how persistent, easily frustrated, sensitive, active, regular, or intense you are, and how you cope with transitions and new situations. Recognizing these traits helps you to understand your child's reactions and identify the emotions that are fueling the behavior. Because temperament is part of who you are, it is often a source of the emotions that fuel ongoing power struggles with your child. If, for example, your child is temperamentally persistent, you might have realized since infancy that this child was more committed to her goals. While other parents easily distracted their toddlers from an electrical outlet, yours kept going back to touch it. Seven years later your persistent child is still sticking to her goals, no matter what the task or issue. Or perhaps when your son was young, you appreciated how easily he could be distracted from the electrical outlet or a particular toy. He wasn't persistent, and it made your life easier, but now that he's in school you wish you could get him to stick to something!

Understanding temperament helps you to step into your child's shoes and experience the world as he does. You become wise to the emotions he is experiencing because you can see the threads that weave through the experiences of his day.

2. Medical Factors: Is Your Child Experiencing Any Physical Symptoms That Would Indicate a Medical Problem?

Medical factors can wreak havoc on a child's behavior. He may not be listening to you because he doesn't hear you, or he may hear you but is unable to process what you've said. Perhaps he is experiencing anxiety or attention deficit disorder. If there is a family history of depression, allergies, or learning disabilities, you might be worried that your child's behavior is tied to these issues. You're not certain what's going on, but you know that despite your best efforts the struggles have continued and you're feeling discouraged, worried about the future, and exhausted. If a medical issue is affecting your child's behavior, it's essential that it be identified in order for you to understand the real fuel source behind your child's behavior.

3. Stress: What Has Changed? Are Your Child's Reactions Unusual for Her?

Perhaps the power struggles with your child are new. You may have rolled along quite smoothly until the move, the divorce, the new teacher, baby, or child-care center. Suddenly the angel who used to live with you has been replaced by a monster you barely recognize. The child who easily went to bed now screams, "Don't leave me!" as the routines you've so carefully created fall apart. And the kid who could do everything won't do anything, even refusing to walk upstairs alone or make his own lunch.

Kids are not immune to stress, and it can affect their behavior tremendously. When your child is stressed, his body is on alert for fight or flight. It's much easier to trigger him. Even the slightest demand may push him over the edge. Recognizing stress symptoms can help you identify your child's fears and anxieties and know when to adjust for a child who is feeling overwhelmed.

4. Development: Does Your Child's Behavior Reflect Typical Emotional Development?

Perhaps the struggles didn't start until your child hit a certain age. It might have been on her second birthday when she first looked you in the eye, smiled, and then did exactly what you asked her not to do. Or maybe the downward spiral began after her fourth or fifth birthday when she declared, "You're not my boss!" Perhaps it wasn't until she turned ten or twelve that your suggestions were suddenly infuriating, and every discussion turned into an argumentative negotiation session.

Every child goes through predictable stages of emotional development. Power struggles often begin when kids move into new stages of development or when stress causes them to backslide. That's why those power struggles tied to development often appear around a child's birthday or half birthday.

When you know what's "normal" development for your child at his age, it's easier to understand the new emotions he's working on and devise more effective strategies.

The Real Fuel Sources

Your thirteen-year-old who is failing to perform in school isn't just being lazy. Your eight-year-old who is calling you every name in the book isn't deliberately trying to reduce you to tears. In order to effectively prevent these and other challenging behaviors, you have to stop and ask, Why is this occurring? What's the *real* feeling and need that is fueling the flames of misbehavior?

The four common threads—temperament, medical factors, stress, and developmental stages—can guide you to the real emotions behind your child's behavior. You can use these threads to unravel the mysteries of power struggles with much greater ease. And once you've identified the feelings, you'll know what strategies to choose. If your child is refusing to eat breakfast in the morning because temperamentally he's sensitive to smells and finds the odor of the banana you're eating nauseating, you'll win his cooperation by eating your banana after he's left for school. But if he's not eating because fear of the bully on the school bus has his stomach rolling, eating your banana later won't help a bit. In order to win his cooperation, you'll have to soothe and calm him and find ways to help him stop the bully. Emotions—that's what these power struggles are all about. The better we understand what we and our kids are feeling, the easier it is to respond sensitively and find effective ways to work together. So let's begin by grabbing the thread that takes us to the emotions tied to temperament.

EIGHT

Why You Blow

Understanding Your Temperament

"Each of us is born into the world as someone; we spend the rest of our lives trying to find out who."

—Dean Hamer and
Peter Copeland,
Living with Our Genes

Lori didn't get it. Weren't all kids supposed to like to go to the park? But when she suggested an outing to her son, David, he'd burst into tears. He didn't want to go. Or if they were out running errands and she suggested that they stop at the library to get a few books, David would insist on going home. Lori loved spontaneity, but with David everything had to be planned or he had a fit. David had reacted this way practically since day one. They were so different, and it was often those differences that got them into power struggles.

Sometimes, however, it was their similarities that got them into trouble. Take the grocery store. Lori hated buying groceries. The smells in the deli department repulsed her, and the lighting was awful. Before she finished shopping, her head would be pounding from the glare. Moving through the store, she seemed to "suck in" the moods of the other shop-

pers. She knew immediately who was in a big hurry, and when someone was impatient with a clerk, she felt their words like a physical blow.
It took every ounce of self-control she had to make it through the grocery store, and, inevitably, that's when David would lose it because he,
too, went nuts with all of the stimulation. She'd try to stay calm and
soothe him, but if he continued to be upset more than a few minutes,
she'd find herself ready to scream as well.

And David didn't give up. Of course, neither did she. They could
debate for fifteen minutes whether there was enough syrup on the pan-
cakes or not, and by then the breakfast was cold. If he asked for a cookie
at eight A.M. and she told him he had to wait for lunch, he'd ask her
again fifty times if it was lunchtime yet.

In her dreams, before David was born, she'd imagined sitting quietly
by the fire reading to her child. In reality she spent hours chasing after
him. He didn't want to be cuddled, except at bedtime for just a few minutes. Even then he often jumped in and out of her lap. The power
struggles seemed inevitable. What she liked, he hated. What bothered
her set him off, too. And no matter what, they both wanted to *win*!

Understanding Temperament

Variety, that's what makes life rich, and when it comes to people,
Mother Nature has provided us with a smorgasbord of styles. The challenge is to enjoy those styles rather than let them pull us into power
struggles.

Even at birth infants express their individuality. Some babies vigorously cycle their arms and legs and let loose with lusty, expressive cries.
Others watch intently, slowly cycling their limbs or letting out a mere
whimper to indicate their discomfort.

Thanks to new studies on identical twins reared apart, genetics
research, molecular biology, and neuroscience, we now know that
many of our personality traits are the result of our genetic makeup.
Researchers call this inborn dimension of personality "temperament."

Temperament describes how we perceive the world and our first and
most natural responses to those perceptions. It includes how sensitive

we are, how we react to new things, our activity level, intensity, persistence, and how easily we shift from one thing to another.

Temperament is not learned from parents or books, nor can the traits be easily controlled through willpower alone. A baby doesn't decide to be active or inactive, she just is. A child doesn't choose to feel the seam in his sock and experience shivers down his spine as a result, it just happens. It's part of who he is, just like the color of his eyes or hair.

Why Temperament Is Important

Temperament is one of the real fuel sources that may lie behind the power struggles you are experiencing with your child. By his very nature, your child may be slow to adapt. If that's true, the odds are that he hates surprises of any kind, and shifting from one thing to another is so distressing that you end up in power struggles. If you're quick to adapt, you don't even notice transitions. Switching plans or stopping one thing and starting another is no big deal. Your child's reaction to change can drive you nuts. Or, if you're like Lori and David, and you're both highly sensitive, then lights, smells, sounds, and emotions can easily overwhelm you, making it that much tougher to keep your cool and stay connected.

By understanding temperament you will be better able to:

- understand the emotions you and your child are experiencing, like the deep distress experienced by a slow-to-adapt child when she has to leave her friend's house, or the exhaustion of the active child who's been forced to sit still for long periods of time.
- predict potential "triggers"—the things that set both of you off.
- select the most effective strategies to help you to eliminate or minimize those triggers.
- maximize the pleasures and reduce the frustrations of working with your child.
- reduce the number of visits to your pediatrician because you understand what's "normal" for your child and therefore worry less.

Finally, understanding temperament allows you to stop trying to change your child or yourself and instead find ways to work together and enjoy each other more.

Understanding Yourself Helps You Understand Your Child

In order to understand the feelings that your child's temperament generates, you need to understand your own temperament. When you can identify your feelings it's much easier to work with your child's.

Take a look at the following temperament chart. Each trait is placed on a continuum—from a mild reaction to a strong reaction or from high to low. Read through the statements listed for each side of the continuum. Think about your first and most natural reactions. Which responses fit you best?

Remember there are no right or wrong answers. Our goal is to gain an understanding of ourselves so we can maximize our abilities as emotion coaches.

---

1. Persistence

If you are involved in a task and your child interrupts or asks for your help, do you find it frustrating and difficult to stop?
If your child tells you no, do you want to push harder for compliance?

easily stop or let go   difficult to stop or let go
don't mind interruptions   want to finish

1	2	3	4	5
low persistence				high persistence

If you're a highly persistent adult, it's likely that you are committed to your goals! You not only like to concentrate on a task, you *need* an opportunity to finish something. When you're focused on your kids, they have your full attention. Nothing can deter you, and when it comes to holding the line and setting a limit, you're confident and willing to do battle.

But there are challenges to this trait as well. When you're focused on a task, those numerous interruptions from children can drive you wild. As your intensity rises, your ability to be a nurturing emotion coach declines. And because you are focused, you might miss cues that the kids' tempers are escalating, or you might try to hold them off with "just a minute" until they're at an explosive level. Sometimes when you're highly persistent, it's tough to be as flexible as the job of taking care of children requires, especially when your child is as persistent as you are and has plans that conflict with yours. It can also be difficult for you to tell yourself you've done a good job when it feels like you haven't gotten a thing done all day.

In order to stay out of power struggles, it's essential that you clearly look at the expectations you've established. Can you truly accomplish all the tasks you've set out for yourself and still nurture your children? Or do you need to cross a few items off the list, remembering that spending time with your kids is essential to your relationship?

My husband realized early in our marriage that he had wed a *very* persistent woman. So every Saturday he'd ask me to make a list of all I wanted to accomplish. Inevitably he'd glance at the list and ask, "Where's the fun?" I'd have to add an interesting activity so that later I could enjoy crossing it off the list! Then he'd read my list out loud, not mocking me, just reading it, and as I listened to him, I always realized I would need a month to accomplish my "to do" list, not a single day. Persistent adults need to remember that spending time with children *counts*! It is an accomplishment. We just have to wait a long time for the final product to evolve.

Recognize, too, that interruptions trigger you. The next time your child asks for help or interrupts you, stop yourself from automatically saying "no" or "not now," which will set both of you off. Instead, stop, pause, breath deeply, and decide: Can you work together? Could you set a timer? Is there a creative solution you can both accept, or is it time to stop and refocus your attention?

If you really do need to accomplish a task and have young children, find another adult who can care for your children and let you concentrate. Everyone will benefit.

When you understand your persistence and the emotions that are generated by it, it's much easier to stay out of those power struggles!

If you're an adult who finds yourself on the low persistence end of the continuum, it's probably easier for you to let go of a task and shift attention to your kids. The frequent demands of young children really don't bother you, and as a result, you can usually stay calm as you deal with the interruptions. If need be, you can stop and start a task ten times. And while you do sometimes feel guilty about the things that don't' get finished, you usually do complete the important things. Give yourself credit for your ability to let go.

Your biggest challenge is holding the line. It isn't that you're a pushover. You're not. You just don't like dealing with the drawn-out battles.

Think carefully about your standards so that when the time comes to hold the line, you're ready and you can do so without feeling guilty. And don't forget to get your backup, that other adult who will support you when you truly need to hold the line.

2. Sensitivity

How aware are you of sights, sounds, smells, textures, or tastes? Do slight noises irritate you? Do you notice subtle changes in temperature or lighting?

not easily irritated by smells, tastes, or noises, etc.; enjoy amusement parks, fairs, etc.	easily irritated by noises, lighting in a crowded store; a child crying or asking questions in a loud voice can drive you wild
can wear clothing of any texture; rarely notice changes in temperature	very particular about how clothing "feels"

1	2	3	4	5
low sensitivity				high sensitivity

If you are a highly sensitive individual, any sensation—a child's shriek, glaring lights, a noxious smell, or a slight rattle—has the potential to trigger you. All five senses may not pose a challenge for you; for instance, you might be bothered by lights but not smells. But whatever offends you does so profoundly. It's nearly impossible to listen to your child or to soothe him when the tags in the back of your shirt are driving you wild or the person next to you is cracking her gum. Add to all the potential sensorial assaults a mess like dirty dishes sitting on the counter, or toys, shoes, and clothes all over the floor, and your intensity rises very quickly. It's likely, however, that all your life you've been told you were too sensitive or picky. So now when you start to feel bombarded, too hot, or irritated by the noises around you, you get frustrated with yourself for being so sensitive. As a result you may be tempted to ignore or deny your feelings until they overwhelm you.

And if your child is also sensitive, you may feel as though your worst nightmare is occurring. You don't want her to suffer the ridicule you've experienced, and do your best to stop her from being *so* sensitive.

If you're a highly sensitive adult, be kind to yourself. Try to remember that high stimulation levels make it very difficult for you to focus on your child. It takes all of your energy simply to manage your own strong reactions to the stimuli. In order to keep your cool and stay connected with your child, monitor stimulation levels and their effects on you closely. Shop during "quiet times" whenever possible. Know when to take a break; leave that family gathering, shopping center, or amusement park *before* you're at your limit. Don't let tags, harsh lighting. or weird noises send you over the edge and pull you into fights with your kids that would never happen if you weren't on stimulation overload.

Most important, appreciate your sensitivity and your child's. Celebrate it! You are who you are. Recognize that it is your sensitivity that allows you to monitor the emotions of others. Few things escape your notice. You sense a problem and can potentially take preventive actions *before* things get out of hand—if you'll respect and listen to your keen senses.

There's little that will trigger individuals on the low end of the sensitivity continuum. It's easy for you to stay calm and focused even in the most stimulating of environments. You can breeze through a shopping mall for hours without feeling barraged.

But sometimes it's hard to be patient or to understand why the texture of meat makes your child gag, or why his shoes have to be tied just right. And you really do not appreciate it when your sensitive child keeps turning down your radio or television because for her it's too loud.

Your greatest challenge is to become aware of sensory stimuli that may trigger your child. Because you do not personally experience the sensations your highly sensitive child does, it may be easy for you to miss potential triggers. Even when you don't sense it, try to affirm your child's feeling. Believe her and be willing to leave when she tells you that she cannot eat in a restaurant because the smell of jalepeños is making her sick. Understand, too, that going to the movie theater, amusement park, or mall is an endurance test, not fun for highly sensitive people. Your sensitive child is not trying to control you when she asks to go home. Truly, the stimuli are driving her wild. And do cut the tags out of her clothing, find socks without seams and buy jackets that feel right. She's not just trying to make you late in the morning; the sensations these articles of clothing create can be unbearable to her.

3. Adaptability

How easily do you shift from one activity or idea to another? How easily do you adapt to surprises or changes in your schedule?

easily cope with surprises	drained by the constant surprises you face as a parent
easily change plans	find changing plans distressful
shift easily from one activity to another	find shifting from one activity to another difficult
adjust quickly to changes in routine or schedule	find changes in your routine or plans frustrating

1	2	3	4	5
adapts quickly				adapts slowly

"Organized" and "predictable" are words that describe individuals who need time to adapt. It's easy for you to establish routines and rituals for morning and bedtime because you like them. If you know what's expected ahead of time, you have little problem adapting to changes. You're less likely to overprogram your child or fill your day with multiple transitions because you don't like them. You like to stay focused and enjoy the moment.

If you're a parent who's slow to adapt, you'll get pulled into power struggles when you're rushed or surprised. Unexpected meetings or appointments, a child who needs pants ironed or a diaper changed at the last minute, or discovering that the car is out of gas are all things that can upset you. You don't want to change your plans and may attempt to stick to your schedule no matter what! That means that when the school nurse calls and says your child needs to be checked for pinkeye today, you schedule the appointment on top of the normal piano lessons, rather than canceling the lessons for that week. The result is chaos, kids and parents on overload shrieking as you all dash down the highway.

Slow adaptability can also pull you into power struggles when your child changes the plans on you. You pick her up from school expecting to have a quiet evening at home. She wants to go swimming at the YMCA with her friends. Rather than shift, your first reaction may be to say no, and the fight begins.

If you are a slow-to-adapt parent, know that the more prepared you are, the easier it is for you to be an emotion coach. Set your clock ten minutes ahead so you always have a few extra minutes and won't feel so rushed. Talk with your kids about the day ahead. Share your plans and ask them theirs. Teach your children to avoid surprising you by asking the night *before* for your help ironing an outfit or packing a lunch. The more surprises you can avoid, the more energy you'll have to be there for your child. When you are surprised, remember to try to pause, take a deep breath, and tell yourself, "This is a transition. Transitions are tough on me, but I can choose how I wish to respond to this one," then decide if you need to shift and how you want to do it.

If you're a quick-to-adapt individual, you don't have trouble with transitions. You are very flexible and are comfortable switching plans at the last minute. You might even find the changes invigorating. You're triggered by those who need more time to adapt. You'd like them to hurry! Your first challenge is to recognize transitions. You probably don't think about them, or how many are in your day, because they don't bother you. Try to remember and accept that others, especially your slow-to-adapt child, can't transition as quickly as you can. She needs you to avoid surprising her. If you will simply forewarn her, and give her time to shift, you can win her cooperation and eliminate the power struggles tied to transitions. When you are quick to adapt, your child may also need a more predictable schedule than you're providing. Remember, too, that spontaneity and surprises are not fun for family members who need time to adapt!

4. Intensity
How strong are your emotional reactions?

other people often don't know how you feel	experience every emotion deeply and powerfully
other people describe you as calm	others often try to convince you to let go of an emotion
you are not easily triggered by the intensity of others	easily triggered by the intensity of others
not easily frustrated	easily frustrated

1	2	3	4	5
mild reactions				intense reactions

Intense individuals parent with gusto! You are passionate and zestful, and everything you do is done with intensity. Your child is loved deeply. When you've hit your limit it's clear—you yell loudly. And there's no stopping you when you're on a roll. You get a lot done!

You realize you've always had strong reactions and because of that you have to work harder not to get triggered. Preventive actions are essential. Regular exercise, frequent breaks, and calming activities need to be part of your day in order to help you manage those strong reactions. Monitor your stress level and your child's because when she gets upset, she can fuel your emotions as well. Because you are intense, your child may never know when you're going to "blow." Remembering to pause helps you to continue listening to your child rather than shutting down or striking out.

If you're not an intense individual, you have a much easier time keeping your cool. It takes a lot to get you going. You tend to be calm. Your challenge is to let your child know you are excited about, happy for, or proud of him. Your demeanor may also be so calm that he doesn't realize when you are angry or really serious about a limit. You have to remember to be passionate about your standards!

---

5. Regularity
How regular are your eating, sleeping, and eliminating patterns?

need to eat at specific times	easily skip meals or change mealtimes
wake at the same time even if you went to bed later than usual	easily adapt bed- or wake times
find shifting time zones or to daylight savings time challenging	easily adjust to changes in time zones
find it difficult to understand how some people can skip meals	find it difficult to understand why some people *have* to eat at specific times

1	2	3	4	5
very regular individual			irregular individual	

Regularity is an interesting trait because there are lots of triggers on both ends of the continuum. If you are an irregular individual, you're flexible. You probably find travel very easy. Switching time zones doesn't faze you. You can sleep and eat, or you can wait if necessary. You realize that being woken at night doesn't exhaust you as much as others. And when a child goes two days without a bowel movement, you don't panic. You know this can be normal.

Your challenge is to work with your regular child. It can be very difficult to understand why he can't wait thirty minutes for a meal and demands to eat something *now*! Or why he can't delay his bedtime or nap to fit with your schedule for the day. It's the schedules and the structure they provide for your child that can frustrate you the most. Since you are most comfortable eating when you're hungry, mealtimes may be unpredictable in your home. And because you're not necessarily hungry even if you're preparing meals, you might not sit down with your child, which may lead to a kid trying desperately to get your full attention. Bedtimes may vary widely as well, resulting in struggles with a child who isn't tired or one who's overtired because his body is never quite sure when sleep time is. While you'll never feel comfortable with the schedules your regular counterparts naturally fall into, you may need to provide your child with a bit more structure. Plan times in the day when your family can connect and be predictable enough so that your child can work with you.

If you're a regular person, you're more predictable. It's likely that your routines are well established. Your child knows exactly when the family will be eating and when nap time and bedtime are. That routine can create a sense of security for him.

But it's frustrating to you when you've got that irregular child who doesn't fall easily into your pattern. You are triggered when your routines are disrupted. You need to eat at set times; otherwise, you get a headache or feel sick. It's hard to be an effective emotion coach when you're feeling faint. If your child hasn't fallen asleep by the prescribed time, you're exhausted. Hanging on for another hour can be torture. And a child who skips meals or has irregular bowel movements can make you hyperventilate. It's hard to understand how this could happen since you can't imagine skipping a meal, or having irregular bowel movements.

When we understand our own and our child's pattern, we are better able to stay out of power struggles!

---

6. Activity Level
How active are you?

find it easy to sit still for long periods of time	find sitting for a long period of time exhausting
quiet and quiescent	frequently fidget
can take or leave exercise	*need* regular exercise
like to stroll	prefer to move briskly

1	2	3	4	5
low activity level				high activity level

Highly active parents have the energy to keep up with busy kids. You enjoy physical activities with your kids and stop frequently when traveling because you need the release as much as the kids do. You understand the strain of sitting quietly through a long religious service and are even relieved to step outside with the high-energy toddler.

It's inactivity that can trigger you. You have a tough time understanding the child who would rather sit than go play ball with you. You're happiest when you're busy and on the move. A "to do" list often runs through your head, especially if you're persistent, too. That's why sitting quietly with a sick child or reading three bedtime stories can be taxing for you. It's hard for you to stop and totally focus on your child. And when forced to sit for long periods of time, like on a plane or in a restaurant with slow service, your intensity rises right along with your high-energy child's.

Low-activity parents tend to be more laid back. You can sit for hours reading, rocking, and holding your child. You don't have to be busy to be happy. Your child knows you're there to come and cuddle with.

Your challenge is to keep up with active kids. They can wear you out! Rest times during the day are just as important to you as to your child. You need some downtime! Trying to keep up with a busy kid and one who refuses to sit quietly in a restaurant can be frustrating. Why, you wonder, can't she sit still like me?

---

7. First Reaction
What's your first reaction to any new idea, place, thing, or activity?

quickly decide what you like and dislike	need time to decide whether you really like something or not
jump at the chance to try new things	prefer a more cautious approach to anything new
like to quickly join in an activity	prefer to watch before joining in
usually agree to let your child try something new	tend to initially say no when your child wants to try something new

1	2	3	4	5
jumps in			cautious first reaction	

Those who have a cautious first reaction like to think before they respond. You're not intrusive. You don't push your child into new things without thinking it through first. You can understand your child's need to watch before jumping into things and are willing to give him a second chance. Once you're comfortable you're just fine and others enjoy your company. But new situations make you uncomfortable. You can actually feel the adrenaline surging through your system when faced with something new. Initially you have to deal with your own reaction, which makes you less available to your child. You also know you've had to cope with a cautious first reaction all of your life and hate to see your child having to work through it, too. If your parents didn't understand your caution, they may not have been able to teach you the steps to take in order for you to feel comfortable entering new situations. Now you're trying to teach your child, and you're not quite sure how. Or you might be tempted to send a strong message—"DON'T be this way!"—and push, even though you know it's not what your child needs. And because you are cautious, when your child asks you if she can do something, it's likely that your first answer will be no!

If you can appreciate your caution and allow yourself and your child to move slowly into new situations, you'll have more energy available for your child. And a simple response, like "Let me think about that," can prevent you from unwittingly falling into struggles with the kid who doesn't take no for an answer.

Bold individuals feel comfortable exploring and discovering because they do not experience strong physiological reactions in new situations. When John Glenn first blasted into space, his pulse rate rose only to 110 beats per minute, in contrast to the 170 of a colleague on an earlier flight. Unlike their more cautious counterparts, people who enjoy jumping into things don't get that rush of hormones that tells them to watch out. As a result, living with them is often an adventure. They like to expose their children to new experiences and opportunities.

If you prefer to jump into new situations quickly, your challenge is to understand that new situations can be stressful, especially if your child is a cautious kid. He needs time to watch before joining an activity, which might be difficult for you to accept. And because you're comfortable jumping in, you may move in so quickly that your child, especially a preadolescent or teen, may find your actions a bit invasive. Teach yourself to pause before you jump in to solve a problem for your child. And think about how many *new* things you're signing your child up for. These actions can reduce the number of power struggles you experience.

Putting It All Together

Now you have it, a picture of your first and most natural reactions. When you understand your own style and your own emotions, it's much easier for you to recognize your triggers, understand those of your child, and find ways to work together. So go back and total your score. Remember there isn't a good or bad temperament. Every style has its strengths and weaknesses.

Total Score		
7–14	15–25	26–35
low-key	spunky	spirited
emotion coach	emotion coach	emotion coach

Once you've figured out your total score, select your top two "trigger traits." These are the traits that are most important for you to honor. The emotions and needs tied to these traits must be recognized and met on a daily basis; otherwise, you get drained and pulled into power struggles.

For example, if you know that you are very persistent, it is critical that you plan in your day the opportunity to *finish* something. You will be more able to deal with the interruptions of your day if you can tell yourself you've accomplished at least one thing.

Or perhaps you know you are very regular. Plan your meals, don't skip them. If you skip a meal, two hours later you're likely to lose your cool. Managing intensity in the face of hunger is a huge effort for people who are temperamentally regular.

If you're intense and active, plan exercise into your day. It's when you know yourself, understand, and accept *your* emotions and needs that you can open yourself to your child's.

Savor Your Successes

Jessica honored her temperament and turned a potential blowup into a successful outing. "I took my four-year-old and his friend to the Children's Museum," she told us in class one day. "I take them there frequently, but on this day it was jammed. There must have been five hundred school-age kids, many of them almost too old to be there. The noise and commotion were overwhelming. When we did the temperament charts, I had selected sensitivity as my trigger trait, but I didn't figure out that I wasn't going to make it through the museum until we were on the top floor. That's when I realized my intensity was rising. I couldn't focus on the kids. I knew I needed to leave while I still had the energy to negotiate with them, get them three floors down, walk them across the parking lot, and get them into the car. I remember thinking, How can we get out of this building without a major fight?

"I told the kids, 'It's getting close to lunch and it's too crowded in here. It's time to leave.' We have a rule that if you leave a place nicely you can go back. Alex knows that, but he's persistent, and that day it didn't work. He had a list of three things he wanted to do. 'Let's try two things,' I said, 'and then leave.' We did that, but he couldn't contain his energy. It was too much to expect him to say, 'Okay, let's go,' but I could tell I was running out of energy to cope. We just had to go. Finally, in desperation, I pulled a coupon out of my purse for a toy store. I said, 'Oh look, we have a ticket to the toy store. We have to go there right now before it closes. I'll bring you back here next week when it's quieter.' It worked. I felt all right about it because I didn't bribe him. I simply gave him information about the next thing that we would do, knowing that it would interest him. We often visit the toy store, but we don't buy. He knows that. We did get out of that building and our fun outing didn't disintegrate into a power struggle because I recognized my trigger and made the decision to get out while I could still hold it together."

Understanding and working with your temperament allows you to identify your emotions and manage them. Often you've been told you should be able to block the noise or skip the meal. It's when you listen to yourself, accept your style, and work with it that you can truly connect not only with your child but with the essence of who you are as well.

Coaching Tips

- Know yourself.
- Accept yourself.
- Honor your feelings.
- Identify your triggers.
- Celebrate the person who lives inside of you.
- Learn more about temperament.
- Read my book *Raising Your Spirited Child*.
- Listen to your feelings.
- Exercise.
- If you're persistent, allow yourself to finish something every day.
- If you're sensitive, avoid overstimulating situations.
- If you don't like surprises, plan your day.

NINE

Why Your Child Loses It

Understanding Your Child's Temperament

"Children are to be discovered as well as shaped."

—*Dean Hamer,*
Living with Our Genes

When Amanda was a child, the annual visit to the haunted house was a family tradition she eagerly looked forward to. Now she was thrilled that her daughter, six-year-old Corrine, was finally old enough to enjoy it with her.

Ever since she could remember, Corrine had heard the stories of the haunted house and had eagerly awaited participating in the adventure. But now that she was here, in the dark depths of the house, she wasn't sure if she liked all of the scary puppets and noises. She held her mother's hand firmly. Ahead of them rose a slimy, bumpy monster on the wall. A deep voice invited passersby to touch it. Her mother reached out to it and squealed with delight as the monster grazed her fingertips.

Corrine held back. Her mother invited her toward it. Corrine yanked away. People behind them pressed forward, reaching to run their hands over the monster's back. They giggled and shrieked as the sensations teased their fingertips. Again, Amanda tried to convince Corrine to touch the monster, but once more she pulled back. It was then that the crowd pushed them into the room of mirrors, followed by the row of coffins with tops that creaked on rusty hinges and headless corpses that rose from their depths.

Finally they stepped out into the light. Corrine sighed with relief. Her mother noticed it and turned to look at her. Corrine wasn't smiling. Instead, she appeared to be in deep thought. When Amanda asked Corrine what she was thinking about, she simply shrugged. In the past, Amanda would have brushed past the moment and left, but that was before she knew about temperament. Now she stopped, looked carefully at Corrine, and said, "I think you're trying to figure out how you feel right now. The look on your face makes me wonder if something upset you?" Corrine nodded.

Knowing that a trigger trait for Corrine was her cautious first reaction, Amanda continued. "New situations often make you feel uncomfortable. Was there something you're thinking you wanted to do that you didn't do because you weren't comfortable yet?" Once again Corrine nodded. "Do you want to go back inside?" Amanda guessed. Tears rolled from the corner of Corrine's eyes. "I wanted to touch the wall," she whispered. "I'll take you back and stay right with you, if you want to try," Amanda offered. And so they did. It wasn't as crowded now. Corrine could stand and scrutinize the wall carefully.

While Corrine stood there, her mother brushed her own hand across the wall and described the sensations to Corrine. "It looks wet, but it's not. It's just shiny," she explained. "You'd think it was cold, but it's actually warm. The texture is rough, but it doesn't hurt my fingers." And then she stopped and waited. Cautiously, Corrine reached out. Quickly she touched one finger to the wall. A huge smile shattered the frown on her face and then she giggled as she placed her entire hand on the wall.

Amanda grinned with pure joy and relief. Before she learned about temperament she hadn't understood Corrine's reactions and too many outings had turned into huge power struggles. Now things were different.

Goodness of Fit

When you understand your own temperament and your child's, you can more accurately identify the feelings and needs each of you is experiencing. You're not left in the dark, mystified as to what's happening. You *know* yourself and your child, and it's that knowledge that allows you to identify the emotions and choose a more sensitive and effective response. Ultimately, it's what Drs. Stella Chess and Alex Thomas call a "goodness of fit" between parent and child that allows you to understand each other's experiences and work with the emotions they garner. And as you make that connection, a whole new world can open up to you, one in which your differences actually enrich your life instead of irritate you.

Your Child's Temperament Profile

Since you already have a profile of your own temperament, let's create one for your child so that you can compare the two. When you and your child share similar temperament traits, the things that trigger your child may also trigger you. You need to know that. But when your child is very different from you, she may be experiencing emotions and sensations that you are not aware of. You need to know that, too. An understanding of temperament allows you to predict your child's typical reaction and makes it much easier for you to monitor your child's emotions and pick up cues *before* he loses it.

As you review the traits, remember there isn't a right or wrong answer, a good or a bad trait. You simply want to create a profile of your child's first and most natural response.

- Review the following statements for each of the seven temperament traits. Think about your child's typical reactions. Which responses fit him or her best?

- Remember there are no right or wrong answers. Every trait has its strengths and weaknesses. Our goal is to gain an understanding of the child who has come to live with you.

---

1. Persistence: How persistent is your child?

easily lets go of an idea or stops an activity	finds it difficult to let go of an idea or activity that he has chosen
willing to accept no for an answer	refuses to accept no for an answer
easily goes along with your plans	wakes up with plans of his own
stops working on a puzzle if a piece doesn't fit	continues working on a puzzle until she figures out how a piece fits
accepts your first answer to his question	asks the same question over and over if she doesn't like your answer

1	2	3	4	5
low persistence, quickly stops			high persistence, pushes to continue	

High Persistence

Even at a very young age, highly persistent kids wake up with plans for things they want to accomplish. That's why it's essential that you ask them what their plans are. Was your child expecting to have Cheerios or Special K for breakfast? Find out, and you may avoid a power struggle at the breakfast table. Persistent children also need to finish the things that are important to them. Telling them they have three more minutes doesn't work. You have to ask them, "What do you need to complete before you're ready to stop?" If it is not humanly possible to accomplish what they want to do in the time available, work with them, explaining that there isn't enough time to read ten more pages, then helping them find a stopping point by saying something like, "I know you'd like to read ten more pages, but there isn't enough time right now. You're a good problem solver, where could you stop now, and how could you finish later?" If necessary, offer suggestions like, "Let's stop at the end of the page, mark it, and then finish the rest of it in the car."

Persistence is a great asset and is a key indicator of future success. But in the "raw" it also leads to kids who refuse to stop and "lock in." That's why you'll want to teach your persistent child to problem solve with you and to focus on what you *can* let them do.

Emotion Coaching in Action

Thirteen-year-old Rachel is a highly persistent youth and so is her mother, Kim. On a recent fall day, Kim wanted Rachel to mow the lawn. Rachel had just sat down at the piano and was trying to figure out a new piece. As a persistent person herself, Kim wanted the lawn finished now! Of course, highly persistent Rachel wanted to practice now! It could have been a huge power struggle, but it wasn't. After learning about temperament, Kim recognized that Rachel wasn't just procrastinating or being difficult. The reality was that both of them were temperamentally very persistent and had tasks they wanted to accomplish. It wasn't easy for Kim to pause, but she did, took a deep breath, then sat down with Rachel to discuss a timeline for the day. It was ten A.M. and at two P.M. Rachel had a volleyball practice. Kim knew Rachel would be too tired after the practice to mow, so she told Rachel the lawn needed to be completed before she left. The limits were set, but within those limits there was room to work together. They estimated that it would take an hour to mow and an hour to eat lunch, shower, and get dressed for practice. That left two hours. Rachel agreed that she would practice the piano for one hour, mow, clean up, and if there was time remaining, she could choose to practice the piano again. Satisfied with their plan, Kim left Rachel alone to pursue her music. She didn't keep coming back to ask when Rachel was going to stop or to yell at her for not stopping. Instead Kim set the timer on the stove for fifty-five minutes. When it went off, she told Rachel she had five minutes to finish up. Rachel did and went out to mow.

But what if she hadn't stopped? you might ask. When you understand how frustrating it is for a highly persistent child to not accomplish her goals and respectfully include her in the planning of a timeline, the odds are she'll work with you. If she doesn't, it's time to enforce the standard that in your family you do work together and you do keep your promises. If she still doesn't stop, consequences may be needed, but ninety-nine times out of a hundred, you'll never have to use them if you've worked with her needs and respected her feelings.

In order to understand and affirm the emotions they are experiencing, highly persistent kids *need* to hear words and phrases like:

- It's frustrating when you have to stop working before you're finished or someone tells you no.
- What are your plans for the day? weekend? holiday?
- This is what Mom needs you to do today; please include it in your plans.
- You are a good problem solver. We can work together.
- I'm trying to understand what is important to you.
- We will save it, and you can finish later.
- How many more before you can stop?

Low Persistence

Kids who are low in persistence are easy to distract from the task at hand. This is great when they are doing something you don't want them to do. It's challenging when you want them to finish something.

Research shows that kids who are low in persistence will persevere when working in groups, near the teacher, or with a friend or tutor. The interaction motivates them and helps them to keep going. As a result they tend to seek the help and support of others and learn to be great team players. Because they often rely on their parents for that help and support, they may experience significant separation anxiety when Mom or Dad isn't available.

Kids who are low in persistence need you to teach them strategies to soothe and calm themselves when they get frustrated. They also need help creating timelines that allow them the breaks they need to manage their frustration and complete a project.

Emotion Coaching in Action

Two-year-old Aaron was a charming, low-persistence kid who was also intense. When the piece didn't fit into his puzzle or the vinyl character wouldn't stick to the window, he immediately quit trying or he'd yell for help. His mother would jump to assist him. But he was becoming a bit of a tyrant, demanding help *now* every time he encountered an obstacle.

After attending my class, his mom took a different approach. The next time a puzzle piece didn't fit and Aaron shrieked, she went to him but didn't rush to fix the problem. Instead she named his feelings. "It's frustrating when you can't get the puzzle piece to fit. When you're frustrated, you want help, but look," she showed him, "if you turn it this way you can get it in yourself." Aaron stopped, shocked by his mother's response. This wasn't normal. He fussed and pulled at her hand. She rubbed his back for a moment to calm him. "It's hard," she continued, "but you can do it. Try again," she encouraged. This time Aaron twisted the piece and slid it into place. He beamed with satisfaction. His mom clapped.

If you've got a low-persistence child, support him with your presence but don't be too quick to take over for him. Instead, point out something small that he can accomplish and let the joy of that achievement spur him on.

Kids who are low in persistence need to hear words and phrases like:

- It's exhausting when you have to work on a difficult task by yourself.
- It's frustrating when you can't finish something easily or quickly.

- Take a break and come back to the task in fifteen minutes.
- When you need help, you can say, "Please help me."

---

2. Sensitivity: How sensitive is your child to sights, sounds, smells, textures, and emotions?

doesn't seem to notice the mood of others	very affected by other people's emotions, especially anger or sadness
not sensitive to pain	very sensitive to pain
rarely complains about textures	refuses to wear clothing that doesn't feel right
doesn't notice noises, smells, etc.	complains about loud noises, smells, or lights that are too bright
eats anything	aware of subtle spices, textures, or smells of food
rarely complains about temperature	is always hot or cold

1	2	3	4	5
usually not sensitive			very sensitive	

High Sensitivity

In cross-cultural studies of temperament the "ideal" child in Italy is highly sensitive, aware of sights, sounds, textures, tastes, and emotions. In the United States kids who are disturbed by sirens, glaring lights, strange odors, clutter, and chaos are often told they are too sensitive. Understanding and appreciating your child's keen sensitivity is the key to working together. She needs you to believe her when she tells you that getting her hair cut hurts, or that the seams in her socks or the tags in her shirt are driving her wild. Help her to find ways to eliminate or reduce the sensations that bother her the most.

Emotion Coaching in Action

January in Minnesota is fun if you like to ski, snowshoe, or ice fish, but for Molly and her family these endeavors were not exciting. Instead they planned a vacation to Mexico where their days could be spent walking on sandy beaches instead of through snowdrifts. Their "ideal" outing almost turned into a nightmare when four-year-old Tim refused to walk in the sand. Tim said that the sand hurt his feet and stuck between his toes. Fortunately, Molly had completed a temperament profile on Tim and knew he was a 5+ when it came to sensitivity. She believed him, carried him across the sand, and laid out a big blanket for him to play on. Over the week, he gradually started venturing from the blanket. When he did and the sand stuck between his toes, she showed him how to brush it off. By the last day he was walking across the sand, not gleefully, but competently, explaining to his mother, "If it bothers me, I can stop and brush it off."

Kids who are highly sensitive need words and phrases like:

- You are very aware of noise, light, colors, etc.
- I think the stimulation in here is bothering you.
- When you hear another child cry, you feel sad too.
- You can feel bumps and seams that I can't feel.
- I believe you.
- How food tastes and smells is very important to you.
- I'm not hot, but you can take off your sweatshirt if you are.

Low Sensitivity

Kids who are not as sensitive to the environment around them are not as easily triggered. Lights, smells, sounds, tastes, textures don't bother them. You can usually get them dressed or serve a new food without much hassle. Their challenge may be in recognizing their own body's cues and in understanding the needs of others. Hunger or fatigue may sneak up on them, unless you teach them to stop and take note of how their body is feeling. And they may need your help to understand that even though they find the carnival rides exhilarating, others may find the experience overwhelming and want to leave.

Kids who experience low sensitivity need words and phrases like:

- Noises, lights, etc., don't bother you, but sometimes they do irritate others.
- It's important to stop and check the stimulation level. How does your body feel?

---

3. Adaptability: How quickly does your child adapt to changes in routines, intrusions, surprises, or transitions?

getting up and dressed usually isn't difficult	getting up and dressed is a hassle every morning
easily falls asleep at night	takes a long time to settle down and fall asleep at night
enjoys suprises	hates surprises
easily switches from one activity to another	switching from one activity to another is a monumental task
able to leave a friend's home	very difficult to leave a friend's home without a battle
enjoys schedule changes on field-trip days	finds the change in schedule on field-trip days upsetting
easily switches clothing from one season to the next	giving up summer's shorts for fall's long pants is a major endeavor

1	2	3	4	5
adapts quickly			adapts slowly	

Adapts Slowly

Kids who adapt slowly make us aware of our overcommitments. These are the kids who let us know that ten transitions in a day are a bit much. It's distressing to them to leave a friend's house or switch from one activity to another. Intrusions upset them. They let us know that the phone ringing, a neighbor knocking on the door, a delivery person's arrival, an unexpected request, or being scooped up for a diaper change or to use the bathroom are all irritating interruptions and unwanted surprises. Settling these kids down for sleep can take sixty to ninety minutes.

Slow-to-adapt kids can teach us to stop rushing! They need to know what to expect; they need time to shift from one thing to another; and they need some warning about what's coming next. Routines give them a sense of predictability that they thrive on.

Emotion Coaching in Action

Every night Liza and her mother Peggy would select Liza's clothing for the next day. Peggy recognized that Liza didn't like surprises, so they'd check the weather forecast and carefully lay out an outfit. Inevitably, the next morning Liza would have changed her mind about what to wear. This infuriated Peggy, who much preferred spontaneity to planning ahead. "What am I doing wrong?" she wanted to know.

"Nothing," I responded. "I suspect Liza just needs even more time to review her decision. Don't stop what you're doing, add to it." Peggy huffed in frustration. So I asked her, "What would you like to do in the morning that you presently don't have time to do?" "Sit down with a cup of coffee," she replied. "All right," I said. "Here's my suggestion, set the alarm fifteen minutes earlier. Get up, make yourself a cup of coffee, take it into Liza's room (Liza wasn't sensitive so the smell didn't bother her), sit on her bed while she lies there and talk about the outfit she's picked out, the plans for the day, and what you know of the weather that morning. This will give Liza the additional time she needs to process her decision, and you'll get your cup of coffee. It won't seem like such a hassle. In fact, this connection will probably soothe both of you and make the transitions from pajamas to school clothes easier."

Indeed, when Liza wasn't rushed, had her mom's full attention, and had time to reflect on her choices and plans, Peggy found her to be much more cooperative. And, thanks to the coffee, Peggy actually enjoyed herself.

Kids who adapt slowly need words and phrases like:

- In ten minutes you'll need to stop and . . .
- Today we will be doing . . .
- That was a surprise. You don't like surprises.
- Change is hard for you.
- You wish you didn't have to leave.
- I appreciate how you remind me to stop rushing.
- Changes in your routine upset you.
- After lunch we always . . .

Quick to Adapt

Kids who are quick to adapt aren't triggered by transitions. They can shift from one thing to another a dozen times a day, without even noticing. This may actually be their challenge, for it is easy for these children to get overcommitted. It may also be difficult for them to understand others who don't shift as quickly as they do. We can help them learn to be more sensitive to others by pointing out transitions and teaching them the importance of forewarning their friends and family members who are not quite as quick to adapt.

Emotion Coaching in Action

Casey was a quick-to-adapt, cheery kid whom everyone loved. Talented and vivacious, her social life was full. And that was the problem—it was too full. Casey was so quick to adapt that she quickly shifted from one activity to another, never stopping to think about whether she really had the interest or energy for the next event. As a result, at thirteen she found herself frustrated and overcommitted. Helping Casey meant making her aware of her quick adaptability, teaching her to slow down a bit, and encouraging her to think before she shifted or committed.

Kids who are quick to adapt need words and phrases like:

- Think about how many things you've agreed to do.
- It's important to forewarn your brother that you're going to quit playing.
- I appreciate how easily you shift from one thing to another.
- Let's slow down.

---

4. Intensity: How strong are your child's emotional reactions?

not easily frustrated	becomes frustrated easily and fiercely
quickly stops crying when upset	can cry for forty-five minutes over a seemingly insignificant issue
others may not even know this child is upset	experiences every emotion deeply and powerfully
not easily upset	becomes upset quickly and unexpectedly

1	2	3	4	5
mild reactions				intense reactions

High Intensity

Children who experience intense emotional reactions are not necessarily loud; in fact, some intense children focus their intensity inward. You can "feel" the emotion radiating from them. They experience every emotion deeply and physiologically. Stress hormones move swiftly and easily through their bodies, and they produce lower levels of soothing agents. As a result they get upset more easily and stay upset longer.

That's why the advice to ignore a child's strong reaction doesn't work.

He's not trying to manipulate you. He truly experiences every emotion as a powerful jolt. Kids who experience intense emotional reactions are triggered and pulled into power struggles when their feelings are ignored or when your intensity fuels theirs.

Intensity reflects a zeal for life. It's essential that kids who are more intense learn how to monitor their emotions closely and discover what soothes and calms them. Clear standards, enforced and modeled by you, are a must! Help them find outlets for the passion that lies within them through sports or the arts.

Emotion Coaching in Action

Tad was a smart kid who experienced intense emotional reactions, especially frustration. He loved to read and play ball, but he hated mathematics. Getting him to sit down and do his math homework was a major battle every night. His parents would insist that he do it. He would adamantly refuse. Then his parents learned about temperament and intense emotional reactions. Instead of insisting that Tad get his math done immediately after school, when he was worn out by his day, they encouraged him to calm himself by going outside and playing. Homework didn't start until after dinner when everyone was relaxed. The session began with reading, which Tad enjoyed and found soothing. Then instead of starting with the toughest problems, his father selected the ten easiest problems for him to do. The simplicity allowed Tad to immediately experience success. He was rewarded with a ten-minute break (another soothing strategy), after which he began the next ten problems. These were a little tougher, but the joy of his earlier success helped him to keep going and manage his frustration.

Kids who experience strong emotional reactions need words and phrases like:

- You experience strong feelings.
- Take a deep breath.
- Put your hand on your heart. Is it beating slowly or quickly?
- Can you feel the volcano inside of you bubbling?
- Take a break and then try again.

Mild Reactions

Children who experience mild reactions don't often pull you into power struggles. They're mellow kids who roll with the punches, which means their needs may go unnoticed. That's why it is important to teach them to recognize their emotions and express them clearly.

Emotion Coaching in Action

Tiara was the youngest of four kids. She was an easygoing, happy kid who was a great joy to her parents. After learning about intensity her mother realized that she was often pushing Tiara's needs aside to deal with her older brother, who was much more vocal and outspoken. Now she consciously takes time each day after school to check in with Tiara.

Kids who experience mild reactions need to hear words and phrases like:

- If that is important to you, it is okay to clearly let others know.
- I will make sure that I plan to spend time with you.

---

5. Activity level: Is your child always busy and on the move, or more quiet and still?

walks when asked	rarely walks, often runs
can sit quietly for extended periods	always on the go, usually squirms or slides out of her chair
doesn't need regular exercise	becomes irritable if confined too long
rides in a car seat without protesting	hates the car seat

1	2	3	4	5
low activity level			high activity level	

High Activity Level

Kids with a high activity level are always on the move. They need to run, jump, and use their whole body in order to feel good. Which means they're great in sports and dance, but they find it difficult to ride in a car, sit down, and eat or get into bed. Whenever they haven't had an opportunity to exercise or have been confined, you can bet their intensity will be running high.

It's often tough to get high-energy kids to bed. They don't like to stop, especially if they are kids who seek stimulation and are happy. Interestingly enough, Sara Harkness found that when high-activity kids who live in Holland start to get restless, their parents put them to bed! The average Dutch child gets two and half hours *more* sleep a day than the average U.S. child. In the United States when high-energy kids start to get restless, their parents find them something else to do.

Researcher Jim Cameron suggests, "High-energy kids fight slowing down to go to bed and often don't even give you cues, like rubbing their eyes, that they are tired." He recommends that rather than letting them stay up till they "drop," establish a regular bedtime and stick to it! Otherwise high-energy kids tend to get sleep deprived. Then they're cranky in the morning and your day begins with power struggles.

Keeping a high energy child in a car seat is also a challenge. The key is to bring along something that's more interesting to play with than the buckles and straps on the seat. A tape recorder, handheld games, or a word game with mom or dad can distract him from the frustration of being restrained.

And when it comes to getting the high-energy toddler to sit at the table, start with "small" expectations. This child is not only temperamentally more active, he's also in a stage of development where his brain is screaming, *Try it*! Seat him at the table and involve him in a conversation. When he wants down three minutes later, let him go, but insist he eat only at the table. A few weeks later aim for five minutes, then gradually, over time, ten and fifteen minutes. Avoid getting into a struggle with him, but do gradually increase the time to sit so that ultimately he does learn how to slow his body down when the situation requires it.

Plan daily physical activities for your high-energy child and frequent breaks when he has to be confined, and you'll find life with him much more enjoyable.

Kids with high activity levels need words and phrases like:

- You are very coordinated.
- Let's go outside.
- Exercise, then do your homework.
- You can lie on the floor and work; you don't have to sit at the table.
- When you start to pick on your sister, I know you need exercise.

Low Activity

Teachers often love low-activity kids. These children are in their seats working instead of running around the classroom getting into trouble. Their challenge may be to get enough exercise. That's why it's important to insist that these children choose at least one physical activity each day that interests them. The exercise can be a group activity or time to be alone. The most important factor is that it happens. If you're a high-energy parent, plan family outings that allow a choice of being active or watching so that you can connect with your low-energy child.

Low activity kids need words and phrases like:

- You like to be still.
- You can choose one activity and then sit for a while.

6. Regularity: How predictable are your child's eating, sleeping, and elimination patterns?

wants to eat at very predictable times	frequently skips meals or eats very little at one meal, then a great deal at the next
needs to nap at specific times of day	can easily delay his nap to fit your plans
wakes up at the same time every day	if left to his own schedule would wake up at a different time each day
needs to eat *now*	prefers to "graze" rather than eat at specific mealtimes

1	2	3	4	5
regular				irregular

Irregularity

Kids who have irregular body rhythms tend to be very flexible. They can easily wait for a meal or skip a nap if you're out and about. The challenge is that you never know when they're going to be hungry or tired. Kids with irregular body rhythms are triggered when they are pushed to eat when they are not hungry or to sleep when they are not tired. If you have an irregular child, create routines that are predictable but flexible. When your child wants a snack at four-thirty P.M., allow him to choose foods that meet his nutritional needs. What difference does it make if he has veggies and dip at four-thirty or veggies at six with his meal? Remember that you control what food is available. If you don't want him snacking on "junk," don't buy it. Acknowledging that your child is hungry affirms his most basic emotions. If he isn't allowed to read his own hunger, how can he be expected to monitor more subtle emotions like irritation or jealousy? If you're worried that your child is eating due to boredom and not hunger, ask him, "Do you want to eat because you're bored, or is your stomach growling?" Teach him to clarify his emotions! Don't get into power struggles about food. Eating disorders are a major health concern for children today. *Do* teach him about good nutrition, *do* make sure healthy foods are available, and *do* plan regular family meals.

If naps are leading to power struggles at your house, create a "siesta" time when everyone slows down, reads, and rests. If your child is tired, he'll fall asleep. If he's not tired, after thirty minutes siesta time is over and it's time to get up and go. By changing your expectations from sleep time to rest time, you'll reduce your frustration and find it easier to stay calm if your child doesn't fall asleep.

Emotion Coaching in Action

Jack was an irregular kid. Even though he was on the lean side, he ate a huge breakfast every day. But after that his mother never knew what he'd want. At lunch he often wasn't hungry. By four o'clock he was dragging and would demand a snack. Dinner varied. Sometimes he ate everything and other times two bites seemed to fill him. She worried about him until she realized he was eating nutritiously. It was the time and amount of food that varied. In fact, his pattern was very similar to his dad's, who was a healthy, strong man. After learning about temperament she planned regular meals, insisting that Jack come to the table, sit down, and talk at least for a few minutes. He could choose what he wanted to eat and how much, but connecting with the family was expected. If he was hungry, Jack ate; if he wasn't, he didn't. Since Jack stayed on his growth curve, his mother stopped worrying and the struggles over eating stopped.

Kids with irregular body rhythms need words and phrases like:

- It's difficult for you to fall asleep.
- You can have a nutritious snack when you're ready.
- This is rest time. You don't need to sleep, but you can rest.

Regular

Regular kids are very predictable. You know exactly when they're going to want lunch, fall asleep, or eliminate. The challenges occur when you want them to adapt their schedule. They cannot. If the need for a bowel movement hits every day at seven-thirty A.M., that's it. They've got to go. If they are hungry at noon, they need to eat or they become irritable and may complain of a headache. These kids need predictable mealtimes and bedtimes. It helps if you understand that to delay eating or sleeping may actually make them physically ill.

Regular kids need words and phrases like:

- Take a snack with you in case you have to wait for lunch.
- Try taking a nap today because you'll be up later.
- I understand you need to eat *now*!

---

7. First Reaction: What is your child's reaction to new things, places, ideas, or people?

jumps right into new activities	initially says no to any new activity, even if it was his choice to sign up
joins in right away	prefers to watch before joining a new activity
enjoys new foods, clothing, etc.	is reluctant to try any new food, clothing, school, teacher, etc.

1	2	3	4	5
jumps in			cautious first reaction	

Cautious First Reaction

Kids who are cautious in new situations are very aware of potential danger. They're the kids whose adolescence is a dream to their parents. While other teens are trying out their independence by plunging into activities without thinking, cautious kids are reflecting before leaping. They don't do dumb things. It's important to know that kids with a cautious first reaction are not lacking in confidence. They simply approach new things thoughtfully. They are triggered when pushed, rushed, or not supported. In order to stay out of the power struggles with this child, slow down, help him understand that new situations make him feel uncomfortable or anxious, and ask him, "What will make it better?" Together make a plan. Would he like to watch first, or take a friend with him? Let him know that you understand his discomfort and are there to support him. A reminder of past successes is helpful, too.

If your cautious child is also very sensitive, his first reaction may not be fear but rather overstimulation. In a new situation too many new messages may be hitting him all at once. If that's true for your child, teach him that just as you can walk into a room and adjust the temperature if it's too hot or cold, stimulation can be managed as well. He can take the deep breath and choose to sit or stand where it is quieter or where the lights are less glaring. By doing so, he can reduce some of the stimulation and make it easier for him to cope.

Emotion Coaching in Action

Leah was a kid who approached every new experience cautiously. Her first public speech was no different. The mere thought of getting up and looking into the eyes of all of her classmates was nearly overwhelming to her. That's when her dad explained that public speaking gives almost everyone the jitters, whether you're cautious or not. But when you are cautious it's even *more* important that you practice your speech thoroughly. Then, don't think about your feelings as fear but rather as overstimulation. You can control overstimulation. Close your eyes for a second. Focus on one person or point in the room for a moment. Allow yourself to adjust.

Leah took her dad's words to heart. She listened to the kids who went before her, telling herself, "I can do this, too." She reminded herself that she'd practiced. She knew her speech. And then she said, "This isn't fear. It's stimulation, and I can manage it!" When Leah's dad picked her up that day from school, they couldn't even pull out of the parking lot until she had shown him the A she'd received.

Emotion Coaching in Action

Tara was cautious about anything new. Learning to use the toilet was a very taxing experience for her. All attempts to use it had ended with tears. She felt much safer urinating in her diaper than sitting on a scary toilet. One summer day she was outside playing in her wading pool when she realized she had to go. She didn't have a diaper on, and the potty chair was sitting right next to the back door. Her mother invited her to try it and Tara agreed. It was the first time she approached the potty without tears. This time Tara urinated right through her suit and was completely amazed. For the next three days, Tara used the potty—but only with her swimsuit on. After three days she took off the suit to use the potty, but she would not wear panties. Instead she stuck to her diaper and simply pulled it down when she needed to go.

Her mother invited her to go to the store to select her own new panties. At the store Tara picked out panties decorated with her favorite cartoon characters, but when they got to the checkout counter, she changed her mind. Her mother did her best to remain cool and calm although she felt like screaming. She held it together and explained to Tara that if they left they would not come back that day. Tara accepted the restriction and walked out. A couple of days later when her grandmother came to visit, Tara suggested, "Grandma, let's go to the store and buy me panties." Off they went. It was a proud Tara who returned home, panties in hand. It took only three weeks from the swimsuit to the panties—not bad for a cautious kid.

Kids who are cautious in new situations need words and phrases like:

- This isn't fear, it's overstimulation.
- I am here. I will help you.
- It's okay to watch first.
- Let's read about it before we go.
- You can take a friend.
- You may feel uncomfortable, but you're not sick. Take ten deep breaths.
- This is just like . . .
- This isn't about lack of confidence. It's just new. Give yourself time.

Quick to Adapt

Kids who jump right into things have a zest for life! They can literally leap into situations, which means you may frequently find yourself at the local emergency room. They're triggered when they're forced to wait extended periods of time for their turn or want to try things the adults consider unsafe. When these kids are little, you can *never* leave them unattended because they'll literally try anything. If these kids are active and persistent as well as quick to adapt, the odds are you'll find them on top of the refrigerator or attempting to "fly" from the roof. As they grow older you'll want to teach them to pause to think before acting and to be good problem solvers. You'll also want to make sure that they learn to swim and develop the other skills they need to be safe. Finally, you'll want to provide them with opportunities to take reasonable risks, because one way or another, they're going to take them! Just remember, someone needs to be raising the next test pilot.

Kids who are quick to adapt need words and phrases like:

- You enjoy adventure.
- Stop, think, then act.
- What's your plan?
- It's very important that you learn to swim, take a first-aid class, etc.

Now you have it, a profile of your child's temperament. Add up your child's score.

Total Score		
7–14	15–25	26–35
low-key child	spunky child	spirited child

Understanding temperament truly allows you to go below the surface to the fuel source, the real feelings and needs that fuel your child's behavior. If your child is intense, you know you have to soothe him and calm him before you can work with him. If your child is sensitive, you can predict that rough clothing, crowds, or family gatherings are likely to trigger him. If he's not persistent, a one-hundred-problem worksheet is going to send him under the table. And because you understand the real emotions, you can select strategies that help him to reduce the stimulation, break the tasks down, and be successful. Understanding temperament allows you to step right into your child's shoe, see the world from his point of view, and stay out of power struggles!

Coaching Tips

- Your child is born with a preferred style of reacting to his world around him.
- When you understand your child's temperament you can work with him more easily and stay out of power struggles.
- Persistent kids need you to ask them their plans.
- Sensitive kids need you to believe them when sensations are bothering them.
- High-energy kids need help channeling their energy
- Intense kids need help learning how to soothe and calm themselves.
- Regular kids need predictable routines.
- Irregular kids need flexibility and to learn about good nutrition.
- Slow-to-adapt kids need to know what's going to happen and time to shift from one thing to another.

- Kids with a cautious first reaction are not being stubborn, they need your support.
- Kids who jump into things quickly need to be taught to think and then act.

I believe working with temperament is so important that I have written *two* books about it. If you haven't read *Raising Your Spirited Child* and *Raising Your Spirited Child Workbook*, I encourage you to do so—whether your child is spirited or not.

TEN

The "Silent Treatment" vs. the Talking Machine

Understanding Introverts and Extroverts

"I thought he was ignoring me. I didn't realize he was thinking!"

—*The mother of an introvert*

Stella slumped into her chair. "How are you supposed to figure out what your child's feeling when she refuses to talk to you!" "Yeah," Lisa agreed, "that's my thirteen-year-old, she doesn't want to discuss problems or talk things out, she never has. She's the queen of the 'silent treatment.' If I try to talk with her, she complains that I'm repeating myself or that I talk too much. And she is always telling me to get out of her space."

"What I'd give for a few moments of silence," Ben sighed. "I've got Miss Motor Mouth living with me. She *never* stops talking. If she has a problem, she wants to discuss it over and over again. How many times can we discuss the fact that she didn't get invited to Katie's birthday party? If she thinks I'm not listening, she'll get right into my face. Sometimes she'll even turn my head toward her and demand, 'Are you listening to me?'"

Believe it or not, the "silent resister" and the "motor mouth" aren't really trying to pull you into power struggles. They're simply processing information and recharging in their own preferred styles.

That's why if you're a person who needs to talk through a problem, you may feel rejected by a child who pushes away from you and puts his hands over his ears when you try to talk about his feelings. He really doesn't hate you. He needs to process his feelings in a style that's different from yours. And if you're the type of person who prefers to pull your feelings inside and think about them, you may feel invaded by your child who has to "unburden" herself every time she's upset. If you don't understand these differences, you can unwittingly trigger each other and end up disconnecting when you're actually trying very hard to connect.

Fortunately, there are patterns to how we process information. Every individual has a preferred style. When you understand your own and your child's preference, you'll know which strategies to use in order to keep your child working with you.

The Theory

More than seventy years ago a Swiss psychologist named Carl Jung developed a theory called "psychological type theory." He suggested that human behavior could be classified into predictable categories or preferences. During World War II the mother and daughter team of Katharine Briggs and Isabel Briggs Myers enthusiastically embraced Jung's work. Their hope was to bring peace to the world by helping people understand and appreciate differences. As a result, they spent more than twenty years developing the Myers-Briggs Type Indicator to distinguish the preferences described by Jung and to help us apply that information to relationships and to stay out of those power struggles!

The psychological type theory was developed separately from the temperament theory discussed in the previous chapter. The two theories work together but describe different aspects of individual differences. Both include a genetic element. Jung believed that healthy development was based on *lifelong nurturing of these preferences, not on trying to change them.*

We don't get to choose our children's type, but we can help our kids understand their style and what they need, and teach them how to work with us, especially if our styles are different. In this chapter I'll describe *introversion* and *extroversion*, whether we need to go inside of ourselves to process information and recharge, or whether we need to go outside of ourselves and reflect. It's these preferences that can help us understand why some kids seem to give us the silent treatment while others never seem to stop talking.

Introversion and Extroversion

It's the extroverts who need to go outside of themselves, talking and interacting with others and the world around them in order to figure out how they feel and to find the energy to cope. Introverts go inside of themselves in order to sort out their feelings. They need space, unstructured time, and quiet in order to polish their thoughts and energize. Introversion and extroversion do *not* describe social skills. Introverts can be very social people and strong leaders. They simply think and feel best when they have the opportunity and space to reflect. Extroverts are not all party animals. If they are temperamentally cautious in new situations, they may be quiet initially when meeting people, but they like to do their thinking by talking. They are energized by interaction and activity.

Most people demonstrate a preference for one style or the other, but each of these traits is on a continuum. You can have a strong preference or a slight one. What's most important is recognizing at a particular moment whether your child needs time, space, and quiet, or an opportunity to talk. If you watch closely your child will let you know her preference, even if she's only an infant.

The Extroverts

Extroverts are the babies who fuss and squirm when you hold them up to your shoulder and are just fine when you turn them away from you so they can watch the world around them. They are the older kids who grab your attention the minute they come home from school or child care by shoving their papers into your face. They need to talk and they need to talk *now*! Too much time alone can leave extroverts drained and irritable. They're the kids who clamor to bring a friend home from school or complain they are bored when there's no one to play with. You may worry about their self-esteem because they rarely choose to play by themselves. When they're upset, they don't want to be alone. They'll follow you around, touch you, and move right into your space. If you want them to take a break, they will—but only if you go with them, which often isn't what you need at all. Ask them how they feel, and they'll have an immediate answer, which may change the more they talk and "think" about it.

The Introverts

Those who prefer introversion go within themselves to process their emotions and recharge. They are the kids who tell you about the bully on the playground three days after they've been roughed up or teased. Ask about their day right after school, and they have a one syllable answer. It's not until bedtime that they're ready for a full discussion, and then you think they're just stalling. If you ask them how they feel when they are upset, they may not be able to answer—until hours or even days later.

Introverts have a strong sense of personal space. If their space is invaded—even by an offer of a hug—they may pull away. It's not that they aren't affectionate; they are. They simply like to choose who and when someone comes into their space. And it's not only their physical space that they like to protect. They may also complain that someone is looking at them, breathing on them, or talking too much!

Noise and crowds drain introverts and leave them feeling cranky. After a hectic day at school or child care, they want to go home, lie down on the couch, and watch a video. They're not unmotivated, they're simply taking a break to recharge and process their thoughts before they begin homework or other tasks. Bringing a friend home from school for a play date can be a disaster—unless you can help them figure out how to put on a quiet video to watch together or get some downtime before the interaction begins again.

How You and Your Child Prefer to Process Information and Recharge

The older you are, the more likely you'll be using both preferences, especially if you grew up with a parent whose preference was different from your own, or have a job that demands a style different from your preferred style. As a result, you may be comfortable using both styles, but you usually prefer one. Our goal with the following checklist is to identify your child's and your own preference—your *first* and most *natural* response. I devised this list for use in my classes. Check those statements that seem to fit you or your child best, the statements that are true for you most of the time. Your behaviors will give you a good idea about your preferences. If your child is able to read, let him complete the checklist himself or complete it with you.

If you or your child prefers extroversion you probably:

_____ need to talk in order to figure out what you "feel."

_____ tend to share thoughts or feelings immediately as they strike you.

_____ need feedback, affirmation that your point of view and feelings are valid.

_____ want *immediate* responses to questions.

_____ figure out how to do things by talking or doing.

_____ need people and activity to feel energized. A day alone leaves you feeling drained and cranky.

_____ ask lots of questions.

_____ get into trouble for talking too much or interrupting.

_____ hate to wait for lengthy directions—you just want to do it.

If you or your child prefer introversion you probably:

_____ need time alone to figure out how you feel.

_____ need time to think before you are ready to talk about your feelings.

_____ share thoughts and feelings selectively, often with those closest to you but rarely with strangers.

_____ feel grumpy and drained after being in a noisy crowd or large group.

_____ need downtime to recharge.

_____ often start talking in the evening after having time to reflect.

_____ learn best by watching, reading, or listening first.

_____ have a strong sense of personal space and do not like to feel invaded.

_____ are often told to "hurry up" or that you're taking too long to make a decision.

Count how many statements you would agree with in each group.

Total

My child	**Me**
Extrovert statements _____	Extrovert statements _____
Introvert statements _____	Introvert statements _____

Coaching the Extrovert

Preventing power struggles begins by working with your child's type rather than against it. If your child prefers extroversion, it's essential that you understand that in order to work with you, your child needs:

- to talk in order to figure out how he feels.
- activities and interactions with people in order to feel energized.
- questions to help him think.

When you honor the extroverts' need to think out loud and to be active, you help them to discern their emotions. You are also helping them keep their energy levels high so that they can more effectively manage their behavior and not get into fights with you.

1. Coaching the Extroverts When They Need to Talk

The voice was tight, the message direct. "I've had it!" I recognized my friend Kathleen's voice and immediately returned her call. When she answered, I simply asked, "Tough day?" She growled in response. "I'm willing to listen," I invited.

"It's Courtney," she exclaimed. "She's unburdening herself again, complaining that she's got too much homework. Her teachers are too demanding. She'll never get all of her work done. I know she needs to do this, and I've listened for a good fifteen minutes. But now, I'm done!"

Extroverts are the kids who need to talk about an issue over and over again until they've got it figured out. Hearing the words come out of their mouths allows them to sort their feelings.

The problem is, the process can be exhausting for the listener, especially if you prefer introversion like my friend Kathleen. An introverted parent alone can never meet the needs of an intense, extroverted child. She'll wear you down to a nub. Your extroverted child needs you to let her talk, and it's important that you do listen to her, but you can also teach her how to express herself without wearing you out.

After our conversation Kathleen and Courtney came up with a plan. Kathleen explained to Courtney that she was an extrovert who needed to talk about her feelings, especially when she was upset. Reassuring Courtney that she loved how willing Courtney was to share her news of the day, Kathleen also explained that she herself was an introvert who became drained by constant conversation. "I can listen for a while," she said, "but then I get worn out. When I get exhausted, I want to yell at you. But you don't need me to yell at you. That would upset both of us. The problem is, I'm out of listening energy, but you're not done talking.

Next time you are upset, you can count on me for about twenty minutes of listening. Then I need a break. We can have a plan that when that happens you can call your dad, speak to a friend, or go exercise. If you don't want to exercise alone, I'll sit by you while you ride the exercise bike, but I can't talk."

Their plan worked because it included strategies that met Courtney's need to talk. It also respected Kathleen's needs. Thanks to their plan, Courtney understood that her mother loved and understood her, and that when her mom needed quiet, she wasn't breaking off. She simply was out of listening energy.

If your extroverted child is exhausting you, help her understand her need to talk, but know it's all right to set some limits that teach her to be respectful of your feelings, too. Let her know that you're good for ten questions, but then you need a break. Or that you'll listen for ten minutes; then set the timer for five minutes of silence.

If you are an introvert, involve your child in extracurricular activities and encourage him to visit friends at their homes. There's no way you can match your extroverted child's need for interaction. Allowing yourself to honor your limits keeps you connected and out of power struggles.

As you listen to your extroverted child, it's important to remember she is "thinking" out loud. Which means she may say things that "come to mind" but do not reflect her true feelings or final decision. As you listen to her ideas, you might be inclined to think, What will happen if she does that? It's important to remember she is only exploring thoughts, not making a decision. That's why when she explodes and declares, "I hate you," or "You can't make me," or "That's stupid," instead of immediately getting angry, stop and calmly ask her, "Is that really what you wanted to say?" Odds are she'll give you a sheepish grin and admit, "Not really." Allowing your extrovert the time to simply "hear" herself and not making judgments about what she is saying allows her to sort out those feelings. Later, when everyone is calm, you can teach her how to assert herself without being disrespectful or hurtful to others. We'll discuss that in a later chapter.

Extroverts also want your feedback—usually immediately—that their ideas and feelings are valid. A simple nod in agreement or "ah-ha" may be all that's necessary, but they do want to know that you are listening! It's learning how to express themselves without interrupting or intruding upon others that is their challenge. So when your little extrovert grabs your face and turns it toward her, you can say, "Stop, that hurts my cheek. If you want my attention, you can say, 'Mommy, please listen.'" If your child interrupts, you can create signals, like a hand on her shoulder that means, I heard you, and I'll give you my full attention in one minute.

As you work with your extrovert, remember she isn't talking to drive you wild—she's thinking and recharging. It's your task as her emotion coach to listen well and at the same time teach her the social skills she needs to work with others instead of overwhelming them.

2. Coaching the Extroverts When They Need Activity and Interaction

"I'm worried about my child," Angela lamented. "She rarely if ever chooses to play alone. Even if she's been with other kids all day, the moment they go home, she exclaims, 'I'm bored!' And then she tries to get me to play with her. I will for a while, but I've got other things to do. Is there any way I can get this kid to play by herself?" "Yeah," Diane agreed, "and how can you get them to work alone? I tell Zach to clean his room, but he always ends up handing me stuff or wanting me to work with him, and we end up fighting."

Extroverts seem to need lots of your attention because they are at their best when working and interacting with others. If you want to win their cooperation, instead of fighting their nature by pushing them to work alone, work with them. Together you can clean their room and then yours. You'll get the rooms cleaned faster, more effectively, and with much less aggravation. And when it comes to homework, instead of sending them off to their room, let them work at the dining room table while you work nearby.

Understand that extroverts can be very independent, they simply think and feel best when interacting with others. Sign them up for group activities, plan social outings with them, and respect their *need* to be with others. This doesn't mean, however, that extroverts can't ever play or work alone. They can. Your task is to get them started by work-ing with their preferred style. That means helping them select an active, hands-on kind of activity such as playing with building blocks, con-struction toys, or art materials. Sit down with them and get them going. Once they are engaged, you can pull out and let them work on their own. If you can, work by them and be ready to stop what you're doing to give them the feedback they need. Know that when they are finished they'll need your attention again because they'll have been drained by their time alone. Older kids will gradually learn to work alone for more extended periods of time, but it's always at a cost to them. They're drained by that time alone.

Know, too, that extroverts learn best when they can get their hands on things and try them. Long lectures or lengthy verbal directions can drive them wild.

3. Coaching the Extroverts When They Need Questions to Help Them Think

Extroverted kids will often ask you for help and then reject your advice. This process can be infuriating, at least it was to Debbie. "My daughter Jessica would ask me to help her decide what to wear," she told us in class one day. "But then she wouldn't like any of my sugges-tions. She'd negate every single one of them. I swore she was just trying to pick a fight with me!"

But then as we talked about extroverts in class, Debbie realized we were describing her daughter. "That's her!" she exclaimed. "Jessica is always thinking out loud. When she was little and I took her on stroller rides, she'd carry on a running monologue. 'There's the house with the green shutters. Oh, and there's the big dog!' Every thought that came to her mind came out of her mouth. Suddenly the insight struck me. She's asking for my help, and I'm thinking that means she wants me to make the decision. But what she *really* needs me to do is help her talk through her decision. So instead of offering suggestions I started asking ques-tions like: 'Do you feel like wearing something cool or warm? Does the outfit need to be layered or not? Do you want something baggy and loose or more close fitting? Are you thinking of bright colors or black and white?' When I asked questions, her intensity dropped. She could hear me, then she started thinking and made her own decision."

In order to avoid those power struggles in the first place, you can teach your extroverted child to say, "I'm having trouble deciding, I need to hear myself think. . . ." Or "Please ask me questions so I can think better." Her clear communication will keep both of you from becoming frustrated. If your child doesn't tell you what she needs, you may have to ask, "Would you like me to ask you questions to help you decide?" Or, "Would you like me to make suggestions?" If your child is just a toddler, you'll have to try offering suggestions *and* asking questions; then decide which strategy seems to be working best.

Coaching the Introvert

Working with your child's type is often like a dance—two steps forward, one back, pause, step again. The more familiar the steps, the easier to dance. When it comes to coaching introverts, it's important to understand they need space, time for reflection, and opportunities to watch or listen before participating.

Recently I experienced a "dance" with a child I'd never met before. I didn't have the faintest idea if he preferred introversion or extroversion, so I had to let his cues tell me which steps to try.

1. Coaching the Introverts When They Need Space— Physically, Verbally, and Visually

I was meeting with the director of a child-care center when suddenly two harried teachers arrived simultaneously at her door. Each had in hand a very angry child. "We need help," they exclaimed, and proceeded to leave the children with us while they returned to their classrooms. The director invited the two-year-old onto her lap and said to Thomas, the four-year-old, "This is my friend, Mary; she can help you." So there I was with a scowling, snorting four-year-old who'd never seen me before. I didn't have any idea what had happened to him or why he might be so angry. But angry he was. If looks could kill, I was dead. He stood just inside the door glaring at me.

The look on his face, the hunch in his shoulders, his arms wrapped tightly around his body, and a growl deep in his throat clearly told me, "I *need* space! Don't touch me!" Ah, an introvert who doesn't like to be crowded and needs some time to think, I decided, and chose not to move from my chair. Instead, I said, "The look on your face tells me you don't want me to come near you." He growled in response. "And the sounds you're making tell me you'd rather I not talk with you, either." He growled louder. "Maybe you'd prefer I not even look at you." He growled once more. "All right," I responded. "I won't touch you or even look at you, I'll just sit here and when you'd like my attention you can tell me." I turned back to my work. I was not ignoring him. I was simply respecting his need for space and quiet at that moment, but clearly letting him know I was available.

Introverts will often pull away from interaction because they need space, time, and quiet to figure out what they are feeling and to pull themselves back together. They aren't deliberately shutting you out, they are recharging. So before you physically move into your child's space to give her a hug, or move in verbally by asking twenty questions, ask her if this is what she would like or read her cues. Even an infant will turn to you or raise her arms, letting you know that, yes, she would like you to come into her space. Or if she doesn't, she'll turn her head away and pull her arms back.

Introverts often get into trouble for doing things that "push" you and others out of their space, like shouting, "Everyone be quiet!" Or they may hit, bite, or growl to clear the space out around them. If this happens, it's critical that you clearly enforce your standards, help them understand the emotion they are experiencing, and teach them what they can do. For example, if your child pushes another child out of her space, you can say, "Stop! You may not push. I think you are needing space. You can say, 'I need space!' But you may not push to get it."

Once I gave Thomas some space, he was more open to working with me; of course, he didn't tell me that with words. Shortly after I turned back to my work at the table, he started to kick the wastebasket. "Stop, Thomas," I declared firmly. "No matter how angry you are, you may not kick the basket. If you're ready for my attention, you can tell me." He growled once more, the scowl still deep. But his arms were no longer crossed over his chest. His cues told me he was a bit more open. Remaining in my chair, physically out of his space, I stepped in verbally. "I'm wondering if something made you sad," I said. He nodded in agreement. Now I was really stuck.

2. Coaching Introverts When They Need Time for Reflection

I had no idea what would have made Thomas sad. "Can you tell me what made you sad?" I asked. He snorted. Ah, he needs time to think, and I'm interrupting him by asking too many questions, I thought. Introverts don't like that. So I said, "You can think about it, and I'll keep working until you're ready."

I waited. I admit it almost killed me. I'm an extrovert who likes to talk things through; it's hard for me to remember that introverts are not wasting time when they are silent. They are thinking! It was even harder for me to wait because I was running out of time. I gave him a few minutes, and then I tried answering my own question by guessing. "I'm wondering if someone took a toy from you." He nodded and snorted once more, but it was a weak snort, the intensity diminishing. He was forgiving me for my intrusion, so I continued. "It must have been a very special toy to make you feel this sad." He nodded once more. This time he didn't growl or snort. We were making progress! I waited to see if he would tell me what toy it was. He didn't. So I guessed. "I wonder if it was a truck?" Finally, he turned and said, "No, it was my dinosaur!" "Oh," I replied. "I can understand how sad that would be. I really like dinosaurs, too. My favorite is Tyrannosaurus rex. What's yours?" "Brontosaurus," he proclaimed, and proceeded to tell me he had a book about dinosaurs in his bag. "You do!" I exclaimed. "Would you like to get your book and read it with me?" He nodded and led the way to his cubby. Once again, I gave him his space, and walked next to him without touching him. When we returned to the office, I asked him where he would like to sit, offering him a chair at the table or on my lap. He chose a chair—still needing more space. Then he opened the book, turned it so that we both could see it, and proceeded to read it with me. It took twenty minutes until he began to laugh, and his body relaxed. It was only then that the teaching and planning could begin. I told him that next time he needed more quiet time he could say, "I'm not ready to talk yet." Or, "I need a break before I can talk about this." He didn't need to snort. Words worked much better. He looked at me, but he didn't snarl. I continued. "I'm noticing that your body seems much more relaxed and you're smiling. Are you ready to go back to your classroom?"

"No," he replied.

"All right," I agreed, realizing he needed more time but also aware of my time limits. I said, "We can read three more pages, then you'll need to go back to the classroom." He agreed, and we read the pages.

Introverts do need time for reflection. Even if it means waiting until the next day to talk through an issue, it's worth the wait. But sometimes there are time limits. In this instance I realized Thomas was relaxed enough that I could set a deadline. It worked. If his intensity had been higher, I may have had to make a phone call and change my plans to give him a bit longer or find someone else who could take over. If neither of those options was feasible, I may have had to take him back to the classroom and help him find a quiet space there. Somehow I needed to help him get his reflection time. He couldn't work with me until he got it. I needed to know that in order to stay out of a power struggle with him.

If you're an extrovert who finds yourself aggravated by the introvert who in your mind is taking too long to make a decision, you should know about a study completed at 3M Corporation. Engineers for 3M were sent out to fix problems for their customers. The engineers who preferred introversion took much longer to complete the tasks than their extroverted peers. However, those jobs completed by introverts had a vastly lower percentage of callbacks than those completed by the extroverts who had finished the jobs more quickly but failed to solve the actual problems the first time out. It's worth your time to give the introverts the reflection time they need! (Ultimately 3M trained their extroverts to slow down and their introverts to give their clients more feedback as to why it was taking them longer. Both types have their strengths and weaknesses!)

3. Coaching Introverts When They Need an Opportunity to Watch or Listen

I still wasn't quite done coaching Thomas. This "diffusing" session had taken twenty minutes. Obviously no one wants to do that every day, so I decided to finish our time together by teaching what he could do to prevent the problem in the first place. "Next time someone takes your toy, Thomas," I said, "you may *not* hit him. You can say, 'I'm not ready to share.' Can you remember to do that?" He nodded. "Let's practice," I said. "Would you like to say those words yourself, or would you like to listen while I say them?" True to his type, he chose to listen. Introverts learn best by listening and watching. I turned to the director. She pretended to take my book. "Stop," I said firmly. "I'm not ready to share!" Thomas listened attentively. "Will you remember to use those words next time someone tries to take your toy?" I asked once more. He nodded, and we walked back to his classroom.

Introverts need to be able to observe and practice privately. They don't like to be put into the spotlight until they choose to be there themselves. That's why some introverts throw a fit when the teacher sings their name in the hello song.

In my classes we never sing a child's name in circle time without first asking his permission to do so. If he says yes, we then ask if he would like it sung softly or loudly. Even the toddlers let us know their preference, and as a result the tantrums don't occur.

An introverted child may also need to be taught how to greet others or enter a large group. If you're an extrovert, you may be tempted to "push her" into a group. But you can actually help her more by respecting her need for space and observation time. Let your child know that she is a person who is happier when she can observe before participating. Teach her to say hello and then to step back out of traffic in order to watch for a moment. She may need to learn to say, "I prefer to watch first," in case there's an extrovet in the room who unintentionally invades her space and tries to drag her into the action before she's ready. When she understands what she is feeling and learns strategies for expressing those feelings appropriately, she'll be working with you instead of embarrassing or frustrating you by running out of the room or hiding behind your body and refusing to talk. Ultimately, she may use those great observation skills to become a strong leader in the group or a fabulous performer.

Plan for Success

It's really tough when kids come at you with scowls, snorts, and shrieks, and you have to help them sort out their feelings or to recognize that they need to recharge. When you understand what type you're dealing with, you have the information you need to know how to approach them and make that connection.

Think about the recent struggles you've had with your child. Now that you know her preferred type—extroversion or introversion—help her plan for success. For example, if your child is an extrovert and has been getting into trouble at school for interrupting or talking too much, you can tell her, "It's difficult for you to wait because when a thought hits you, you want to share it. You get excited, and you want to talk. When that happens you can hold up a finger to let others know you want into the conversation, but you may not speak. You can say, 'I'd like a turn.' Or, 'Excuse me, please.'"

If your child is an introvert and has been getting into trouble for pushing or shoving when he feels crowded or disappears when he needs a break, you can let him know that in a crowded classroom he may feel uncomfortable and need space. Teach him to say, "I need space." Or to ask the teacher if he can step into the bathroom or run an errand to the office in order to take a break.

Working with your child's preferred style keeps him open to your guidance. It allows you to teach him what he might be feeling and how to express those feelings respectfully. It's this coaching that will stop those power struggles before they ever start.

Coaching Tips

If you or your child prefer extroversion:

- Honor your need for conversation and activity.
- Be sensitive to the need of others for space and quiet.

- Understand introverts are not wasting time or rejecting you when they are quiet. They are thinking and recharging.
- Enjoy your ability to easily converse with others.
- Recognize that you are drained by too much time alone.
- Seek feedback. Needing and enjoying feedback is not an indication of low self-esteem.
- Remember to stop and listen.

If you or your child prefer introversion:

- Honor your need for space, reflection time, and observation. Plan it into your day.
- Understand extroverts are "thinking" when they're talking and what they initially suggest may not be their final decision.
- Be sensitive to others' need for conversation and activity.
- Enjoy your observation skills and ability to carefully think things through.
- Recognize that you are drained by large groups and interaction.
- Learn to say, "I need to think about that."
- Let extroverts know that you have heard them and are thinking about your answer.

ELEVEN

Too Sensitive or Too Analytical?

How We Make Decisions

"Naw . . . tellin' the truth is good, Joey.
I just overdid it a little."

—*From* Dennis the Menace,
by Hank Ketcham

Marnie glanced up the stairs just as her ten-year-old daughter, Tory, walked down. "Good morning," she called to her, then added, "your bow is crooked." Tory walked over to the mirror and fixed it. Moments later eleven-year-old Kelsey came down. Marnie also greeted her and noted that she too had a crooked bow, but Kelsey's reaction was totally different from Tory's. Instead of going to the mirror and fixing it, Kelsey burst into tears and wailed, "You don't love me!"

Marnie was flabbergasted by Kelsey's reaction and immediately realized that somehow she'd unwittingly triggered Kelsey again. It was a common occurrence.

Later that day the differences in the girls' reactions were evident again. After school each of them had brought home a friend. A hot game of Monopoly totally engrossed them, until suddenly Marnie heard Tory's voice sharp and accusing. "Kelsey, you're cheating!" Kelsey burst into tears. Marnie pulled the two of them into another room and demanded to know what was going on. "She gave Sarah fifty dollars to get out of jail," Tory declared. "Sarah was broke. She should have been out of the game, but no, Kelsey slipped her a fifty! That's cheating!" She glared at her sister. Kelsey sniffled, "But, Mom," she explained, "if I didn't give Sarah fifty dollars she'd be out of the game. She couldn't play anymore. I didn't want her to be sad or to just have to sit there while we finished the game. That would feel awful."

Two kids, two very different responses. Years ago, I would not have recognized their differences nor the value of both of their approaches. But today I could, because of the Myers-Briggs research. Today I recognized that Tory's preferred style is *thinking*; Kelsey's is *feeling*.

Figuring out what you feel starts by talking if you prefer extroversion, or reflecting if you prefer introversion; but it doesn't stop there. In their research Katharine Briggs and Isabel Briggs Meyers also discovered that people make decisions about the information they've received. For some kids, like Tory, those decisions are guided by the "facts." Thinking types are influenced by what "makes sense to them, and what they believe to be truthful and just." If the bow is crooked, you fix it. If you're broke, you're out of the game. You respond to the facts.

Others, like Kelsey, immediately experience and respond to the feelings of the situation. They don't just hear the fact that their bow is crooked, they feel criticism from their mother and are hurt. It's the feeling types like Kelsey who step right into the emotions and can actually experience the feelings of others around them. Their decisions are guided by what "feels right" to them. As a result a rule that leads to someone feeling left out needs to be changed.

It's the differences between the thinking types and feeling types that can be most painful when misunderstood. Frequently the feelers are viewed as too sensitive, while the thinking types are criticized for being too analytical or insensitive. It's essential that we remember that both types experience strong emotions and feel deeply. But what triggers them and what they need to stay connected are very different.

Thinkers and Feelers Are Born, Not Made

"We can't go home yet!" Jennifer wailed when her mother told her they'd run out of time shopping at the mall and needed to leave to pick up her dad from the office. "But you promised I could buy a toy. You said it's important to tell the truth and keep our promises!" Jennifer continued. "We can call Dad and tell him we'll be late picking him up. You promised!" Thinkers use logic to make a decision and solve problems. They convince others by "proving" their point. Thinkers also need to understand "why" to feel comfortable and are easily upset if they make a mistake or fail. When their team loses, they need to analyze what could have been done better and to lay out a plan for winning next time.

Feelers make decisions by considering the impact on other people. They convince others through persuasion. If Jennifer's sibling was a feeler, she'd probably say something like, "Jennifer, let's go get Daddy. He's got more money and then we can buy a bigger toy!" Feelers need harmony to feel comfortable and are upset by conflict. If their team loses, their first response is to cheer everyone up.

During the preschool years children explore their preference for thinking and feeling. All children will explore both preferences, but during the school years they will begin to find that they prefer one style to the other. This preference is as innate to a child as gender or eye color.

When your child is upset or needs direction, it becomes especially important to respond to her preferred type. If your child is a feeler, she needs your sympathy and empathy in order to hear you. If you try facts and logic or move into a solution too quickly, you'll set her off and disconnect. If your child is a thinker, she may pull away from your warm hug or tell you to "cut the sympathy" and help her fix the problem instead. Knowing whether you and your child need to deal with facts or feelings first is essential for effective emotion coaching; otherwise you can unwittingly pull yourself into power struggles.

Identifying Your Preferred Style

It is possible to do a formal assessment of your child's preferences, but we're going to let your child's words and actions give you the information you need. If you watch and listen closely, your child will show you whether she is using her thinking or feeling preference. This awareness will help you know where to start when things are sizzling. Think, too, about your own preferences. How you and your child work together is most important.

If your child is a thinker she probably:

_____ is an excellent critical thinker who is able to quickly analyze the facts, see the flaws in ideas, people, or things, and can't resist offering solutions or suggestions for improvement, i.e., You're holding the gerbil the wrong way. Logic guides her decisions.

_____ finds it easier to explain what happened than how she feels about it.

_____ needs to know "why" things are done and loves a good debate. This is the child who gets into trouble for taking an opposing stance or asking, "Why do I have to do that?" She becomes upset if you answer, "Because I said so!"

_____ values justice and becomes alarmed if something is unfair. When playing a game, she will insist that everyone play by the rules, even if that means someone is "out." She is incensed if you break a promise.

_____ hates to feel incompetent and becomes upset if you try to review her mistakes with her or suggest other strategies.

_____ does not want to talk about feelings when she is upset and may reject your comforting hug, cover her ears with her hands, and refuse to talk at all.

_____ highly values truth and may get into trouble for being too blunt. When asked to be more tactful she may say, "Do you want me to lie?"

If your child is a feeler he probably:

_____ is very sensitive, experiencing strong emotional reactions to anything including sad movies, or hurt feelings. He is also very aware of the emotions of others. As a result he may feel great about winning a game but worry about how the loser feels.

_____ needs to work through his emotions before he is ready to problem solve and may say something like, "I got a C on my math test. I'll never be accepted into college. What good would a tutor do? I'm a complete failure."

_____ highly values harmony and will avoid confrontation or conflict even if it means giving up a toy or letting someone else make the choice.

_____ may experience stomach or headaches if there is conflict at home or in the classroom.

_____ is easily hurt by criticism and may immediately ask if you love him when you reprimand him.

_____ is deeply concerned with how decisions affect others and may change the rules of the game if following them would mean someone was "out."

_____ needs to know others like him in order to perform well.

Count how many statements in each group describe your child's typical reaction.

Thinking statements _____
Feeling statements _____

Your child doesn't get into power struggles with himself. So go back through the statements and this time check the ones that fit you best. What's your total?

Thinking statements _____
Feeling statements _____

If you are uncertain of your child's preferred style after reading through the statements, you may need to tune in more closely in the next few weeks. Watch and listen carefully, and he will show you his preference.

Remember these traits are on a continuum. You and your child may demonstrate a very strong preference or a mild one and can also learn to use both. Ultimately, the best decisions are those that consider both facts and feelings. We just need to remember that the thinking types work best when they can analyze the facts first and the feeling types need that Band-Aid on their feelings *before* they're ready to problem solve with you.

Coaching Your Thinking Child

While every individual is unique, there are some common strategies that can help you stay connected to your thinking child and out of power struggles.

1. Deal with the Facts First

Four-year-old David's sister was very frustrated with herself. "I could kick myself in the head!" she exclaimed. Her mother responded, "That's why God put our feet so far from our head. So we wouldn't do that." David listened intently and then offered, "I could do it for you." David wasn't intentionally being insensitive, he simply responded to the facts and came up with a solution.

It's the thinking types who tend to stand back from a situation, look at the facts, take an objective view of the situation, and come up with a solution. Their decisions are guided by logic. The image that comes to my mind is that of a cat approaching a puddle. When a cat approaches a puddle it prowls the edges, slapping the surface with one paw, testing, jumping back, pulling away. It's edgy, wary of jumping in. When upset, thinking kids like to step away from their feelings, which means they sometimes may not address the feelings that are truly fueling the problem. That's what happened to Ben.

He was a thinker who wanted to win a place on the student council. But that day at school he'd overheard other kids saying they were going to vote for Nathan. Frustrated and scared, his anxiety rose. He didn't want to lose! But even more than that, he didn't want to cry, nor did he want to admit his feelings of vulnerability. By the time he got home a volcano was brewing inside of him. His mother noticed it and tried to offer him a hug, but he pushed away from her. When his brother wouldn't give him a turn shooting the basketball, he attacked. His mother had to pull him off his brother and send him into the shower to cool off. An hour later as she sat by him in his room, she asked him why he'd been so upset, but he couldn't tell her. She tried once again to offer him a hug, but he pushed her away. Frustrated, she started to reprimand him. How could she help him if he wouldn't let her? Then suddenly she remembered the discussions in class about thinkers and feelers and realized that her son was responding as a thinker. Immediately she switched tactics and said, "Tell me what happened." Ben started describing the conversations he'd over heard at school. "I want to win!" he declared. "Nathan's giving out suckers and all the kids are saying they'll vote for him. It isn't fair."

It's the thinking child who covers her ears and turns away from you when you try to talk feelings with her, especially if she also prefers introversion. In fact, if you attempt to give her a hug or discuss the feelings when her intensity is high, she may strike out at you either with her fists or with words. She doesn't want to go into those feelings at first. She prefers to stand back and look at the situation more logically. If your child rejects your overtures of sympathy, simply say, "Tell me what happened." If that doesn't work, try asking questions. "Did someone say something you didn't like?" Or, "Was something unfair?" Stick to the facts even if your first inclination is to teach her about feelings and relationships with others. Later you can deal with the emotions and teach her that it's not all right to attack others when she's frustrated or scared.

2. Let Them Feel Competent

When Kim saved her five-year-old son from being hit by a swing, instead of being grateful, he demanded to know why she had done it.

In fact, he pulled away from her warm hug and walked back past the swing! "If I hadn't known he was a thinker," she said, "I would have been furious, but I realized he hates to look incompetent and by 'saving him,' when other kids were watching, I'd embarrassed him. He had to prove that he could handle it."

Thinking kids do *not* want to feel incompetent. They highly value achievement and as a result are often their own toughest critic. That's why criticism given *after* a situation upsets them deeply. They hate to review their mistakes. When you try to discipline them or practice a different response with them, they may tell you that you are the meanest parent in the world, refuse to listen, or explain in detail why their actions were correct.

In order to keep them working with you, set goals *before* they start an activity. For example, you might say, "You're running for student council. Here's the plan. If you win, it's important that you be courteous to the losers and tell them that they ran a good race. If you lose, you need to congratulate the winner. When you come home, if you're feeling badly, you can go for a run or take a break in your room, but you can't come home and yell at us."

If you do need to review a situation, you might say, "What happened today can't happen again. Let's talk about what we can do differently next time." Then focus on setting up a plan for the future! Avoid dwelling on past mistakes or you will lose your thinking child.

And don't forget to validate her competence. When Helen returned from a walk with her neighbor she found her nine-year-old daughter, Janey, crying and screaming hysterically at several neighborhood children. The other kids were arguing that Janey had pushed another child into the water. Janey was screaming, "No, I didn't. I didn't do anything wrong. This isn't fair!" Helen recognized a thinking kid in action. "I realized that Janey would argue to the death," she said. "I was afraid she'd end up alienating the entire neighborhood, so I dragged her into the house away from the commotion. I wanted to talk with her about the importance of getting along with others, but I knew if I started there she just get more upset. I remembered how important it is for her to feel competent, so to calm her I said, 'You're someone who really values truth. That's such a great quality, an important characteristic. You have the courage to stand up for what you believe. The world needs people like you.' She calmed down immediately, and I knew that later I could teach her that maybe next time instead of shouting 'That's not true!' she might say, "I'm sorry if you thought I pushed you, I never intended to.' Or, 'That's not the way I saw it, but I'm sorry if you did.'"

When you're working with your thinking child, make your comments specific. General praise is suspect to her. She wants to know specifically what you like or what she has done well. Comments like "Great idea" or "You jumped one hundred times" mean much more to this child than "Super!"

Thinking kids need direct coaching when it comes to identifying and acknowledging feelings, especially those that make them feel vulnerable. Admitting that they made a mistake or apologizing takes a great deal of effort. You'll have to teach them how important it is to do so and then help them to do it.

3. Justly Apply Rules

Three children were playing at the Play-Doh table. I was a visitor and didn't know the rules. So when another child came to the table, I asked, "Does anyone have extra Play-Doh so Alyssa can play, too?" Clair turned to me and matter-of-factly informed me, "The rule is only three children may be at the Play-Doh table at one time. Alyssa will have to wait."

Thinking kids value justice. They become alarmed if rules are changed or something seems unfair. The principle of fairness is very important. When playing a game, thinking kids will insist that everyone play by the rules even if that decision means that someone is out or unhappy. Statements like, "You don't like it when the rules are changed" can be very effective. If your child rejects your statements, try using questions like, "How did you see it?" or, "Are you trying to understand why the rule was changed?"

In school it's essential that thinking kids know the criteria for evaluation and grades. They also need to know what the rules are and that they will be enforced for all kids.

It's the "gray" situations that can throw off the thinking kid. He likes to focus on the facts. Sometimes you have to teach him directly the importance of considering the feelings of others and adjusting those rules when doing so would not hurt the good of the group.

Twelve-year-old Lindsey had been very focused on facts. "Feelings don't matter," she declared to her mother. "A rule is a rule. If you're out. You're out. That's it." Her mother realized there were times that adjusting for the feelings and needs of others was important, so she said to Lindsey, "I know you've moved your bedroom downstairs and have it all set up, but your brother's coming home from college and the fact is he's older than you and has lots of stuff. I think you should move back upstairs to the smaller room and he should have the larger room downstairs for the summer." "That's not fair!" Lindsey declared. "I worked hard setting that room up. It's mine."

"But the fact is he's older," her mother continued, "and he has more stuff."

"That's not fair!" Lindsey protested again.

"Oh, so you would like me to consider your feelings in making this decision?" her mother asked.

"Of course!" Lindsey declared.

"So feelings matter?" her mother asked.

Lindsey huffed and puffed but ultimately realized from her mother's example that some rules are "gray" and that it really is important to consider the feelings of those involved and adjust them accordingly.

4. Explain Why

"Look at the big white snowman," Joe remarked to his six-year-old daughter as they drove by. "It's black," she retorted. Later he said, "It's time to go to bed." "But why do I have to go to bed?" she questioned. "Because we have to get up early for work and school," he replied. "But why do we have to go to school and work?" she asked.

It's the thinking kids who can often pull you into what feels like an intellectual trap. A good debate can be pure joy for thinking children. They may freely choose to take an opposing position simply to check it out. It's important to remember that when they are asking questions, they aren't just debating, they are trying to clarify the facts, analyze them, and understand why. They are offended if you respond to their "Why" by saying, "Because I said so." Firm-minded and unwilling to accept an answer until the facts prove it or until they fully understand an issue, it's often the thinking kids who get into trouble for questioning authority. That's what happened to Victoria.

She was six and in trouble when her mother called me. "It's the 'mouth,'" she said. This time the teacher had said, "Victoria, the order for your shorts came in, put them in your backpack." Victoria was a competent kid who prided herself in knowing what was going on in her life. Her mother had not told her to expect an order. She responded to her teacher by planting her feet, folding her arms, and stating firmly, "Those are not my shorts!"

Offended by her tone, the teacher replied, "Victoria, these are your shorts. Put them in your backpack now!"

Not easily swayed from her position, Victoria held her ground, repeating, "They're not mine!"

The teacher charged on, "Victoria, put the shorts in your backpack and sit down!"

At this point Victoria, knowing that physical might was not in her favor, complied, but the battle was not over. Walking to the cloakroom she mumbled, "Fine, but they're not mine!"

The teacher called her mother. Her mother called me. "Help," she declared. "How do I teach my daughter to back off?"

How different this scenario might have been if the teacher had recognized a thinking kid and had said something like, "Oh, you didn't expect this order. The shorts came on a back order. I was surprised, too. Would you like to check the address label? Or would you like to call your mother and check with her?" Later, when the intensity was down, the teacher could have talked to Victoria about the importance of a respectful tone and given her more suitable words to use that wouldn't "push buttons" for adults. How much better if Victoria had known to say, "I wasn't expecting an order; may I check with my mother?"

Understanding why is very important for the child using his thinking preference.

5. Teach to Be Truthful and Tactful

Kelsey's friend was terribly upset that she'd gotten into trouble for forgetting an assignment. Kelsey listened to her woes and then responded, "Maybe you should have written it down." Kelsey's mother was mortified. "How can she be so insensitive?" she asked. "Kelsey has very strong feelings herself; doesn't she care about those of others?"

Because they value truth, thinking kids can get into trouble for being blunt. They tend to step back, analyze a situation, and matter-of-factly respond. They don't mean to hurt someone's feelings; they are just looking for solutions and being honest about what they perceive to be the facts.

During class one night Dave started to laugh. "My son must be a thinking kid," he said. "The father of a neighbor died, and I had my kids write sympathy notes. Kenna, my little feeler, wrote, 'Dear Dick, I'm very sorry that Grandpa Dan had to die. I loved to ride in the golf cart with him.' Brad, my thinking kid, wrote, 'Dear Dick, I didn't know him as well as everybody else. I remember him driving the golf cart. I was too young to remember riding on the tractor with him, but my mom told me I did. That's it for memories from me.'

"I thought he could do a little better then that," Dave said "so I said to him, How about a little more compassion." He responded, 'Dad, do you want me to lie? I really didn't know him very well.'"

You can count on factual kids to be straightforward and may have to teach them specific phrases like, "That's interesting," instead of, "That's stupid." Or, "I didn't see it that way, but I understand that you did," instead of, "You're wrong!"

Coaching Your Feeling Child

Communicating with feeling kids requires a very different approach from the one that thinking kids need. In order to keep them working with you and to help them understand their emotions, feeling kids need these types of responses.

1. Validate Their Feelings

Eleven-year-old Jason was sitting all alone in his room when I walked in. I knew there had been a conflict with his friends, so I asked him what had happened. When he told me, I temporarily forgot everything I've ever known about individual differences and totally discounted his feelings by remarking, "Oh, Jason, those are your friends. I'm sure they didn't mean to hurt your feelings. You need to go and tell them they hurt your feelings so that they won't do it again." Fortunately Jason was a very forgiving child. He didn't blow up on me. Instead he lamented, "I know, Mary, everyone always tells me that I need to go and talk with them, but right now I'm feeling so sad, would it be all right just to be miserable for a while?"

What Jason taught me at that moment was that feeling kids need to climb into those emotions, wrap them around, and thrash in them before they're ready to let them go. If you're a factual person, you may feel their response is an overreaction or that they are being too sensitive and emotional. But telling them to ignore their feeling or stop feeling that way doesn't work. They have to experience that disappointment and frustration before they are ready to problem solve with you or listen to your advice. When you respond empathetically, they'll work with you. If you try to talk them out of their feelings, their intensity will skyrocket.

In order to stay connected, you might say something that invites your child to share with you how she is feeling, like, "I'm so sorry that happened." Or asking questions like, "Is it upsetting you that someone's feelings were hurt?" "Did that hurt your feelings?" "Would you like a hug?" or "Is the fighting bothering you?" As you work with her, step into her emotion to connect and explore those feelings with her. Avoid minimizing or discounting the emotion or you'll miss its importance and depth. Hold your advice for later. Remember, if your child is an introvert, you'll have to give her time for reflection before she'll be ready to talk with you.

Irene found this information very helpful. Her three-year-old son had been a terror to get dressed. "He can't make up his mind," she complained. Since she was a factual person, initially she had tried logic as she worked with him. "I told him," she said, "either you choose or Mommy will choose." When he couldn't make a choice, she'd say, "Okay, Mommy will make it for you." He'd end up a screaming heap on the floor. "Now I realize he's a real feeling kid, so the other morning instead of being my rational self, I stopped and said to him, 'It's frustrating when you can't make a decision.'" He listened and stopped fussing.

If you are an introvert or a more factual person yourself, and your feeling child's venting is exhausting you, you can let her know your limits and encourage her to find other listeners besides you. Remember, too, that not every emotion needs a solution; it may simply need to be expressed.

According to Myers and Briggs, about 40 percent of males and 60 percent of females are feelers. If you have a feeling son, it's important to recognize his preference. He's dealing not only with his strong emotions but also with societal stereotypes of what it means to be "a guy."

2. Find Solutions That "Feel" Right for Everyone Involved

Children who prefer to sort through the feelings first are very aware of the body language and nonverbal communication of others. They are so observant and perceptive that they'll notice the slightest expression or movement. For example, your son may tell you his teacher has "yelling" eyes. When you look closely, you'll realize she does! Even if your child is not the child being yelled at in class, he may be the one who is suffering from headaches and stomach aches. The conflict in the classroom upsets him.

Because they are so aware of emotions, feeling children strongly consider the impact of their decisions on other people. At school or on the play ground, they're the children who give up the toy rather than fighting for it. They are the children who change the rules to ensure that everyone can stay in the game or will get a turn, which infuriates their more factual counterparts and leads to accusations that they're cheating. They may also get into trouble for "fudging" the facts or using lots of words if they feel the truth will upset you. That's what happened to Kate's daughter.

"She's incredibly sensitive," Kate told us. "Courtney doesn't want to hurt my feelings. Last year she wanted to quit piano, but she couldn't bear to tell me. So she wrote me a note that said, 'I really want to quit. I hate it. I'm crying as I write this note, but if you really want me to continue I will.' "

I suspect Bobby McFerrin is a feeler, too. When he first started conducting the St. Paul Chamber Orchestra, he admitted in an interview that he found the task very difficult. "I could sing for them the way I wanted them to sound," he said, "but there were times I actually needed to tell them things. I sought the counsel of one of the members. She told me, 'Go ahead and tell us what you want. We're used to being told what to do.' He was amazed. 'You mean,' he remarked, 'that I can just say I want it this way and I don't have to worry that the second chair trumpet player won't like me?' "

How decisions affect others is very important to the feeling individual. That's why it's essential that as you problem solve with them, you take the time to look at each possible solution and make sure it feels right for everyone involved. Kate found this to be true with her daughter Christine.

Christine's classmates complained about her sloppy work habits. She was keeping too many things on their shared work table, they said. Christine told them she understood and would try to work on it. "They hurt my feelings," she told her mother. "I was so sad." Her factual mom brainstormed options with her. Christine rejected each potential solution because they didn't "feel right." Suddenly she announced, "I have a pencil holder that is broken. I could throw it away. That would give people more space. I think it's all right to leave my water bottle there, everyone else does, and we could try a rule that everyone has two things on the table." She stopped looked at her mom and inquired, "Mom, it doesn't hurt your feelings if I don't use your solutions, does it?" Her mother reassured her that it was fine. Christine's eyes lit up as she exclaimed, "I think we can work this out so everyone will be happy!"

What's most important to kids using their feeling preference is that solutions feel right and make other people happy even if those solutions don't always seem logical to the more factual types.

3. Reassure Them That They're Liked

In order to perform their best, feeling kids need to know they're liked. That's why building a relationship with your feeling child is essential for winning their cooperation. Yelling at them, getting tough, or criticizing doesn't work. They need a gentle touch, positive words, and the reassurance that they have done well. Your disapproval saddens them and may actually stop them from performing. They need to hear that you love them, empathize with them, and care before they are ready to listen to your advice.

"Oh, that's why teaching my son how to tie his shoe was so different from working with my daughter," Suzanne exclaimed in class. "I matter-of-factly taught my daughter to make a loop, wrap it around, pull it through. She practiced and pushed herself to learn. But my son fussed throughout the entire lesson. He turned away and moaned that it was too hard. When I stopped and said, 'It's all right, you'll learn. It's kind of scary, but you have time,' he started to practice. First he had to know that I wouldn't get angry at him. When he knew he had my support, making a loop was easy. After he learned to tie, he came running to me and exclaimed, 'I can tie my shoes and I can help others because I know there's lots of kids who don't know how to tie yet.'" The feeling child needs to know you like him before he's ready to perform for you.

If feeling children think their teacher doesn't appreciate them, they're likely to be so stressed that focusing and performing can be very challenging. In school, feeling kids need a harmonious climate, lots of positive feedback, personal greetings, group projects that children work on as a team rather than competing, and opportunities to change the rules if enforcing them would hurt someone's feelings.

4. Teach How to Be Assertive

Feeling kids value harmony as a very valuable trait, but sometimes that desire for harmony can make it difficult for them to assert their own needs. That's what happened to David.

"You're describing my son!" Bob exclaimed in class. "Last week I told the kids that they could pick out a bag of candy. My daughter Megan asked David what he wanted."

"I don't care," he said, "as long as it doesn't have nuts in it."

"How about chocolate kisses?" Megan continued.

"That's fine," David replied. "Everybody loves chocolate."

"No, we'd get more pieces if we bought red licorice," Megan replied, "and they won't melt."

"Sure," David answered. "Everyone would like having as many pieces as they wanted."

"Oh, look, here's peanut butter cups. They're on sale!" Megan squealed in excitement. She turned, holding a bag of licorice in one hand and the peanut butter cups in the other. "Which ones do you want to get?" she asked David.

"I don't care; you can decide," he answered.

But Megan knew that wasn't entirely true. David didn't like peanut butter either. If she picked peanut better cups, he wouldn't like them, even if they didn't have nuts in them. She tried to push him to be more specific.

"I really don't care," he protested. "Really!"

"But you do and you're not standing up for yourself!" she retorted and turned to complain to her father, "If he won't stand up for himself, he won't get what he really wants."

It may be that David is getting what he wants. Maybe he doesn't care about the candy as much as he cares about harmony with his sister. If that's true, then it really doesn't matter what kind of candy they buy; but if he does prefer one over the other, then David needs his dad's help learning that he can assert his own needs and still live and work harmoniously with others. His dad might teach him to say, "Let's check our budget and see if we could buy two smaller bags of candy so we could each choose our favorites." Or, the licorice gives us more pieces and is cheaper even if it isn't on sale. By learning to be a creative problem solver, David can learn to solve problems in a way that maintains harmony *and* allows him to assert his own feelings and needs.

As you coach your feeling child, teach him that it's important to be honest about his emotions. Help him to choose words that will "feel" right yet truly express his feelings. Explain that it is helpful if he addresses an issue before he is really angry about it because sometimes he waits too long, then moves right into being aggressive instead of being assertive. Let him know, too, that sometimes a bit of "disharmony" can actually lead to greater harmony and better decisions when we're honest with our feelings and solve problems together.

5. Teach Them to Look at the Facts

The best decisions consider both feelings *and* facts. Once you've helped your child to explore her own feelings and brainstormed solutions that would feel right for everyone involved, try saying something like, "I have some other thoughts, would you like to hear them? Or once she's had a chance to vent her feelings, then ask, "What do you think?" Use this phrase as an opening to go back and review the facts with her. Help her to analyze the logic of potential solutions so that her final decisions include feelings and facts.

The Short Cut

If all of this seems a bit confusing, don't worry about it. When your child is upset, simply ask him, "Would you like a hug?" Or say, "I'm so sorry that happened." If he responds to your empathetic response, keep going, putting a "Band-Aid" on those feelings. But if he rejects your offer of empathy, switch to a thinking strategy and say, "Tell me what happened." Considering your child's preference for dealing with the facts or feelings first is a critical step to keeping those lines of communication open and your child working with you.

Putting It All Together

Initially, when you're trying to decide whether to respond to your child as an introvert or an extrovert or to approach her with facts or feelings first, it may seem complex, but it really isn't. You're just making two decisions—to talk or to reflect, and to address the facts or the feelings first. One day, to demonstrate how simple this idea was, I divided the parents in my class into four groups: introvert thinkers, introvert feelers, extrovert thinkers, and extrovert feelers. They started teasing one another, each group declaring their superiority. I found their comments startlingly different yet all very insightful and helpful. I thought I would include them for you so that you might better understand your style, your strengths, and the things that might pull you into power struggles when you're working with your child.

Extroverted Feeling Parents

You are very aware of and sensitive to feelings and are comfortable talking about them. When you have a problem, you like to talk about it, sometimes over and over again, with anyone who will listen. If you have an introverted, thinking child, be careful not to invade him. Offer your hug, but respect his need for space. When he does come to you, stop what you're doing and listen because he's only going to want to talk about his issue one time. Once he can read, relay information to him via the written word. Be careful not to ask too many questions. If your child prefers extroversion and thinking, expect debates. Understand that this child is trying to understand the facts and doesn't mean to offend you. You'll have to work hard to hold the line with him because a little conflict doesn't bother him as much as it bothers you. Teach him to value harmony as you do, and to give him phrases he can use that will help him learn to be more tactful.

Extroverted Factual Parents

You're great at analyzing situations and coming up with solutions, but you may need to hold back on giving advice until your child is truly ready. Recognize that your feeling child needs his feelings validated. He doesn't want to be argued out of them. Know, too, that when your feeling child comes at you with strong emotions, you may feel defensive. All those feelings are a bit overwhelming to you. Take a deep breath, pause, and remember that he's not trying to attack you; he's venting his strong emotions, and he's not going to die. Later you can teach him how to vent without triggering others. Recognize, too, that when you have a problem, you prefer working with someone who will help you to analyze a problem and come up with solutions. You don't like too much empathy or sympathy.

Introverted Feeling Parents

You are very tuned in to the emotions of your children. Humor is often one of your greatest resources. You can use it skillfully to bring harmony back to a situation. Your challenges are not to take on your child's emotions as you work with her and not to be offended by your straightforward-thinking kid. It's also important that you get enough space and quiet to meet your own needs. You need that reflection time to be able to perform at your best.

Introverted Factual Parents

You are very observant of things that are not fair. It's your extroverted-feeling child who can really wear you down. Help this child find others who can be a sounding board for her so that she doesn't exhaust you as she processes her emotions. Your extroverted kids may also need more feedback from you than you are accustomed to providing. Remember, the feelers need to know you like them, and the thinkers want specific feedback. Know, too, that you need space and quiet in order to perform at your best.

When you know your preference and your child's, you'll have a much easier time getting under the surface to the real feelings and needs; doors will open, lights will go on. Use this information to help you understand what your child is experiencing and why you are responding as you are. Knowing yourself and your child keeps you connected.

Coaching Tips

If you or your child prefer thinking:

- Recognize your need to consider the facts first.
- Find others who will enjoy a good debate with you.

- Allow yourself to linger with your feelings longer.
- Once you've analyzed the facts, remember to check the feelings.
- Validate the emotions of others; avoid trying to argue them out of their feelings.
- Let others know you're trying to figure something out so that they don't feel invaded by your questions.
- Understand you're more comfortable planning for "next time" than reviewing your mistakes.
- Know that sometimes saying you are sorry is very important.
- Ask others to give you a chance to tell them what happened.
- Remember that not every emotion needs a solution.

If you or your child prefer feeling:

- Find others who will validate and respect your feelings.
- Recognize your need to find solutions that consider the feelings of all.
- Consider your own needs as well as those of others.
- Once you've explored your feelings, check the facts.
- Understand thinking types also have feelings; they simply explore them differently than you do.
- Let others know you are not ready to problem solve yet, but you will be.
- Know that being sensitive is a "gift."
- Appreciate your ability to create harmony.
- Remember that disagreement can often lead to greater harmony.
- Offer support to others, but understand that you are not responsible for their feelings.

TWELVE

When the Struggles Are More Than Normal

Recognizing Medical Issues

"My child is a child first; he happens also to have a medical
condition."

—*The mother of three sons*

All parents experience bad days, but for Amy it was different. A nagging
sense of defeat haunted her. There wasn't just one thing that she could
put her finger on. The issues with her son seemed to be compounding,
one thing adding to another. She knew she was a good parent. She provided her kids with a loving home. There were limits, structure, and
routines, but still the power struggles with her son, Bobby, occurred day

after day. Mornings were the worst. Every day she'd vow to keep her cool, but inevitably she'd end up yelling and nagging. The initial fight was about getting out of bed; from there it rolled to getting dressed, eating breakfast without getting in and out of his chair twenty times, and brushing his teeth. The other kids could complete the morning routine in forty-five minutes. Bobby needed at least two hours. But it wasn't just the mornings that were an issue. In school his teacher noticed he was "zoning out." He wasn't finishing assignments, and the notes for parents that other kids were bringing home never made it to Bobby's house. He didn't get in trouble for running around the classroom or talking out of turn, but some part of his body was in constant motion. And by the middle of the year his reading scores were lower than average despite a very high IQ. He was frustrated with his failure, but when she asked him if he was paying attention, he'd get angry and insist he was.

For Sarah the bad days were different than Amy's, but they, too, were chronic. It was the anger that frightened her the most. She'd adopted her daughter, Anna, when she was two. Not only was Anna intense, but she could go completely ballistic three or four times a day, one tantrum rolling into another, sometimes lasting for up to three hours. Her shrieks were ear piercing, the violence frightening. Totally out of control, she'd tear things off of walls, head butt, or bite anyone who tried to stop her.

Sometimes your gut tells you that your child is different from other kids. There's something that's just not quite right. You're fighting over things other people with kids this age aren't, and the struggles are more frequent, intense, and long lasting.

You know about temperament and have realized that your child is more sensitive. But she doesn't just complain about the tags in her clothing or the elastic at her waist, she refuses to wear *any* clothing and has started turning down play dates because to go to someone's house means she has to wear pants.

Maybe you recognize that your child is more perceptive, but you've seen him look right at you when you've asked him to get dressed and then go off to do something else as though he hasn't even heard you. You know he can hear you. His hearing has been tested, and yet the connections just aren't being made.

And then again maybe you've realized that your child is slow to adapt. He doesn't like change. Before he can stop playing he has to line up his toys just so. Without his "ritual" he is distraught, but the "ritual" is growing longer and more complex. It's beginning to take up so much time that it's interfering with your day.

Everyone has suggestions for you. If you'd just be tougher or provide more structure, they advise, but you already feel like you're a drill sergeant living in a boot camp. Even professionals have minimized your concerns, assuring you it's just a stage.

But you know in your gut it's not. You child is dealing with something more than temperament or normal development. You can't quite put your finger on it, but it's there and it's real. You desperately want to be wrong.

Your emotions fluctuate from worry to fury. Guilt grabs your gut. Are you doing something wrong? Did you make him this way? Deep inside, you know you didn't, but you don't know how to help him. No matter what you do, it doesn't seem to be enough. The behavior isn't changing. Then you get angry, furious that this is happening to you. At moments you are certain that your child does have control of herself and is just choosing not to behave. But deep down you know that isn't true either. In the end it's the fear that's the worst, fear that somehow you are failing as a parent and letting your child down.

The Invisible Medical Issues

What I've learned over the years is that usually your "gut" is right. When, despite your best efforts, the bad days are far outnumbering the good ones, there very likely is something more going on with your child. Often that something more is what I call the "invisible" medical issues.

Medical factors can play a significant role in behavior issues with kids. There are the typical illnesses of childhood that can make your child temporarily cranky, irritable, and hard to deal with, but once the cold is over or the ear infection cleared, your child is back to his normal sunny self. But "invisible" medical issues can wreak havoc on your child's behavior and your relationship with him because they don't go away. That's why it's essential to seek professional help when your head tells you you've used all the normal emotion-coaching strategies and your gut tells you there's still something more.

Identifying the invisible medical issues isn't easy. Doctors often call the identifying behaviors "shadow symptoms" because they're fuzzy and often misinterpreted. Teachers will tell you your child is being lazy or not really trying. Others see the behaviors as intentionally "irritating." It's likely that you'll run into many dead ends before you find your way. But your child needs you to be his advocate, to believe in him and trust him. He isn't out to get you. He doesn't want to fight with you every day, and he *does* want to be successful. Truly he is doing the best that he can. There are things that he needs to learn, things that he needs help overcoming. You're his teacher. But when a medical issue is involved, the wiring systems get more complex and the teaching becomes more challenging. You need to have more tricks up your sleeve in order to stop the struggles. Fortunately, there are professionals who can help you to identify the issues you're facing; provide you with information, strategies, and treatment options; and, most important, support you on your journey.

Recognizing Invisible Medical Issues

In this section I'll describe for you behaviors often tied to invisible medical issues. This list is in no way comprehensive or to be considered a diagnostic tool. It's simply a description of behaviors I commonly see that lead me to advise parents to seek a complete medical assessment for their child. If what you are experiencing is different from what you see listed, trust your gut. Keep searching to find the answers you and your child need.

As you read through the list, you may realize the "symptoms" are often similar to the normal temperament factors you've just read about. But the behaviors fall along a continuum. Some fall into what's considered a "normal" range. On a continuum this might be from 1–5. *What sets the behaviors that reflect a medical issue apart is their* frequency, intensity, *or* duration, *the* combination *of symptoms, and/or a* family medical history. On a continuum these behaviors would fall in a range from 6–10. For example, the child who has to line all of his toys up just so may be demonstrating a normal need for order, but when his rituals begin interfering with normal everyday life and there is a family history of obsessive compulsive disorder, it's likely that the behaviors move out of what is considered the normal "1–5" range and into more of the problem or disorder range of 6–10. If this is the case, emotion coaching alone is not going to be enough to get you out of the power struggles. You need outside help and resources. Often, too, a child experiencing difficulties in one area is likely to have problems in others as well. For example, a child diagnosed with depression may also have an anxiety disorder, obsessive compulsive disorder, and/or attention deficit disorder. So if you're gut is telling you there has to be something more that's fueling your struggles, read through the following descriptions. If one or more strikes you as "fitting" your child, pick up your telephone and contact your pediatrician, school psychologist, or some other professional who can help you. All families have problems, but it's healthy families who know when to get help.

Attention Deficit Disorder (ADD or ADHD)

Sam was a very capable kid who also happened to be impulsive. Without thinking, he'd take a toy from another child. His teacher had worked with him for months, each time making it clear that it was not acceptable to take another child's toy and telling Sam that he needed to ask, "May I have a turn?" They'd even practiced saying the words and handing one another toys, but still Sam didn't get it. It was as though he knew what he needed to do, but he just couldn't stop himself long enough to do it.

Carrie wasn't impulsive at all, but she often got into trouble for daydreaming or tuning out. She once told her mother, "It's as though there are a hundred radio stations playing in my head, and I don't know which one I'm supposed to be tuned to." As a result she often failed to follow directions or complete assignments.

It was David's activity level that got him into trouble. He'd fidget so much that he'd fall right out of his chair. He couldn't settle himself at night. And he was the proverbial motor mouth, talking constantly, interrupting others with seemingly little regard for their frustration with him.

Three different kids, but what all of these children have in common is attention deficit/hyperactivity disorder (ADHD). This condition fits all three because there are actually three subtypes of ADHD, including: attention-deficit/hyperactivity disorder, combined type; attention-deficit/ hyperactivity disorder, predominantly inattentive type ADHD-pi; and attention-deficit/hyperactivity disorder, predominantly hyperactive-impulsive type.

Obviously all kids are energetic, and at times impulsive and inattentive. High-energy kids who don't have ADHD are always on the move and often grab things before they learn to stop and ask. Extroverts often say what's on their mind. Perceptive kids may get lost in their thoughts and forget things. But for kids with ADHD these behaviors are so intense and frequent that daily life is significantly disrupted. They forget things *every* day, even failing to turn in assignments they've completed. Or their energy and fidgeting keep them from completing tasks—even those they're interested in doing. Relationships with peers are disrupted because they miss social cues. For instance, they may fail to pick up the look on someone's face that suggests, You shouldn't have said that, or You're standing too close, or You're speaking too loudly.

It's true the diagnosis of ADHD can be very subjective. For this reason a complete evaluation conducted by a professional team, consisting of a pediatrician and psychologist and ideally a speech therapist and occupational therapist along with reports from home and school settings, is essential for an accurate diagnosis of ADHD. ADHD-pi is usually not evident until a child reaches school age, but ADHD may be evident in a child as young as two years old. It is my hope that a new test developed by Dr. John Gabrieli of Stanford's Department of Psychology, which uses a brain scan to identify a biological "signature" of those with attention deficit, will soon be more readily available.

If your child's energy level, impulsiveness, or inattention is constantly pulling you into power struggles, look for the real fuel source.

You don't have to scream every morning. Your child can be successful in school and with friends. Treatment may include behavior training like all of the strategies included in this book. For example, daily exercise to direct his energy; picture charts or charts with words written in different colors to help him remember what he needs to bring home from school; games that ask him to stop, think, and ask himself, What will happen next, in order to teach him how to manage his impulses. Environments with just the right amount of background noise and lighting may help him stay focused when he's working on a task. In addition to these strategies, however, it's likely that your child will need medication.

Remember, your child doesn't want to fight with you. He isn't just being absentminded, mean, or lazy. This truly is a child who is desperately asking for help. He knows he's different, but he doesn't know why. He needs you to help him define what's wrong and to find the strategies that work at home and school. Most important, he needs you to love him for who he is and to see his creativity, ability to see outside of the box, and energy as gifts he can learn to channel.

Sensory Integration Dysfunction (SI)

It was textures that drove Haley mad. She refused to eat any kind of meat, complaining that it was too stringy. Clothing was a huge issue. The only way her mother could get Haley to wear socks was to vigorously massage her feet first. At school Haley refused to finger paint and hated worksheets that included any kind of pasting. The struggles were constant, time consuming, and exhausting, especially when other people told her mother she should just force Haley to comply.

Sadie loved finger painting. The trouble was she didn't just paint the paper, she painted her arms and face, rubbing the paint along her skin and reveling in the sensation. Whenever the paint was available, Sadie was in it up to her elbows. She was also the kid the teachers couldn't get off the swings. She seemed to crave movement and would swing hard and long. On the days it was too cold or rainy to go outside, Sadie was miserable.

Peter loved the swings, too, but more often than not he got into trouble while lining up to go outside. That's because he'd literally bounce off the walls or tightly squeeze the child in front of him. His shoes were never tied because he liked them loose. And it wasn't unusual for him to clown around and "stumble," then roll on the ground, seemingly enjoying the sensations.

Many kids are temperamentally more sensitive, but for some kids the intensity of their sensitivity has a significant impact on their daily lives. If this is true for your child, you may be dealing with behavior that is actually a disorder. Sensory integration disorder, also called sensory integration dysfunction, is the inability to process information received through the senses. According to Carol Kranowitz in *The Out-of-Sync Child*, "The red flags of SI Dysfunction are a child's unusual responses to touching and being touched, and/or to moving and being moved."

Initially the behaviors of kids with SI dysfunction resemble those of kids who are temperamentally sensitive. But kids experiencing SI don't just need comfortable shoes like the sensitive child, they can't stand to wear any shoes. They are dealing with more than temperament.

The lines defining SI dysfunction are fuzzy. Sometimes children experiencing SI dysfunction are *over*sensitive and choose to avoid sensations. At other times they may be *under*sensitive and seek sensations. What seems to be most important is that they have *control* of the sensations bombarding their body.

For example, a child experiencing SI dysfunction may refuse to have you push her on the swing but will choose to lay stomach first on the swing dangling her feet, then swing for an hour. That's because she's in control of the movement. Or a child may run to you with open arms begging for a tight bear hug. When you respond, she'll squeeze you so hard it almost hurts. But if you come up behind this child and unexpectedly hug her, she may throw a fit or even hit you. She wants to control the touch.

A child experiencing *over*sensitivity doesn't like to be touched, hates to get dirty, and is intolerant of the most minor of irritants. This is the child who doesn't like to swing, climb, slide, ride in the wagon, or run, and may avoid physical activities. He commonly experiences motion sickness and covers his eyes or ears if there's too much stimulation.

Because his mouth may also be very sensitive, brushing his teeth can be a huge battle and the texture of foods can be a major source of irritation. Smooth, familiar yogurt may be fine, but lumpy foods like cottage cheese may be detestable.

Children experiencing *under*sensitivity may actively seek sensations or just sit because their bodies are not processing the stimulation around them. If they seek stimulation, they may look like Sadie, coating their entire body with paint while the other kids simply finger paint with it. They may chew on inedible objects like shirt cuffs and love to swing or spin for extended periods of time. It's these kids who turn up the television and speak in a booming voice, unaware that they're hurting other people's ears.

If your child is in trouble because he can't walk from his desk to the front of the room without bumping into ten other desks or kids, you may have a child experiencing understimulation. He seeks stimulation, especially pressure, and gets it by bumping, hitting, or jumping.

Some kids with SI may crave one sensation and detest another. And sometimes kids with SI have good days when systems are working well and bad days when nothing seems to connect. This can be confusing since one might expect that if your child has this disorder there would be problems every day. The reason he doesn't is because on one day he might have gotten up early and then jumped around for twenty minutes before he got on the school bus. Because of the jumping his body is now able to regulate the motion and noise of the school bus and he does just fine. However, the next day you might be rushing in the morning. He doesn't get to jump, and as a result can't stand the motion and noise of the bus. By the time he gets to school he's fit to be tied and hits the first child who comes near him.

Most family doctors have not received training in SI dysfunction, which contributes to a lot of misdiagnoses. SI kids are frequently mislabeled as having attention deficit, but the treatments are different. Medications are not used in the treatment of SI dysfunction. Instead you and your child will learn noninvasive strategies: brushing techniques (to desensitize the skin), bear hugs (for pressure), joint compression, jumping, chair push-ups (putting your hands on your chair and lifting your body), and other sensory motor activities. You'll also discover simple strategies like having your child sit at the end of a row or stand in the back of the line so that he has to take in stimulation from only one side of his body, or keeping a Koosh ball or worry stone in his desk at school or in his pocket to use when he starts to feel fidgety or irritable.

So if you and your child are constantly fighting because he squeezes other people, refuses to tie his shoes or even wear shoes, take another look. This may not be a child who is intentionally trying to be aggressive, nasty, or noncompliant. This may be a kid who is trying to calm down his nervous system.

When you understand SI and work with your child to help him integrate the sensations he's experiencing, you'll discover that those long-standing power struggles have disappeared. Suddenly you can enjoy the new awareness of stimulation your child brings to you. Your life is richer because of it.

If you think your child may be experiencing SI, consult an occupational therapist. They are professionals specifically trained to help you and your child learn adaptive strategies that help the nervous system work more efficiently. You can find one through your school, doctor, health insurance company, or the Yellow Pages.

Language Problems

Becca didn't listen. It wasn't that she couldn't hear. Her mother knew she could. She'd had her hearing tested, but Becca didn't do what she was asked to do or answer questions. For example, her mother could lay out colored blocks. Becca would quickly and accurately name the colors of each. But if she asked Becca to hand her the green one, Becca wouldn't. It was as though she was playing a game, but the game was no longer fun. It was worrisome.

From the outside it looked like Becca was just being stubborn or uncooperative, but the reality was even though Becca could hear, she couldn't figure out what the words meant.

Ben's issue was different. He understood the questions adults asked him, but he didn't talk. At preschool his teachers thought he was being manipulative.

Individual differences in the rate of speech and language development can be substantial and still fall within what's considered a normal range of development. However, experts estimate that 3 to 5 percent of all children may be affected by language disorders. For some kids, like Ben, the disorder relates to expressive language. Other kids, like Becca, are experiencing what's called mixed receptive-expressive language disorder. They speak, but they don't understand the meaning of the words.

If you are frustrated because your child isn't listening to you or refuses to talk, step into her shoes. Understand that your words are important to her. She wants to communicate with you. If she's not, it's not because she isn't trying. It's because something is wrong.

When a child is two years old, strangers should be able to understand what he is saying 50 percent of the time. By age three that rate climbs to 75 percent. If he constantly searches for words—for example, instead of saying refrigerator, he says something like "the thing that keeps things cold," or if you are giving him clear directions and he just isn't responding while other children his age are—it's time to seek help.

Language delays or disorders of any type affect impulse control. Being able to express oneself verbally is an essential element of a more thoughtful and suitable response. A speech therapist can help you determine if your child has a language disorder, and can give you the techniques you need to connect with her. You don't have to struggle. There really are effective strategies that can help you. Don't delay; early intervention for language problems is critical. Once again, you can find the help you need through your local public school or pediatrician's office.

Anxiety Disorders

Allison was a worrier. This didn't surprise her mother because she came from a family of worriers. But Allison didn't worry just a little, she worried a lot. She needed to know where she was going—not unlike kids who are temperamentally slow to adapt. But she also had to know how long they would be gone and exactly what to expect. Even when she had that information, however, she still wasn't calm. In first grade she asked her mother, "What if I come home from school and you're not home?"

"What could you do?" her mother asked. "Go to Kim's house," Allison replied. "Good idea," her mother said. "But what if Kim wasn't home?" Allison continued. "Go to Sarah's house," her mother suggested. "But what if Sarah *and* Kim weren't home?" Allison pushed. The discussion continued, each time Allison adding another "what if." Finally, her mother said, "There are four school-age children in this cul de sac. All of them have someone home when they get off the bus. It would *never* happen that no adult was home in the cul de sac." But the worry bothered Allison. She didn't want to ride the bus. She didn't want to go to school. Worry upon worry piled up.

Four-year-old Patrick was attending preschool. Initially he was excited to go, but upon arrival he shut down, stopped talking, then fell onto the floor curled up in a fetal position with his eyes shut. He didn't respond to the teacher's words. He didn't even look at her, but ten minutes later he got up and was all right.

Everybody knows what it's like to feel anxious—the butterflies in the stomach before a first day at school or when you have to give a speech. Anxiety can make you gear up and prepare and help you to cope. But those with an anxiety disorder experience extreme worry that disrupts daily life. Anxiety disorders aren't just a case of "nerves"—the anxiety can be paralyzing. You can't think, and you can't function.

General anxiety disorder often appears in childhood and adolescence. It affects more females than males and tends to run in families. It is exacerbated by stress and often is also linked with depression.

When kids experience anxiety, adults often misinterpret their behaviors, thinking the kids are being stubborn or trying to get out of going to school, riding the bus, or participating in the field trip. But they're not just trying to pull one over on you. Anxiety is a medical issue that requires treatment. If your gut says your child's worries are more than the average child's, consult a psychologist. You can learn strategies to help your child be successful. That's what Terry did.

Leta was eight when she started experiencing significant separation anxiety at school. They had just moved, and she didn't want her mother to leave her. Tears streamed down her face at the mere thought of going to school. "I can't!" she desperately declared. Through her pediatrician

Terry found a psychologist to help them. First she learned that Leta truly was anxious. She wasn't just trying to be difficult. Together they set up a plan for success that included vigorous exercise before school. Then they bought Leta a textured locket that felt good to rub. In the locket they put a picture of their family. A box with a lock on it was also purchased, and Leta was asked to draw pictures or write stories about her worst fears. These fears were then locked away in the worry box where they were contained. She could take them out and talk about them if she wished, but then the pictures were locked back in the box. Leta and her mother also wove a cloth bracelet for her. Mom slept with the bracelet so that it smelled of her. When Leta felt anxious, she could put it up to her nose and smell her mother.

Finally they set up a schedule for adapting to school. The first day Leta and her mother went to school together. Mom stayed the entire day. The next day she stepped out for fifteen minutes at ten o'clock. Leta knew this was part of the plan and that during the time, if she felt anxious, she could rub her locket, look at the picture it held, or touch her bracelet. Gradually Mom extended her absences, always remaining in the building, always telling Leta exactly when she would return. Most important, she let Leta know that she could do this, that she was a capable kid. It's true Terry had to take time off from work, but by taking the time to work with Leta instead of resisting her, the morning struggles diminished rapidly as well as the number of distraught phone calls that had interrupted the day. The plan hasn't been 100 percent effective—Leta is still anxious—but Leta *has* learned strategies for coping with her anxiety, and she's feeling more comfortable every day.

You, too, can help your child learn to live with a brain that's a bit more on alert. Knowing that you understand and are willing to support her will keep her working with you, even when the going gets tough.

Depression

What struck Terry about her daughter was that the childlike joy was simply not there much of the time. This was so different from the child she knew, and it worried her. Depression can be hard to diagnose in children. The symptoms are different from those in adults, and are more intermittent. Depressed kids may experience spurts of energy followed by lethargy, bouts of sadness followed by periods of happiness. They may experience inattention or an inability to make decisions, but not all of the time. The most common and consistent symptoms are extreme irritability and negativity. That's why they can pull you right into power struggles. They're sleeping for longer periods of time and won't get out of bed, or they're barely sleeping at all. You can't get them to eat, or they're craving junk food. Their poor attitude drives you wild. But this isn't just a bad mood, it's ongoing. This is a child experiencing depression.

Depression is often misdiagnosed as attention deficit. Teachers complain that the child is daydreaming or inattentive. He isn't getting things done and isn't well organized. Disagreements with peers are frequent. The difference between attention deficit and depression is that attention deficit is usually an ongoing problem. It was an issue in second grade and is still an issue in fourth. Kids experiencing depression have done well in earlier grades, then suddenly run into problems.

Significant stress, like parents' divorce, loss of a job, or death, can trigger depression, but sometimes it just happens. In order to recognize it, you'll want to look at your family history. Depression runs in families.

If your child seems to be experiencing so much anger and resentment that everyday activities are affected, then it's time to consult a professional who specializes in treating children with depression. Remember your child doesn't choose to feel this way. He doesn't want you to feel angry or disappointed because of him, but he doesn't know what's wrong or how to change things. He needs your help, guidance, and understanding to regain his energy and sense of joy. When he does, the power struggles will disappear.

Obsessive Compulsive Disorder (OCD)

Aaron was trying to write out his multiplication tables. He would complete a row, then stop, and yell at himself, "Stupid! Stupid! Stupid! How can you be so stupid!" Violently scratching out his mistakes he'd rip holes in the paper and destroy it.

Aaron is a child experiencing obsessive compulsive disorder, or OCD.

According to the National Institute of Mental Health, at least one-third of the cases of adult OCD began in childhood. At the extreme end these kids have to write things on a page in just a certain way. Even if they are almost finished with an assignment, they'll rip up the entire thing and start over again if they make a mistake. It's hard for them to get things done because they get stuck on little tiny details. Things *have* to be done a certain way. Or they *have* to be the first in line, first to answer, or first in anything. When it doesn't happen, they are terribly upset.

Children with OCD suffer intensely from recurrent, unwanted thoughts or rituals that they feel they cannot control. They may get into trouble for not listening because they are obsessing in their mind. They're counting to a certain number over and over or saying a specific prayer. On the outside it looks as if they're unfocused, but on the inside they're focused on every single word.

Many kids with OCD have an overwhelming fear of germs. It's not uncommon for them to need to wash their hands until they're raw. Along with rituals of handwashing may be counting, checking, or cleaning—all in hope of feeling more comfortable.

All children enjoy rituals. It's not uncommon for a preschooler to demand the same book night after night or to go on eating jags during which he wants to eat only one type of food for a period of weeks. However, when the rituals require more than an hour of attention a day, the sense of perfectionism is debilitating your child, he is fearful that if he doesn't complete his rituals something bad will happen, and/or there is a family history of OCD, it may be time to explore whether you're dealing with a kid who is experiencing OCD. Treatments for OCD combine medications and behavior therapy. Your child will deeply appreciate your help in easing his fears.

Autism and Other Pervasive Developmental Disorders

He was wailing, deep sobs choking him. His mother sat on the floor nearby. He didn't want to be touched. "What do I do?" she asked me. "He'll do this, just lose it, and I can't comfort him." Her eyes filled with tears. "I'm his mother, and I can't figure out how to comfort him."

"What soothes him?" I asked. "Nothing," she responded. "Does he have a blanket or a pacifier?" I asked. "He's got a blanket," she said, and went to get it. He took it and pulled it over his head.

Autism and other pervasive developmental disorders, PDDs, are neurobiological in origin. Children experiencing PDDs do not use adults as resources to help them meet their needs. They do not seek interaction.

For example, a normal fourteen-month-old child who wants something from a cupboard whimpers or goes to an adult to get attention. It's likely that a child experiencing autism, however, would go straight to the cupboard and try to get what he wanted on his own. He doesn't know that an adult could help him.

The severity of autism varies widely. Some children are more severely impacted than others, which affects what treatments might be suggested.

Some kids with autistic behaviors have limited language skills, but not all. Kids with Aspberger syndrome, a type of autism, have higher verbal skills but still have issues with social interaction. Their language development is often out of sequence. Most children learn the concept of "one" before learning to count to ten. Children with autism learn out of sequence. They can count to ten but don't know what one cookie is. Or they can recognize a word but don't understand what the word is.

Ritualistic and/or repetitive behaviors are also common to kids experiencing autism. You may see unusual posturing or finger movements, rocking, or looking or playing with a toy in a unique, repetitive way. That's what two-year-old Mindy did. Whenever she finished with a toy, she dumped it behind the stereo cabinet. This didn't seem too unusual since all toddlers dump toys, but then Mindy started dumping *every-thing* behind the stereo cabinet, including her dinner plate when she finished eating.

It's kids with high functioning autism that are often the most challenging for parents and teachers because they look normal but have difficulty with written and verbal language, organizational skills, social skills, and interpreting the emotional and verbal cues of others. These problems make success at school and peace within the home challenging, which is why you find yourself in power struggles day after day.

If your child's behavior strikes you as unusual, or if you find it extremely difficult to soothe him and connect with him, seek a professional assessment. Help may be as close as your public school's early-childhood special-education office.

Attachment Disorders

During infancy a child's most critical developmental task is to learn that he can trust his caregivers to respond sensitively when he needs it. When this doesn't happen, he mistrusts others and may become hyper-vigilant, depressed, angry, or he may fail to thrive.

Attachment disorders occur in a variety of situations. Sometimes a parent experiencing depression or other medical issues hasn't been able to respond consistently. Extended separations or hospital stays can cause attachment issues. Children who have been moved through the foster care system or adoption process with attachments formed then broken may also experience symptoms. Frequent changes of caregivers, or moves that separate family members at critical points in a child's development, or a shift from one culture to another, can also affect the formation of a strong sense of attachment.

It's the severity of the behaviors that raises a red flag for attachment disorders. If your child's life experiences include a significant loss or separation, exposure to an adult she could not trust, or the unavailability of a consistent, sensitive caregiver during her early years, seek professional help and intervention.

The most common symptoms in young children are problems with feeding and weight gain. Other kids may be angry, hypervigilant, and lack empathy for others. This is the child who responds to a crying child by hitting him, or not only shoves back the child who pushed him but rams the child into the wall. Bedtime is a nightmare for kids with attachment issues. Separating causes them to panic, and the battles can go on for hours. It's these kids who are often better behaved with strangers than with their family members. Once there is any hint of intimacy, they pull back, ready to do battle. Kids with attachment issues will test and push limits, trying to find out if they really can trust that you will not abandon them. They also vehemently fight limits and guidance because they do not trust you to have power over them.

Hoarding or stealing can also be an issue for kids with attachment disorders. Because they don't feel safe or connected to others, they may hide food or clothing or steal without any thought as to the impact of the loss on others.

Children with attachment disorders can learn to trust again and to be empathetic. Don't let the intensity of your child's anger and pain disconnect you. Seek professional help. Your child can be successful—it's not too late.

Encopresis

Encopresis is a physical problem that often leads to huge power struggles. The official definition of encopresis, or fecal soiling, is the regular (at least once a month) passage of bowel movements or smears of feces (not just stains from inadequate wiping) into clothing, pajamas, or other inappropriate places by a child over the age of four years. These bowel movements are not voluntary, and the most common cause is severe, long-standing, unrecognized constipation. Encopresis is more common among boys than girls.

When a child experiences constipation or retains his stools because he's uncomfortable using a public rest room, a large mass of feces gradually collects in the rectum. As it sits inside of the body, it gets dry and dense, making it more and more difficult and painful to pass. The fear of pain causes the child to withhold even more. Finally, the external sphincter and rectal muscles tire from continual stretching, and stool leaks out. This constant stretching may also lead to nerve fatigue and the child no longer consciously feels the urgency to defecate. The result is a school-age child who may be having accidents at school, on the bus, or at home.

You may think your child is deliberately soiling when in reality it's taking every ounce of his self-control to avoid having accidents in front of his friends. Encopresis starts out as a physical issue but can become an emotional one if not recognized and treated. If your child is experiencing toileting accidents, consult your physician about encopresis. He isn't just being lazy or stubborn. He is a child who needs your help and understanding. Be his emotion coach, work with him, and stay connected.

This is in no way a complete list of potential medical issues that can affect kids' behaviors. Enlarged adenoids and tonsils may disrupt sleep, leading to sleep deprivation. Fluid in the ears and undiagnosed ear infections can cause language delays and coordination problems. Fetal alcohol syndrome, Tourette's syndrome, growth disorders, diabetes, thyroid problems, and many other medical issues can significantly impact your child. When your child's behaviors leave you puzzled and at wits' end, don't give up. It's essential that you seek help. This may not have been your dream, but it doesn't have to be a nightmare.

Seeking Help

When you realize that the power struggles you are experiencing with your child are more than normal, it isn't easy to pick up the phone and ask for assistance. This isn't the way it was supposed to be. Your dream shatters, the pieces splintered and sharp. But know as you call that you are doing the right thing. The earlier you seek help for your child, the better. You are taking the steps to help him understand the emotional and physical sensations that he is experiencing and to teach him effective management strategies. You are your child's emotion coach, but you don't have to be the only one. You don't have to do it alone.

Talk with your physician, health insurance provider, or local public-school-district special-education office. Help is available to you. Schools are required by federal law to provide services for children with special needs. Many, but not all, of the invisible medical issues I've described for you do qualify a child for services.

As you seek help look for the following:

- a team of professionals who work specifically with children
- a thorough, multifaceted evaluation
- support and encouragement

The Importance of a Team Approach

Many of the invisible medical issues include very similar symptoms. You need and want an accurate diagnosis and quality treatment recommendations. The team conducting an evaluation may include a pediatrician, speech pathologist, psychologist or psychiatrist, and/or occupational therapist; together they will provide you with a very thorough and broad analysis of the issues. While medication may indeed be part of your child's treatment, you want a plan that includes more than management of medications. Behavior training is also an essential part of treatment. Medication alone is *never* enough.

Children are not miniature adults, and working with kids under seven years of age requires very skilled practitioners. Preschoolers cannot tell you with words what they are experiencing. The professional has to be able to interpret a child's behaviors. That's why your team must include people who see hundreds, maybe thousands of children each year and know the difference between temperament, normal growth and development, stress, and potential medical issues. If your child is elementary age, be sure to include your school professionals on your team.

Getting a Thorough Evaluation

Invisible medical issues cannot be accurately diagnosed with a fifteen-minute conversation in your pediatrician's office. A complete evaluation includes reports from you, your child's teachers, and child-care providers. One of the professionals on your team may also conduct an observation in one or more of the settings. Your family's medical history is also vital. You know more about your family's history and your child's than you might think, but it may take a competent professional asking the right questions and allowing enough time for you to come up with key pieces of information. If your child is adopted and you do not have a complete family medical history, it's worth your efforts to learn as much as you possibly can. Finally, an evaluation conducted over a period of weeks rather than hours also helps to discern an ongoing problem versus a stress issue or a developmental growth spurt.

Finding Support and Encouragement

You have the right to expect that the professionals you work with will be nonjudgemental and supportive of you and your child. Together with this team, you will be making decisions that are critical to your child's well-being now and in the future. It's important that you trust and respect them and sense that they realize you know your child better than anyone else. Don't be afraid to get a second opinion. Find the team and treatment plan that fit your family.

Allow yourself time. You don't have to rush to make a decision. Initially when you find that your child has a medical issue you're likely to grieve. Elizabeth remembers vividly the day she learned that her son had attention deficit disorder and her daughter an anxiety disorder. "A team at the university tested the kids," she told me. "We'd been back and forth numerous times over a period of about six weeks. When it was finally time to review the reports and make recommendations, I remember sitting at the table with three or four professionals. They were considerate and kind people, but I felt so small. Thank God my partner was with me. After they reviewed the reports and told us our options, I remember being asked if I had questions. I couldn't think of one. I was numb. I guess they expected that reaction because they introduced us to Christine, our contact person. She gave me her card and told me, when I was ready, to call her with my questions.

"I walked out. By the time I got to the car I was sobbing. I couldn't call Christine. At least not until I called a good friend whose son has attention deficit. When she answered the phone, I sobbed again. She told me, 'There's lots of things you can look at. Take your time. You can decide. Taking medication doesn't necessarily mean taking it for life. And if it works, it's wonderful.'

"I needed to hear it from a friend whom I respected more than just in that cold setting with those people telling me what they knew about my kids."

Draw your friends and family members around you. Consider joining a support group with other parents whose children face similar challenges. Knowing you're not alone gives you the energy you need to help your child the most.

Focusing on Your Child

Your child will always be a child first. He is not an attention deficit child. He is a child who also happens to have attention deficit. Always keep that special, unique person in mind. Let go of the expectations that are unfair to your child. Discover his gifts and treasure them.

Kim Cardwell advises, "Look at the positive things your child brings to your family. This may be the child who comes up with solutions or ideas no one else would have devised. Then again this may be the child who has forced your family to slow down and connect more, allowing you to appreciate each other even more." Don't let an undiagnosed medical issue disconnect you from your child.

Coaching Tips

- Understand all the issues your child is dealing with in order to be a more effective emotion coach.
- Listen to your intuition.
- Recognize behaviors that are more frequent, intense, or long-standing than "normal."
- Seek help.
- Create a team.
- Treasure the unique gifts of your child.

PART FOUR

Developing Competence: Teaching Life's Essential Skills

THIRTEEN

Stressed-Out Kids

Learning to Deal with Life's Ups and Downs

"You can't be brave if you've only had wonderful things happen to you."

—Mary Tyler Moore

One of the most unusual phone calls I have ever received jarred me from my reverie at six-forty one morning in December. When I picked up the phone, the caller desperately asked, "Is this the woman who wrote the book?" "Yes, I write books," I replied tentatively, not quite sure what to make of this.

"You've got to help me!" the caller pleaded.

"I'll do my best," I stuttered, still groggy with sleep.

"It's my four-year-old," she continued breathlessly. "He's whacking baby Jesus with a pirate's sword!"

I have to admit I was taken aback. In more than twenty years of working with families, I had never run into this problem before. I was speechless and stumbled. "Does he have a history of going after baby Jesus?" I asked, unable to think of a more intelligent question.

"No," she replied seriously, "but he's always been intense."

I paused, trying to get my wits about me. The caller filled the gap in the conversation. "This is serious! The church across the street just put out their nativity scene. Every time I turn around he's out the door whacking baby Jesus with his pirate's sword. I've sent him to time-out. I've taken away his sword. It doesn't matter. He picks up pencils, rulers, anything he can get his hands on, then dashes out the door and across the street. This is a small town; people are starting to talk!"

My mind raced. Why would a child be whacking baby Jesus? He must be very angry about something, I thought, and asked, "Has your family experienced any significant pain or stress lately?"

"My father died six weeks ago," she replied softly.

"Was your son close to him?" I questioned.

"Oh, yes," she answered. "They saw each other every day."

"What did people tell him when Grandpa died?" I asked. She paused, sighed deeply, and slowly responded, "That baby Jesus took Grandpa to heaven."

This child was grieving, but he didn't know how to tell his parents. Instead, he acted out. Kids don't tell us when they're experiencing emotional pain and stress. Instead they whack baby Jesus with their pirate's sword, whine, complain, beg for help with anything and everything, or become downright nasty. It's easy to immediately slip into the intimidator's role in response. And to make matters worse, 90 percent of the time our kids stress is tied to our own. Trying to cope with our own inner turmoil and at the same time be patient with our kids can be a huge challenge. And even if our child's stress isn't related to our own, it still distresses us because we hate to see our kids hurting.

Learning how to deal with life's ups and downs is an essential life skill. When you understand the physiology of stress, it's easier to be the sensitive emotion coach that your child needs and stay out of the power struggles.

The Stress Hormones

If a parent tells me his child has been awake thirty minutes and has already been sent to time-out three times, I always ask about the family's stress level. That's because researchers have found that when we're stressed, our bodies become aroused, ready for action. There are actually two arousal systems: short term and long term. The short-term system is activated when your child spills a glass of milk or drops her Tonka truck on your toe. You quickly get intense and just as quickly get over it. The long-term system of arousal is governed more by longer-acting hormones. This system goes into action just as fast, but it's main by-product is a brain chemical called cortisol. Cortisol keeps the brain on alert and lingers much longer in your system. Because cortisol remains in the system even during sleep, it can make you and your child much more vulnerable to blowups.

When you're stressed, cortisol levels rise, which leads to neural static. You can't think, and you forget things. You're more excitable and more sensitive, which can disrupt sleep and make crowds unbearable, noises louder, and surprises harder to handle. The cycle feeds itself—you get more stressed out and your brain reacts by releasing more cortisol. That's why the more stressed the child, the less he'll sleep; and the less sleep he gets, the more cortisol his brain produces. The result is a kid who wakes up ready to battle.

Recognizing the Behaviors That Signal the Emotions of Stress

Stress sneaks up on us, and as a result we often don't even realize it's taking its toll. Kids never say, "Gee, Mom or Dad, I'm really hurting." Instead they throw tantrums, hit their siblings or the neighbor kids, forget their homework, start having toileting accidents after having been trained for two years, complain of headaches and stomachaches, and refuse to sleep in their own bed or to go upstairs alone. You probably have a few words you could use to describe a child who acts this way, but "stressed out" probably isn't the first to come to mind. That's why it's important for you to recognize some of the typical stress behaviors. As you read through the following scenarios, you'll also notice that adults exhibit many of the same behaviors when their cortisol levels are high. Recognizing stress behaviors helps you to realize that your family has not been taken over by extraterrestrial forces. Neither you nor your child is a monster—even if it sometimes feels that way—but you are stressed.

Typical stress behaviors fall into two basic categories: *regressive* behaviors and *aggressive* behaviors. You and your child may find your stress behaviors falling into one category or the other, or you might demonstrate a combination of both. No one will demonstrate every one of these behaviors, nor is the following list comprehensive. The most important thing is that you recognize stress behaviors when you see or hear them.

Regressive Behaviors

Some regressive behaviors often exhibited by parents and kids who are stressed include these:

Lethargy and Apathy

Judy sighed, "My daughter and I had a huge power struggle yesterday morning. It really scared me. I got so angry I hit her. I have to be out of the house by seven A.M. My husband and I are separated, so it's just my daughter and me. I needed her to get in the shower, but she wouldn't. She just laid on the couch in a fetal position, hugging the cat, refusing to listen and do what she was told. I can't do it all alone. She has to help me, but she wouldn't. That's when I lost it. I finally just hauled her out of the apartment. When we got home that night, I felt terrible. I asked her, 'Why was it so important to you to lay on the couch with your cat?' She turned to me with big brown eyes and whispered, 'My daddy gave me my cat and my daddy doesn't come home anymore.' Here I'm thinking it's an affront of my parental authority or I've produced a lazy, irresponsible child, and the kid is grieving!"

Stress robs kids of energy, making it very difficult for them to comply with requests and perform even the most basic of tasks. They're tired and want more help from us. The trouble is that frequently when our kids are this stressed, so are we. They need our help, and we barely have the energy to get ourselves out of bed. Recognizing as signs of stress lethargy and kids curling into a fetal position when they're upset helps us to keep our cool and realize our kids aren't just being lazy. It's this recognition that allows us to stop threatening them with punishments and instead ask, "How can we work together to make things better?"

Difficult Separations and Disrupted Sleep Patterns

"When my husband was sent to Haiti with the army reserves for six months, I couldn't get my kids to follow routines, especially at night-time. They clung to me all day and refused to let me out of their sight. Each would have to be put to bed ten times or more, and I had to lock them out of the bathroom just to brush my teeth. The whole time I was in there, they stood in the hallway pounding on the door and screaming."

Fear is a lousy companion and fear of abandonment or loss can turn normally independent kids into very needy people. Sleep patterns become disrupted, so children wake frequently. Bedtimes and dropoff at school or child care can become major struggles as your kids fight to stay connected to you and reassure themselves you will not abandon them. When you need them to be independent, they are most dependent, and the fights begin.

Falling Apart Over Seemingly Insignificant Things

Six-year-old Katarina was bubbling with excitement. Today was the Valentine's party at school! Running to meet the crossing patrol at the corner, she suddenly realized that she'd forgotten her stuffed animal. She burst into tears, plopped down on the sidewalk, and refused to go with the patrol. Her mother, Annette, pulled her up and told her to go, but she wouldn't. Knowing she'd left younger kids in the house and not having enough time to deal with this, Annette took Katarina home again. At home Katarina cried and cried. She hadn't slept well. Her dad was gone. He usually helped her get dressed in the morning but he hadn't been there. Katarina was so worried that without his help she might be late that she'd slept in her clothes. And her clothes didn't feel right. Instead of her normal pants and T-shirt she was wearing party clothes. The schedule was going to be different that day, too, and she didn't know when she was going to get to eat lunch. In the end, all of the excitement was just too much and a missing stuffed animal put her right over the edge.

It's hard to imagine why some seemingly insignificant little thing or an innocent request like, "Put your paper in the wastebasket" or "Pick up your bag," can result in a complete meltdown for your child. That's why it's important to remember it's not the "little thing" that took her down. Stress is cumulative. One thing adds to another. The cortisol levels rise and overwhelm her, and once she begins to lose it, she can't easily stop. The same is true for you. On a normal day a request to have a sandwich cut in triangles wouldn't phase you. When you're stressed, it can turn you into a shrew.

Fearfulness

Jacob was eight and suddenly throwing terrible tantrums ten times a day. The last one occurred when he wanted his mother to sit on the landing while he went upstairs. "This was ridiculous," she said. "He's gone upstairs a thousand times without me sitting on the landing, but suddenly he was demanding that I stay there and wait for him. I took a firm stance and held my ground. He ended up screaming for an hour. Is he manipulating me?"

In the end we discovered that Jacob wasn't manipulating his mother at all. He was responding to a news story—the recent murder of a child in her home.

At some point, kids begin to realize that those news stories they hear about are happening right in their own community. Suddenly they're afraid to go upstairs or downstairs or even to the bathroom alone. They have to work through this new awareness and feel safe before they're ready to venture on their own again. Your anxiety rises with your child's. Are you doing something wrong? Why is your normally independent kid suddenly so dependent upon you? Guilt plagues you and the tension rises.

Forgetfulness and Indecisiveness

It was seven forty-five A.M. The school bus had just rambled past my window when the phone rang. It was my "other kid" from down the street. (We're not related but I'm his backup mom.) "I've got a problem," he said.

"You just missed the bus?" I guessed.

"Worse than that," he said. "I can't find my folder, and it's got my report in it. It's due today, and I need it to pass eighth grade. It's hopeless. I'm going to flunk. My dad and sister are already gone. Will you please help me?"

I jumped into a pair of jeans and went to help him look. We searched the house but found nothing. He couldn't remember for sure if he'd had the folder at home or not. He thought he had, but he wasn't quite sure. He didn't remember the last time he had it. I knew we were in trouble. "Let's go to school and check your locker," I suggested. And there it was right where he'd left it.

An irresponsible kid or a stressed-out one? I knew for a fact that this young man is hardworking, responsible, and bright. So I asked him about his school, sports, and music schedule, and about what was going on lately. It took only a few minutes for me to realize he wasn't irresponsible but he *was* stressed.

Two-year-old Ben didn't forget things, he just couldn't make up his mind. He started waking up in the middle of the night, but when his parents went to comfort him, he'd say, "I can't be held." They'd put him down, and then he'd wail, "I need to be held." And so it went. He wanted the light on, then off, then on again.

Stress dumps cortisol into the brain, which disrupts and hinders the thinking process. That's why when a child experiences stress, her school grades often drop. The neural static created by cortisol actually makes it more difficult for her to learn because she can't think, problem solve, or process information as well. It's also this overload of cortisol that can make it diffcult for you to think clearly, make a decision, or remember things as well.

Reversion to Younger Behavior and Becoming More Dependent

Ricky had given up his pacifier on his third birthday, but four months later when his sister was born his mother kept finding him in the crib with the baby, pulling the pacifier out of her mouth and sticking it in his! After removing him time after time to no avail, she finally told him, "If you need a pacifier that badly, you can have it until your fourth birthday." And that's what he did. On his fourth birthday he dropped it in the garbage.

Sometimes we just need to be babied. When kids are stressed, it's not uncommon for them to suddenly want the blanket they gave up months or even years ago, start talking like a baby, demand to be picked up and carried, or want a bottle just like their infant brother or sister.

Toileting Accidents

During a period of economic recession my phone was ringing off the hook. The callers were parents of four-year-olds who were wetting. All of the kids had been dry for months, some for nearly two years, and suddenly they were having accidents. Their parents were frustrated and furious. Why, they wondered, was this child suddenly urinating on the floor? My response to their question was a question of my own: "Has anyone lost a job?" I suspect the callers thought that I hadn't heard them correctly or that I was off in another ballpark. Inevitably, I'd have to ask my question again, and after a moment they'd tell me, indeed, their partner or they had been terminated. And then they'd ask incredulously, "How did you know?" When a breadwinner loses a job, there's major stress in the household. Four-year-olds often wet when they're stressed. I suspect that cortisol is at work here, blocking the processing of information. Since the linkages aren't all that strong yet for four-year-olds, their brain stops being able to read the signals for a full bladder, and they have an accident.

Aggressive Behaviors

Some aggressive behaviors often exhibited by parents and kids who are stressed include these:

Aggression and Opposition

Tad's day-care provider had warned his mother that if Tad didn't settle down, he'd be expelled. Tad had become a terror. He'd mimic directions instead of complying with them. He'd stick out his tongue and call the other children and adults stupid. He was hitting, pulling hair, throwing things, and one day he even bit another child. After three moves, the loss of a favorite nanny, longer work hours for Mom and Dad, and two new day-care centers, the cortisol levels were so high in Tad that a mere look could put him on the attack.

Striking out is a common stress response for anyone because the "thinking" brain that inhibits our behaviors gets overridden by the "fight-or-flight" response.

Demanding Control of Anything and Everything

Laura came home from school, demanding a snack. When her mother started making it, she insisted that her bagel be cut in a certain fashion. Then she didn't want the jelly her mother had pulled from the refrigerator, she wanted a different brand. Her mother gritted her teeth and took a deep, slow breath. "Laura," she replied, enunciating each word carefully, "what happened today that made you feel so powerless?" Laura's eyes filled with tears; then she blurted out, "I got a B on my speech, and I thought I was going to get an A. And the eighth-graders were really mean on the bus. They think they're so cool because they're going to be in ninth grade and the year is almost over. They were pushing people around and saying you can't sit there. I hate those eighth-graders!"

When kids are experiencing stress, it's often because they are feeling powerless. As a result they become demanding and argumentative, wanting to control something. They'll order people around, even telling them that they can't drink out of a particular glass! Or they'll refuse to accept decisions made by others and declare instead that *they* will decide, whether it's what restaurant the family will go to or what coat they will wear. Believe it or not, this isn't a future dictator. It's a stressed-out kid. You might notice that you, too, start barking out orders when the stress levels rise. Like your child you'd like to control something, too!

Looking at these behaviors you may realize that you've never thought about kids and stress. You might have imagined that your toddler was too young to understand that Grandpa died or that Dad moved out. But even infants sense the stress around them and their brain automatically puts them on alert. The cortisol levels rise, and the behaviors that confound you appear. How, you might wonder, are you supposed to know if your child is really stressed or just acting up? Remember, the emotion coach *knows* kids aren't just out to get them. There's a feeling or need fueling this behavior. When you see behaviors that indicate your child might be stressed, an understanding of events that cause stress for kids can help you confirm your hunch.

Experiences That Create Stress

Some stressful events are very obvious, such as a new sibling, a new teacher or child-care provider, a move, a divorce, the start or end of a school year, a death, or a major illness. But here are a few that may surprise you.

Birthday Parties

Research has shown that birthday parties are one of the most stressful events in a child's life. Watching someone else open all those gifts and cards can unravel even the calmest kids!

Bad Weather

It was ten days after the blizzard of the century when my phone started to ring. House-bound parents were fed up, and so were their kids! Trapped together in houses and apartments, they'd had more together time than they could bear. Routines had been disrupted, school had been canceled, and even getting to the grocery store was a major endeavor. Once the streets were opened the typical thirty-minute commute was still taking ninety minutes. Parents were late and frustrated even before they arrived at work. The four-year-olds started wetting, the six-year-olds were slugging it out, and the ten-year-olds were ordering everyone around.

And then there were the floods and tornadoes. They hit at night, which played havoc with sleep patterns, raised the fear levels, and sent kids flying into their parents' bedrooms for months afterward. Even after parents got their kids back into their own beds, a year later when the wind started to blow, the kids were upset again. Think about significant storms or weather changes. Have they raised your child's stress level?

Holidays and Travel

Holidays and traveling are supposed to be fun, which is why the stress they create can sneak up on you. You want to ignore it. You're supposed to be having fun, but the disruption of routines, guests, and new foods can raise stress levels quickly and leave you in full view of all of the relatives or the public at large dealing with a kid flooded with cortisol.

Parents' Travel Schedules

An increase in a parent's travel for work can also create signficant stress for kids. Schedules become more unpredictable and parents more harried. If you listen carefully, your child will let you know that you are overcommitted.

Toilet Learning

If you think about it, why would anyone want to give up the close intimacy of diapering? You get your mom or dad's full attention and a soft, cushy diaper. Toilet learning is hard work. It demands attention to one's body and independence. It's stressful. Add to it a new preschool or a baby brother, and the meltdowns can be terrific.

Growth Spurts

Chad was just about to turn five. Three weeks before the big day he started what his parents referred to as nuclear meltdowns—major tantrums over anything and everything. He'd wake up crabby, couldn't make a decision, and was incapable of doing things he could do three months before.

It's when you've been sailing along quite smoothly and you suddenly feel like you've been blindsided that the odds are you're dealing with a growth spurt. Suddenly the kid who was so competent needs help with everything. His moods are mercurial, and tears are a constant companion. He's demanding and rude and when you look at the stresses in your life, you don't really see anything happening that would stress him out. Except that his birthday or six-month birthday is within the next six weeks.

Kids go through growth spurts about every six months in the early years, and every year as they move toward adolescence. During this time the old systems fall apart before the new ones work. The process usually lasts about four to six weeks. It's exhausting to *everyone* because the only thing you can really do is maintain your standards, nurture more, and wait it out. Growth spurts disappear as suddenly as they appear. One day you realize that your child has achieved a whole new level of skills. The monster is gone, replaced by a very enjoyable kid.

Letting Go of "Lovies"

Kids reach a certain age and adults decide it's time for them to be finished with bottles, pacifiers, nursing, and even favorite blankets. The key to letting go of "lovies" is to work with your child to help him find another way to soothe and calm himself. Without a substitute, he's left without his favorite soother, and the stress levels can rise quickly. So when you wean your child, don't stop holding and rocking him. If you take away the pacifier, offer him oral alternatives like a straw with his drink. If you toilet train him, cuddle him after he uses the potty and tickle his toes at bathtime. When your child is too big to be held on your lap, sit on the edge of her bed and scratch her back.

Invasive Medical Practices

Doctors are sworn to help their patients, but sometimes the tools and techniques they use are frightening and painful. For a young child, being held down and hurt by a trusted adult—even if it's to save her life—can be a traumatic experience. Be aware that if your child has experienced major medical interventions she may be stressed and need more support from you.

Visitations

Leaving one parent to return to another is a very challenging experience for kids. The rules change from one house to another, and separation means letting go. It's important to recognize that when your child returns from a visit, if she's acting out, beneath her anger may be stress.

Bullies

Bullies are a major source of stress for kids. While it is common to tell kids to stand up for themselves or to ignore the bullying, the latest research on bullies demonstrates that adults *must* step in! It's adults who must clearly enforce the standards that everyone will be treated respectfully and that bullying will *not* be tolerated. A child alone cannot stop a bully.

Young Siblings Starting to Walk and Talk

Your child may have been infatuated with her sibling when he was a baby, but once that baby starts to move and talk, it's another story. Suddenly the older child finds her space invaded. It can be a very frustrating and irritating experience. Tempers may flare.

Once again, my list is not comprehensive, but I hope it gives you the idea that kids, even infants and toddlers, experience stress. You may also realize that many of the events that stress kids also stress you, leaving all of you more vulnerable. Each event taken alone may be manageable, but stacked together (the vacation *and* the birthday party), they may overwhelm all of you. When you recognize events that are potentially stressful to your kids and to you, you can take a proactive approach.

Check the stress levels in your home. What has your child been doing and saying lately? Are you seeing stress behaviors? What about you? If people are stomping and screaming at your house, take note. The behavior isn't about purposefully being mean and nasty. This is not the time to mete out punishments or to pull apart. It's time to hunker down and address the *real* emotions that are fueling those behaviors—emotions like fear, sadness, worry, disappointment, grogginess, and that general feeling of being overwhelmed.

While recognizing your child's stress is a very important step, you won't want to stop here. In order to stay out of the power struggles, you need to know what strategies will keep your child working with you.

Enforcing the Standards

It's difficult to feel sympathetic toward a kid who has just smacked you in the face and called you stupid. That's why your first response in any situation is to enforce your standards clearly. No matter how stressed your child is, he still cannot strike out at you, call you names, rudely order you around, constantly talk like a baby, or forget his homework every day.

Remember as you enforce your standards that if you don't want your child to be slamming doors and calling people names, you can't either. He's watching you!

And because those hormones are pumping through his brain, you also can't just tell him to stop. You have to go to the next step and help him understand what he needs and teach him what he *can* do and say. Fortunately there are ways to get your needs met as you meet his. When you and your kids are stressed, here are three things to remember:

- Nurture more.
- Create stabilty and predictability where you can.
- Create rituals that connect you.

1. Recognize the Need to Be Nurtured

When Kate is stressed, she can actually feel the rush of hormones surging through her body. It jolts her from her sleep. Instantly she's on alert, wide awake and tense. When her husband senses her wakefulness, he reaches over, slips an arm across her, and pulls her into him, her back pressed against his chest. The comfort of being tucked there is immediate. Her heartbeat slows. She knows she's not alone, and she falls back to sleep.

Kate's husband is already taken—we can't have him, but we can acknowledge that when we're stressed we need more nurturing, and so do our kids. Stress disrupts our basic sense of security, and your child needs you to help her feel secure, just like you did when she was a baby. And she needs you to do it *proactively*.

Proactively means recognizing the stress behaviors and the situations that cause stress for your family and *consciously* making the decision to slow things down and nurture more. It may seem difficult to do when you're stressed, too, but we can all learn from Kate's husband that it's the small gesture that can really make a difference. Little things such as asking your child if he'd like help, or offering to carry him before he asks you to. It's essential that you offer support *before* your child asks for it because by doing so you allow him to make the decision: "Yes, I need support right now," or "No, I can do this on my own." He feels empowered and secure.

As you work with your child take the time to savor his presence. Revel in the memories of your child's infancy. Sing the lullabies you used to sing. If he's having difficulty separating from you, tell him before you leave a room that you are going and ask if he'd like to come with you. Absorb the joy he finds in being with you. These small, thoughtful actions and words will communicate loudly and clearly to your child, "I am here. I am available. You can trust me that I will not abandon you in your distress."

As you provide the support your child needs, let him know that *soon* he'll be able to do these things on his own. Your reassurance will give him hope and remind you that you are not fostering dependence. You are supporting him while he needs it.

Since you will not always know when your child is feeling stressed, it's also important that you teach your child to respectfully ask for what she needs with phrases such as "Please hold me"; "I'm feeling overwhelmed, will you help me?"; "Please sing to me"; " I need help relaxing, would you rub my back?"; or "I just need you to be close." Be a role model. Ask the other adults in your life for what you need, too.

Confirm His Feelings

"Mommy, are you sad?" "Daddy, are you mad?" Kids ask the honest questions, and we're not quite sure how to answer them. We don't want to burden them with our problems. We are the adults, after all. But it's also important to be honest with your kids. When your child senses that you are upset but you deny it, he learns that he can't trust his gut. Better to confirm his perception by saying something like, "You're right. I am upset. Some things are happening at work. But you don't need to worry about it. Mommy and Daddy will take care of it."

Your honesty allows your child to confirm his perception. He feels more confident because he can trust his gut. At the same time you're not laying the responsibility on him, and that's an important point.

Help Him Name His Feelings

Danny was afraid of dogs, but his teacher didn't know this until she brought her docile Labrador to class. "I hate dogs!" Danny shouted. "I won't come to circle. You can't make me!" If his teacher hadn't been so observant, she would have heard only his words and may have thought he was being oppositional and defiant, but she had seen the quick flicker of fear in his eyes. Instead of immediately reprimanding him, she said softly, "This is a big dog. I'm wondering if he makes you feel uncomfortable." "I hate dogs!" Danny retorted. "It's all right for you to stay back and watch for a while," she told him, recognizing that he was probably frightened and an introvert who needed time to process that emotion as well as a thinker who didn't want to admit his vulnerability. She didn't tell him that he was afraid; instead, knowing that Danny was listening, she proceeded to tell the other children how she had gotten her pet as a puppy and how afraid she had once been of dogs. Then she showed the kids how to pet the dog and invited those who wanted to, to touch him. Danny watched. Tentatively he moved closer but still did not come into the circle. His teacher smiled at him and turned her attention back to the other children. When all but Danny had petted the dog, she sent them on to play and then invited Danny to bring the dog's leash to her. He did, then reached down and quickly touched the dog's back. "It's all right to be cautious," his teacher said. "He's a big dog. Some people may be frightened by him." Danny simply listened. Later she asked him, "Do you think you were afraid?"

Coaching your child doesn't mean telling him how he feels. You're merely giving him information, asking questions, and offering examples so that he can decide himself. When it's stress behaviors you're seeing, remember the emotions are very likely to be fear, worry, exhaustion, sadness, indecisiveness, hurt, or disappointment. Because stress triggers the fight-or-flight response, it's likely that the most obvious emotion is anger, but anger is a secondary feeling. Something else like fear or worry often precedes it.

Create an Allotment of Mental-Health Days

Bill found his son, Michael, slumped in the chair, tears trickling down his cheeks. This was not his usual cheery, self-sufficient, independent kid. "I was so suprised at first," he said, "I couldn't believe the wet streaks on his cheeks were actually tears. But they were. I sat down next to him. 'What's up?' I asked.

"'I'm just so tired,' he groaned. I nodded, remembering the trip to visit grandparents in another town, two baseball games, early risings to finish homework. There was good reason for fatigue.

"'Do you need to sleep longer?' I asked him. He nodded. 'Can I have a mental-health day, Dad?' he asked, knowing that every year we allow our kids two days on which they can say, 'I just need to stop and rest.' I reminded him that he'd have just one more mental-health day left.

"'I know,' he said, 'but I really need it.' I agreed, reminding him that when he awoke there was to be no watching television. He was to catch up on his homework. He agreed and fell back to sleep.

"He awoke at noon, hauled himself out of bed, and started reading. A shower and lunch were his only other activities. When I came home, it was as though a new person had come to reside there. This one was rested and pleased with himself that his homework was done. The next day he was up and out as usual, no complaints and no stalling. One day was all he needed to recuperate."

You might be thinking, If I allowed my child mental-health days, he'd want one every week. My experience working with families is that kids don't abuse them. They hoard them.

2. Create Stability and Predictability Where You Can: Routines Matter

Often when we're stressed, it's because things are happening that are beyond our control. Surprises become the "norm." The demands overwhelm us and the predictability and regularity of our day goes by the wayside. Meals go unplanned, car-pool plans collapse; bedtimes are thrown into chaos. When predictability disappears, kids go on alert, ready for fight or flight, and so do you.

Even on your most stressful days take a few minutes at night or in the morning to think through your day. This will really help. Where will your child be going? Who will be picking him up? Will your partner be home tonight? Will you be there in the morning when your child wakes up? Will your child get the downtime in the morning that he's used to, or do you have an early meeting so you will be dropping him off early as well? Are you going home right away after picking up your child or running errands? Talk through the plans with your child and your partner. Predictability doesn't mean inflexibility. Alter plans as needed, but remember that the more you and your child know what to expect, the less energy you have to expend being alert.

Ultimately you can teach your child to ask, "What are the plans for the day?" As he grows older he can also create plans for himself. This predictability gives him some control, eases distress, and lessens his need to control something else!

3. Create Rituals That Connect

The average American parent spends twenty-two minutes a day interacting with his or her child. When we're stressed, the odds are that we spend even less time. William Doherty, author of *The Intentional Family*, says, "In today's stress-filled world we have to intentionally plan family rituals that bring us together."

Terry was a single parent who worked full-time. She didn't have a lot of extra time for "nurturing and connecting" with her child. Mornings with her two-year-old daughter Tamara were a nightmare. Initially Terry would get herself up, shower, dress, and then wake Tamara. She'd change Tamara's diaper, dress her, and give her a quick snack. Within fifteen minutes they'd be out the door heading for child care. But Tamara hated it and screamed in protest every morning. She wanted to play. She wanted to be with her mother. By the time they separated at child care, both of them were in tears. It was a lousy way to start the day.

In class Terry recognized that her daughter's difficulty separating was a stress behavior very typical for her age. She realized her daughter needed more connection time with her, but she couldn't figure out how to fit it in.

David, another parent in class, suggested that she just try to make the normal routine special. He explained, "When Gayle and I were expecting our first child, we were talking with my brother and his wife. Gayle was going to nurse and take a six-month leave from her job. I was going to be working more overtime to make up the difference. My sister-in-law said to me, 'Oh, David, then you'll have to make bathtime your time with the baby.' I have to admit I found her advice more intimidating than inviting. I had *never* taken care of a baby, much less bathed one. So when my son was born, I approached this task very tentatively. And it wasn't easy. My son's a very sensitive kid. He didn't like being undressed for his bath. The water had to be just the right temperature, and washing his hair was a major feat. But I kept working on it. By the time he was a year old he trusted me. He'd hold his little washcloth over his eyes while I washed his hair, and we'd splash together. I'll always be grateful to my sister-in-law. The connection was worth it, and because bathtime is Daddy's job, we make that connection even during the busiest times."

Terry took David's advice. Instead of waking Tamara at the last minute, she woke her earlier and plopped her into the bathtub with her yellow duck. Tamara had always loved her bath. It soothed and calmed her. While Terry did her hair and makeup, Tamara played and chatted with her mom. When Terry was finished, she dried off Tamara with a fuzzy towel, dressed her, and ate a quick breakfast with her. Forty-five minutes after waking, Tamara would exclaim in delight, "Let's go see my teacher!" Terry hadn't done anything that she wouldn't do during a normal day—she'd just done it differently. The connection of bathtime in the morning brought them together, eased the stress of separation, and allowed them to start their day with smiles instead of screams.

When you're stressed, your family needs those connections more than ever. When it's time to make dinner, try to work together. Put the preschoolers up to the sink and let them scrub fresh vegetables or wash the pots and pans. They'll love it. Older kids can mix up the muffins, set the table, dim the lights, and light the candles. There's nothing like candlelight to settle things down.

Look around you. What needs to be done? How can you do it together? That's the key—be together. If the laundry has to be folded, why not dump it in your child's room and sit and fold it while he falls asleep. You'll get the laundry done, and he'll get the connection that he needs so he won't have to cling. Need to pay the bills? Give your child all the junk mail to open up and play office with while you're working. If your child is older, invite him to bring his homework to the dining room table so you can sit together as you both work. Push the fears and hassles of the day into the back corners. Don't let those forces pull your family apart. Consciously create rituals that bring you together in good times and in bad.

Adjust for Individual Differences

How we cope with stress varies with our temperament and our type. The introverts in your family are going to need more space and quiet time. The extroverts are going to want to talk things out. Recognize your differences. For the introverts, eliminate as many outside commitments as you can. Extroverts, give yourself permission to use the phone and talk with others. Be careful not to wear out your introverted family members.

And if you or your child are temperamentally more intense, know that daily exercise will be even *more* important to you. If you're more sensitive, sensorial stimulation, especially noise, will make you edgier. And if you're slow to adapt, know, too, that transitions become more challenging. Slow down, allow more time, and you'll ease through this challenging period.

Allow Time

Learning to deal with life's ups and downs isn't easy and takes time. If your child is dealing with a significant issue, there won't be a quick fix. It may be a tough six months or year before you see progress, and you may need to seek professional help in the process. And because kids are developing, they often have to revisit a major stressful event at each new developmental milestone. That means that if your child was six when you divorced, when she reaches preadolescence, she may very well have to process her feelings about it all over again at a higher level of thinking.

Don't lose hope. Know as you work through those stressful events that the research on resiliency demonstrates that kids who have experienced tough times are actually stronger adults. They've learned that no matter what happens, they can handle it! Mary Tyler Moore says it well: "You can't be brave if you've only had wonderful things happen to you."

Savor Your Successes

Hannah was seven. Her parents had divorced when she was two. She lived with her mother but spent weekends with her dad. Typically when Hannah returned to her mother's on Sunday night, she was distraught. She was hungry and tired. Inevitably, her mother ended up spending the whole evening just trying to stop the screaming and crying.

Learning about stress behaviors gave Mom a whole new perspective. Suddenly she realized that the transfer from one parent to another after a visitation was a very stressful event for Hannah. She used her new awareness to turn this exhausting experience into one that was reasonably manageable.

Talking with Hannah, she helped her understand her emotions by saying, "When you've been with your daddy, it's hard for you to leave him. You love him. But you love me, too. When you can't be with both of us at the same time, it's frustrating and sad to you. All those feelings are inside of you when you come home."

Mom also realized it was critical that she reinforce her standards, so she said, "When you come home, no matter how upset you are, it isn't all right for you to call Mommy names or to scream for hours."

Then together they talked about what Hannah could do with all of those emotions. They planned a hot bubble bath for her, along with an immediate snack. Hannah could expect that her mom would sit with her while she lounged in her bath so they could talk. Finally they clarified what else they might do that night or who might be coming over. Hannah knew exactly what to expect. All attention was focused on helping her to cope with that difficult transition, and, most important, she knew she could count on her mother to be there when she needed her the most. Hannah was learning that even when there are things in our life that we don't like and that we wish we could change, we can still find ways to cope.

Coaching Tips

Kids don't tell us that they're stressed. Instead they throw us their most challenging behaviors. Our job is teach them how to cope with life's ups and downs—even when we're stressed, too.

When your child is stressed:

- Teach your child to recognize stress behaviors.
- Talk about the emotions she's experiencing such as worry, sadness, disappointment, exhaustion, grief.
- Understand her indecisiveness and forgetfulness; offer extra support.
- Nurture her more. She really does need to be held, massaged, or carried.
- Maintain routines and let her know what to expect.
- Create rituals that connect you.

When you're stressed, too:

- Recognize your stress.
- Allow yourself to slow down and ask for help.
- Understand you need more nurturing, too.
- Take time to exercise.

FOURTEEN

I Will! I Won't!

Balancing Boundaries and Independence

"Our family needs to be a safe place to practice, to explore, and to accomplish."

—Mary, mother of two

Nicholas was two and a climber. The three-foot toy shelf in front of him provided a challenge too compelling to resist. He pulled himself up, plopped down on top, and beamed brightly. He'd done it! His mother, Eileen, watched and smiled. The shelf was sturdy, anchored to the floor, and empty. He was safe, and there wasn't anything that could be harmed. So she let him climb.

But then he started to swing his feet. Bang, bang, bang his heels struck the shelf. Eileen walked over, bent down, and gently laid her hand on his feet, stopping the swinging. Then she let go. "You may sit quietly," she told him, "or I will put you down. What do you want to do?" She let him know he was making a choice. He could choose to sit on the shelf, or, if he banged against it, which would damage it, he would have to get down. The choice was his. She would enforce it.

He looked at her, a glint in his eye, then swung his legs. Once again

Eileen laid her hand on his feet stopping the swinging. Letting go she said, "You can kick the floor, not the shelf." She even showed him what she meant by sitting on the floor and striking her heels against it.

He paused, contemplated, then looked right at her and banged his heels against the shelf again.

"Next time you can try again," she explained as she stood up and lifted him down. He bellowed in response. "Now you're mad," she explained. But his anger didn't frighten her. Empathizing with his frustration, she reassured him, "You'll be able to try again later." But for now, there would be no more climbing on the bookshelf.

Eileen was an emotion coach. She understood that once a child starts to walk, a window of emotional development opens when it is essential that he learn: What can I do? What can I make happen? And, what are the rules around here? I like to think of this process as learning the "dos and don'ts" of life. The window for these important lessons opens during the toddler years, but it doesn't close there. Your child continues to figure out what he can and cannot do throughout his lifetime.

Like Eileen, you are faced every day with requests from your child who wants to try things that you aren't sure you want him to do. And, like Eileen, you have to make a decision. Is this the time to let her do it or to hold the line? As you make your decision you are laying the foundation for self-discipline. When you say yes, you give her a sense of autonomy, a chest-pumping pride of achievement, a glowing sense of capability. When you say no, you are teaching her when and how to stop herself. These two decisions are essential elements of emotion-intelligence coaching. The challenge is to get the percentages right, because too many nos result in kids who are too afraid or ashamed to try, and too many yeses lead to kids without the ability to stop themselves. It's the balance that leads to kids who feel competent, capable, and ready to decide what they can and cannot do—even when you're not around.

Keep Your Cool

The trouble is, kids don't understand that this is a major stage of emotional development and that their brain is practically screaming, "Do it!

Try it! Find out what happens!" Instead they act it out. When they're little, they'll throw, climb, grab, test, leap, push, and investigate, and then look right at you as though to say, What happens now? They demand to cut their own cheese with the sharp knife, and they stomp their feet when you say no. Or they refuse to get in the car unless you let them open the door, then throw a fit if you try to help them. If you're in a rush to get to work, it's inevitable that they'll want to zip their own jacket or tie their own shoe. As they grow older the requests change. Soon they are demanding to ride their bicycle miles across town, stay overnight at a friend's house, ride the city bus years before you think they are ready, or pierce their body. It can be exasperating, and so can the flip side of this stage of development—the child who is too afraid to try. The one who declares he *won't* jump in the pool, refuses to let you leave his side, or insists he is incapable of completing his homework or going to summer camp.

Take that deep breath, count to ten, and remember, this is not a blatant case of insubordination. This is a child figuring out what he can and cannot do. During this stage he needs you as his emotion coach to help him:

- learn to stop himself by teaching him what he *can* do.
- identify and understand the emotions he's experiencing.
- support him when he fears he *can't* do something.

Step One: Learning to Stop Oneself by Learning What to Do

Whenever your child asks to do something—whether it's a request to open the garage door, use an ax or hammer, stay out past midnight, climb up the ladder to the roof, eat cookies for breakfast, or sleep in your bed—you have to make a decision: Is this the time to hold the line or to let go? Over the years the answers to these questions inevitably change. They depend on the child and his age, the situation, how much time you have, the values of your family, and other extenuating circumstances. Unlike standards that remain the same no matter what the age of the child or the circumstances of the situation, there are no hard and fast rules for making these decisions. And therein lies the dilemma.

As you make your decision for your child, it's important for you to remember that someday your child will be on his own and these decisions will all be his. Your task as an emotion coach is to ensure that he feels capable of making these decisions and has the skills to do so. The process is a gradual one. Initially you have to decide what your child can and cannot do, but over time that balance of control gradually shifts toward your child. That's why it is essential that you teach him *how* you are making these decisions. What information or guidelines are you using when you decide to stop a behavior, and what he can do instead? This may seem like a ridiculous thing to do when your child is only eighteen months old, but the reality is that, while he may not fully understand what you are saying now, your words are laying the foundation for later. The three-year-old who is taught about safety as well as stopped from climbing to the roof becomes the sixteen-year-old who realizes that climbing a river bluff isn't the smartest thing to do even if all of his friends are doing it and no adults are around to stop them. It's true that teaching your child why you are stopping him and what he can do instead does take more time; that's why it's essential to remember you are building skills for a lifetime. Your words and actions ultimately allow your child to be able to make these decisions on his own instead of fighting about them with you. In the long run, your efforts will save you a great deal of time and worry!

While every parent will have individual criteria for deciding what kids can and cannot do, the parents in my classes tell me they think about rules of etiquette, safety, family values, and individual needs and differences.

The Rules of Etiquette

Kids are not born knowing that you're not supposed to spit on the floor, write on the walls, run through restaurants screaming wildly, grab someone else's toy, throw food on the floor, screech into the telephone when your mother is talking to someone, walk across other people's furniture, climb on tables, take things that don't belong to them, or rummage through other people's cupboards. These are social rules that govern behavior. Your kids are unaware of these rules, and you have to teach them.

When your young child wants to do or does something that breaches the rules of etiquette and is disrespectful, it's time to step in and stop him. Use the same steps that you use to enforce your standards. Make a thoughtful decision about what you're going to stop and be consistent. Tell your child to stop, and match your words with action by getting up and helping him stop. But as you do stop your child, remember that he doesn't know better. He's innocently testing the waters. When you stop him, you don't have to be a bear.

Sixteen-month-old Stephanie ate like a little trooper. But when she was finished, she'd look right at her mother and then gleefully flip her plate onto the floor. The dog would come dashing to gobble up the spoils. It was an amazing experience. Stephanie had discovered that with one small action she could make her mother jump and the dog leap. The power of her action fascinated her. She had no idea that it wasn't good manners to throw food on the floor. And so when her mother told her to stop, she'd turn around and do it again. But her mom was an emotion coach. She watched Stephanie closely. When she saw the glint in Stephanie's eye, she grabbed hold of the plate and removed it, saying, "We don't throw food on the floor. We say, 'All done!' And Mommy will come and get your plate." Then she calmly took Stephanie out of the high chair. Stephanie protested, but Mom didn't stop there. She held Stephanie to calm her, and said, "It's hard to stop. You were having fun, but we don't throw food." Then she helped Stephanie get a biscuit for the dog. Stephanie learned not to throw food, but she also learned how she *could* get her mom's attention and even bring the dog running.

When your child breaches the rules of etiquette, you must step in and stop him, but as you do, you can also teach him what he can do. He can't draw on the wall, but instead of punishing him, show him where he *can* draw. Get large pieces of newsprint or set aside part of the basement wall for him to create a chalk mural. If he's running across the chairs in an auditorium, stop him, but show him how to help the janitor by folding all of the seats up. If you don't want your four-year-old to change her clothes ten times a day, that's fine, but remember she needs to practice, so how about three times if she also learns to put the clothes away? You don't want your child to scream in the restaurant, so teach him how to join the conversation. He can't run through the grocery store pulling products off the shelves, but he can help find specific items and put them in the basket or sit in the cart and eat a cookie from the bakery while you shop. When your child understands the rules of etiquette and what he can do, he gains a sense of competence.

Safety

Noah was a climber who also happened to be fascinated with the spice cabinet. He'd figured out how to pull down the oven door and use it to climb up to the spice cupboard where he found lots of little bottles and cans. It was so fascinating to him that if his parents turned their backs, even for less than a minute, he was up onto the stove and into the spice cabinet.

Little kids don't know what's safe and what's unsafe. They don't know that stoves can be dangerous even if they are a stepping stone to a very exciting place. They don't know that electrical sockets are potentially life threatening. It's your role to determine what's safe.

When your child is young, you must hold the line on safety. There is no negotiation. You're the one who has to insist that he wear his seat belt or stay in his car seat even if he'd like to move around. You are the one who has to ensure that he uses a bike helmet, stays with you in the parking lot, and does not climb up on stoves. But ultimately, as your child grows and develops, he will have to make the decisions about what's safe and what's not safe by himself. It's your job to prepare him.

Being Safe Doesn't Mean Smothering

It was spring and eleven-year-old Joel was late in returning home for supper. When he finally arrived home, his mother demanded, "Where were you? I was worried."

Joel explained that he and his friends had ridden over to the university where there were ramps to ride up and down. The problem was that the university was way out of his established boundaries and meant crossing a very busy street. The year before his parents had set bike boundaries with him, figuring out who he needed to see, where he needed to go, and what busy streets needed to be avoided.

"I don't remember your boundaries changing," his mother said sternly.

"But Mom, I'm a year older now," he reminded her. "My boundaries should be bigger. I did just fine."

It's at this point that many children would find their bicycles confiscated for the next three weeks, but Joel's mother was an astute emotion coach who immediately recognized this was a child who temperamentally was very persistent and a risk taker. She had to work with him. So she said, "We have to be able to trust you, Joel. Next time you are to ask us before you take off and we'll work with you." Then she took him to the busy intersection and "tested" him, asking him to demonstrate when he would choose to cross the street. When he showed good judgment, she then brainstormed with him the other things he needed to think about in order to be safe, like riding in a group, wearing a helmet, and taking a water bottle along on long rides. Then she gave him permission to expand his boundaries.

The night he was late, Joel did get a cold supper, and he did do the dishes, but the little roamer stayed connected to his parents. During the rest of the summer he respected his expanded boundaries and told his parents where he was going. It may not surprise you to know that today Joel is a young man who climbs mountains and leads backpacking trips into the wilderness. But before he goes out, he makes sure someone knows where he is going and that he has the equipment and training he needs to be safe.

Even for kids who are not risk takers by nature, it's still important to gradually expand their boundaries in order to give them a sense of competence. Recently I had the opportunity to visit the child-development center at Patagonia, a company that manufactures and sells mountain-climbing equipment and outerwear. I was incredulous when I saw the jungle gym in the toddler's playground. It was huge. A similar version would never be found even in an elementary schoolyard in Minnesota.

At Patagonia, the elementary-age kids even had their own climbing wall!

I turned to the center's director and asked, "How can you do this?" She smiled at me. "Remember, almost everyone who works here is a mountain climber. They want their kids to be strong and to take reasonable risks. The jungle gym reflects the company's philosophy. There's only one rule: No adult may place a child up on the gym. The child has to be able to get there herself. Our role is to support her, but she does the rest."

Support is important as your child ventures out and discovers what she can do. Meeting challenges is vital to feeling confident, but it doesn't mean you abandon your child and let her "find out the hard way." The key is to show her what she needs to know to be safe and to stay with her to guide her.

If you were taught that the world is a scary place, it may be difficult to let your child do things that were forbidden to you. For example, if you weren't allowed to use tools or test your skills paddling a canoe, your first reaction might be to say no when your child asks to do these things. But before you automatically stop your child and step right into a power struggle, ask yourself, Is this an opportunity to teach him about safety procedures? Can you make adjustments that will keep him safe, yet encourage his curiosity and build his confidence by letting him do what he wants to do?

For toddlers that means allowing them to be curious, while keeping them safe.

Noah's parents ended up tying shut the oven door, but they also put together a basket of empty spice cans and stored it in a lower cabinet where he could explore to his heart's content.

Older kids need the opportunity to find out how things work. That's why when Rick built his own home, his three children, ages four, six, and nine, were active participants. "I couldn't worry that they were going to turn on the saw or climb up ladders," he said, "but I also didn't want them to be afraid. So I took the time to teach them. First, I insisted that they had to ask before climbing up a ladder. They could climb, but I had to be there. I showed them how to go up and to go down, and then I stood behind them, ready to catch them while they practiced. They were also not to touch the saw unless I was with them. I demonstrated where they could and could not put their hands when they were around it. And I explained that after cutting something the blade was hot. I knew Jake wanted to touch it and test it. So I let him hold his hand over it to feel the heat. After that I didn't have to worry about the kids. They spent hours with me hammering, digging, and climbing up the ladders, and they never ran into trouble."

Family Values

There once were two brothers who were both Olympic ski-jump champions. It all started during elementary school when they pulled the mattresses off their beds, laid them in the yard, and then jumped off the roof onto them. Their parents were also adventuresome types who not only allowed them to do it but helped them stack the mattresses. My kids are downhill skiers but not jumpers. I have to admit I'd have stopped them from jumping off the roof onto their mattresses even if they'd wanted to. Today, my kids are not champion ski jumpers. Theirs are.

Every family has its own set of values. You get to decide for your family what your values are. It's these values that you'll turn to when your child asks questions like, "Can I stay up with you until you go to bed?" It's your decision. If you want time with your partner after the kids go to sleep, then you may not allow your child to stay up. That means you'll have to set a bedtime limit and work with him to get him to bed as well as teach him that time for adult relationships is important, too. Or you might decide that you've got four kids to put to bed and it's just easier for everyone if you simply turn out the lights and call it a night together. If you're doing so early enough so that your child isn't becoming sleep deprived, this strategy may work just fine for your family.

And what about sleeping in your bed? Thousands of families are practicing the "family bed," where kids and parents sleep together. (Around the world this is actually the most common practice.) But many families find this arrangement uncomfortable and insist that their kids stay in their own rooms. Still other families fall somewhere in between, teaching their kids to go to sleep in their own beds but allowing them to come into the parents' room in the middle of the night. There isn't a right or wrong practice as long as the strategies you use are respectful of your child's need for rest and security, and your need for privacy and rest. No matter what decision you make, the most important factor is that you consistently enforce it. As you do, teach your child why this rule exists in your family so that he can make it his own. You aren't just the big person who steps in and stops him. You are his emotion coach helping him to understand why he needs to stop. If you simply say "Don't" or "Because I said so," your child doesn't learn how or why you're making a particular judgment.

Ultimately, your child will figure out that not all families have the same rules. When he argues that his friend gets to stay up until ten on schools nights, you can let him know it doesn't matter. In your family nine P.M. is the rule because that's how much rest your family needs. Or you can choose to look at the rule with him and decide if he is now old enough to begin making decisions himself about his bedtime. Just be sure he knows how to make that judgment according to how much rest his body needs and not by what's on television. By teaching him how you are making your decisions, you allow him to be more capable.

Individual Needs

Eleven-year-old Elizabeth is a very sensitive person, and when she plays the radio at bedtime she tends to get stimulated and can't fall asleep. Therefore, her parents decided not to allow her to listen to her radio in bed, but taught her instead to turn on a fan. When her nine-year-old brother, David, plays the radio, it soothes and calms him and he quickly falls asleep. So David is allowed to play his radio and is even encouraged to turn it on in the middle of the night if he wakes from a bad dream and has difficulty falling back to sleep again. Same parents, same question: "May I play the radio?" But two different answers for two different children. So how do we address the cry "That's not fair"?

Being an emotion coach means helping your children to understand themselves, their own emotions, and their own needs. What's effective for one child may not be for another, which means you cannot always treat your children exactly the same. You will treat them respectfully and fairly as individuals, but you will not treat them exactly the same.

That's why Elizabeth's parents will teach her that she is very sensitive. Playing the radio keeps her awake. They aren't just being mean to her; they are helping her to understand what she needs to settle down and fall asleep. Knowing your child helps you to choose your battles and find alternatives that fit her best.

When You Don't Want Your Child to "Do"

In class when we talked about the importance of stopping kids' inappropriate actions but also teaching them what they could do, Suzanne groaned. "Letting kids do is exactly what our power struggle was about yesterday. I had been visiting my sister with my twins. When we left, it was raining. I grabbed each child by the hand and dashed to the car. When I opened the door, my son stopped dead in his tracks. He refused to budge. He wanted me to shut the door so that he could open it himself. I didn't want to let him open it himself. I felt like he was controlling me! It was raining, and I was getting soaked. Even if I did let him, I've got two three-year-olds. His sister would insist on a turn. I'd be there another ten minutes opening and shutting doors. I didn't have that kind of time, and anyway they might slam each other's fingers in the door."

No one wants to stand in the rain and get soaked. No one wants to feel like their child's servant. Time is a limited resource, and it is our job to keep kids safe. Once again, you get to make the decision.

If Suzanne had to pick up her son and physically put him in the car so that they didn't get wet, she could say, "I know you wanted to do it. You like to do things for yourself." And while she may not be comfortable letting him open the door then, she might offer that he could do it when they got home and were parked in the garage. If her main concern was safety, she has two choices. When it's not raining, she could teach each of the kids how to open and shut doors safely. Or she could simply say, "You wish you could and someday when you're older, you can."

It's true there are times when you don't have time to allow your child to do, but if you find yourself constantly telling your child, "No, not now," "I don't have time," "Let me," "I can do it faster, or better," it may be time to stop and reflect. Am I supporting my child and encouraging him as he learns to do? Sometimes a small change in your schedule can stop these power struggles before they ever start.

Allow Time

Many power struggles occur when you're rushed and trying to do for your child what she wants to do herself. If you recognize that buttoning her own coat, pulling up her own zipper, packing her own backpack, or opening the door is essential to your child's healthy emotional development, it's easier to slow down and allow that extra ten minutes in the morning. It's true, initially it will take more time, but ultimately it will save you time as you reap the rewards of having a child who is more capable and competent. Interestingly enough, the more you allow your child to do, the less intense his reaction when you have to say no. That's because he knows you listen and support him most of the time; as a result, he's more open to working with you.

Plan for Success

Once while I was traveling in France I noticed a banner hanging across a mountain road that read, "Warning: Danger of Death." I think of that sign every time I stand behind a parent with a two-year-old in the checkout line at the grocery store. Why don't they just hang up a banner that reads, "Warning: Parent Torture Chamber." There are certain places, like the grocery store checkout, where you can predict a child determined to do is going to get into trouble. There are so many things to touch, bags to fill, shelves to explore, choices to make, and carts to push—all while parents are preoccupied. This is a prime battle ground. If you know what's ahead, you can plan for it. This is the time to whip out of your purse or pocket the box of raisins you've brought along to keep little hands busy and eyes focused. Or to plan ways for your child to help. If it's a self-serve grocery, can she pull out the bags? Can she help fill them?

Think about the power struggles that happen over and over in your home such as your preschooler jumping on the bed while you're trying to nurse the baby. It's hard for your child to wait her turn and see the baby get all of that attention. She wants to *do* something. So plan activities that allow her to sit on the couch next to you where you can cuddle her and play with her as you nurse. Or, if every time you get on the phone chaos erupts, create a phone drawer with fun things that your child gets to use only while you're on the phone. If your six-year-old kicks the back of your seat every night during the drive home, buy a handheld video game that he gets to play only in the car, or tapes for him to listen to that soothe and calm. Help your child figure out what she *can* do in these situations and avoid those power struggles!

Step Two: Identify the Emotions

Stopping isn't easy for your child, even when you are also teaching her what she can do. It's frustrating and disappointing when her desires are thwarted. That's why it's essential that you also help her to understand the emotions she is experiencing so that she can find a respectful way to redirect them.

A huge oak tree had blown down in Sandy's backyard. The neighborhood kids were having a blast exploring the top reaches of the tree, which in the past had been the domain of only the birds and squirrels. In class, Sandy explained, "I caught my ten-year-old Nicole at the door ready to go out and climb in her clogs. I told her that she had to wear rubber-soled shoes so that she wouldn't slip. She snorted at me and started to go out the door. I stayed cool, but I stepped in front of her at the door and repeated, 'Nicole, it's your choice. You may climb in tennis shoes, or you may choose to stay in the house and wear your clogs.' She yelled at me, 'You're mean.' I breathed deeply. 'Nicole, you wish you could go out in your clogs. When you are excited to do something, it's hard to stop and think of another choice,' I replied. She turned and ran out of the room. I heard her crying, but I stayed calm. I knew I was doing the right thing. This was a safety issue. I wasn't going to change my decision, but I also understood that she's a very persistent person. It was hard for her to stop and make a different choice. I gave her time. Taking a break is the best way for her to bring down her intensity. I think she sensed my confidence because five minutes later, she came out with her tennis shoes on and went outside."

Sandy was an emotion coach. She stepped in and stopped her daughter, matching actions with her words. She allowed time for the intensity to come down and articulated the emotions that Nicole might be feeling.

Look at what you're telling your child when you have to stop her. Does she have the vocabulary to voice her dismay? Here are a few phrases I've collected. As you review them try them on for yourself. Think about what words you appreciate hearing when you don't get to do what you had your heart set on doing.

When your child has to stop

It's hard to stop.	You really wanted to do that.
You wish that was a choice.	That was frustrating.
You wanted a turn.	It's difficult to wait.

Thinking about these words and the emotions they reflect helps you to recognize how important it is to your child to do and try things and how difficult it is to stop. It changes your perspective and keeps you connected.

Come Back to Coach

Later that day, when Nicole came back inside, Sandy knew her work was not yet finished. "I'm glad you chose to wear your tennis shoes for climbing," she said, waiting for Nicole's response and to also check on her intensity level. Nicole's answer was light: "Yeah, the tree was really cool." Sandy decided to continue, "Next time you are angry, it's important that you choose words to explain what you are feeling. You can tell me you don't like that choice. But when you say, 'You're mean,' my feelings get hurt, and my impulse is to stop listening to you." Nicole nodded.

Step Three: Supporting Your Child When He Fears He Can't Do

Sometimes the struggles with your child aren't about stopping her from doing something, nor are they about allowing her to do things. Instead, your struggles are about trying to get your child to do. When your child won't do, it's important to remember he isn't just being lazy or obstinate. It is essential that you look for the real culprits! Some feeling or need is stopping him from doing, and he needs your support more than ever.

Help Your Child Manage the Intensity

When I was a child, every summer I sewed an outfit to enter in the 4-H competition at the fair. It was not an easy task. Matching plaids, getting seams straight, putting in zippers were hard work. Sometimes the task was downright overwhelming. When I'd made a mistake for the third time, I'd start to lose it, and that's when my mother would send me outside for a break. While I was gone, she'd rip out the seam so that I could start over fresh when I came in. She never actually sewed any of the outfit, she just got rid of my mistakes. To this day, I remember what a relief it was to take that break and to have her support.

Learning new skills is tough. Your child needs to hear from you that her performance and skills will improve with practice. When you recognize that she's starting to get intense, insist that she take a break, even if you have to physically take her hand or pick her up. Remember, as her emotion coach, you're her ally, helping her to manage those strong emotions so that she can do.

You also might try breaking down the task into steps, allowing her to feel a sense of accomplishment with each completion. As I was sewing, the completion of a dress seemed like an overwhelming task when I looked at three yards of material and a Butterick pattern. That's why mother would help me set goals for the day such as laying out the pattern, cutting out the pattern, finishing three seams, putting in the zipper, or putting in even just one side of the zipper, or sewing on four buttons. Each time I reached my goal, I got to celebrate and take a break! It's true it took me weeks to finish the projects, but I did and that's what's most important. Think about how you can help your child break down those homework assignments, or make manageable the steps he could use to clean his room.

In Order to Do, Your Child Has to Feel Safe

When parents and kids come to my classes, they spend forty-five minutes playing together; then if the kids are comfortable, we separate. One night all of the kids were ready to separate except two-year-old Jason. When his dad attempted to leave the room, Jason started to scream. Huge tears rolled down his cheeks. The teacher let Dad know that this was a very common reaction for two-year-olds and invited him to stay with Jason, but Dad was upset. He wanted to go to the discussion group and didn't appreciate having to stay in the children's room with Jason. "Why is he being such a wimp?" he asked the teacher. "What's wrong with him? Why won't he play with all these toys?"

Before kids are ready to venture out, explore their world, or test their skills, they have to feel safe. Megan Gunner, from the University of Minnesota, conducted a test in which she separated nine-month-old babies from their mothers for thirty minutes. Half were left with very attentive caretakers who responded to all of the child's moods. The other half were left with a caregiver who was inattentive and unresponsive unless the child actually fussed or cried. While alone with the caregiver, the child was exposed to something startling. The study revealed that the level of the stress hormone cortisol rose dramatically in the saliva of the kids with the inattentive caregivers. But cortisol levels did not rise in those kids who had an attentive caregiver whom they trusted. Remember, high cortisol levels affect our ability to function well. So if you want your child to feel comfortable venturing away from you, you have to help her feel safe and thus lower the cortisol level in her body.

Be a Security Post

The second week of class I invited Jason and his dad to sit with me on the floor of the children's room. Jason gave me a look that clearly expressed that he needed space. I pointed it out to his dad, who agreed that, indeed, Jason did like his space, as did his he and his wife. It was a family trait. I advised him to explain this need to the adults who might care for Jason so that they didn't move in on him too fast.

Jason seemed to appreciate that I respected his wishes because moments later he chose to move into my space and hand me a cookie cutter. I took his offering and asked the dad if Jason had a "lovie" that soothed him. Indeed he did, a teddy with a silky tummy that Jason liked to rub. We retrieved it and laid it on the floor. Jason picked it up and clutched it to his chest. He stood there a few minutes looking around the room. Soon he started venturing out. His dad remained seated on the floor. When Jason came back to check in, his dad gave him a hug but didn't engage him in play. We did this for four consecutive weeks. Dad seriously wondered if he'd ever get to the discussion group. I assured him that he would and that there wasn't anything wrong with Jason. He just needed a bit more practice. It wasn't until the fifth week that Jason ventured out more than fifteen minutes without checking back in. When this happened, I told Dad, "This is your big day. Go ahead and tell Jason good-bye."

"He's happy, shouldn't I just sneak out?" he asked. "No," I explained. "Jason needs to know he can trust you. Don't sneak out." (You'll be able to use this when he's a teenager and you want to tell him, I never snuck out on you, you can't sneak out on me.) "When you go, say good-bye and remind him that his teachers will be here for him, and that he's got his teddy. Tell him you'll come back when it's time to leave."

He did just as he was instructed. Jason whimpered, but he didn't cry. He rubbed the spot on his teddy, then came to me when I started blowing bubbles for him. After only a few minutes he went back to playing with the blocks and continued playing until his dad came back.

All kids go through stages of separation anxiety. It's normal, and it signifies that they've attached to you. They know they can count on you, and it's a big world out there. When you allow your child time to become comfortable in a new situation and connect with the caregiver who will be with him in your absence, he can relax and do.

Feeling safe isn't important just for younger kids. Older kids need your support, too. Leah was thirteen when she flew from Minnesota to Washington, D.C. for a ten-day vacation with her aunt. The first day in Washington, her aunt took Leah and her eleven-year-old cousin, David, to the Holocaust Museum. In the middle of the museum David became ill and asked to be taken out. Leah wanted to finish going through the museum, so her aunt told her to meet them in the rotunda. When she finished, Leah couldn't find the rotunda. She asked a guard for directions, but he sent her in the wrong direction. Frantic, she searched for her aunt, who was also looking for her. Finally, after fifteen long minutes, they connected. But suddenly Leah no longer felt safe.

The next day Leah and her relatives left for the Maryland coast. The ocean waves were huge after a storm, and the thought of ten days away from home was more of an adventure than Leah could endure. Homesickness struck hard. She called her mother, crying, "Please, let me come home." This wasn't a simple matter. Leah had arrived on a charter. A plane ticket home would be very expensive, and returning to Washington would mean an eight-hour roundtrip for her aunt. Leah's mother explained, "If you absolutely need to come home, we'll bring you, but it will cost a lot and disrupt your aunt's vacation. How else can we help you feel safe?" Leah said, "Can I call you whenever I want?" Remembering the typical camp policy her, mother said, "I think this will just make you miss us more." But Leah said, "No, I need to talk with you." So her mother relented. The first day Leah called every hour. The second day she called six times. But by the third day she checked in only twice. Each time her mother reassured her, "You can do it; stay busy. If you need to come home you can, but I think you can work this one through." Leah did, and when she arrived home, she was actually beaming. "I did it!" she exclaimed to her mother. But to do it she had to reconnect with her mom and feel safe. (The phone bill was a tenth of what an airline ticket would have cost.)

As you work with your child, know that she does want to venture out. But she has to feel safe first. You are not coddling her when you stay with her or allow her to check in with you. Be available, but don't smother.

Nudging Isn't Pushing

I always like to ask my audiences about how they learned to ride a bicycle. No matter what age they were—and the ages range from three to adult—there usually was someone who supported and helped them. But sometimes there's someone who learned to ride because their brother dared them.

When it comes to trying things, sometimes kids need a little nudge. A nudge is not a push; it's an invitation. Take toilet training, for instance. There are some kids who are really smart. They don't want to give up their diapers. Think about it. Why would any rational person want to give up the intimacy of diapering to sit alone in a little room over a pool of cold water that you could fall into at any moment. But, alas, even though the diaper companies are making bigger diapers, someday you still have to learn to use the toilet. For these kids a "nudge" may be in order. A nudge looks like this.

In the morning when your child wakes and it's time to change his diaper, you ask him, "Would you like to use the toilet today before I change your diaper?" The choice is his. If he says no, you just change his diaper. But as you do it say, "Someday you'll choose to use the toilet because that's what big people do." The next day ask again, "Would you like to sit on the toilet or just change your diaper?" The choice is still his. If he says no, you change the diaper, but again you say, "*Someday pretty soon* you'll choose the toilet, because that's what big kids do." Plant the seed, and one day when you ask, he'll say yes. When he does, let him sit there. If he doesn't do anything and wants to get off, let him, saying, "Someday you'll be able to sit on the toilet and go."

How Can We Make It Better?

Nudging may also include a little problem solving with your child. When Leah was desperately homesick, her mother asked, "What will make it better?" Stan used that same strategy with his five-year-old son, Paul.

Paul was toilet trained, except he would have a bowel movement only in a diaper. When he felt the urge to defecate, he would ask for his diaper. His parents had tried telling him there were no more diapers. But Paul would become hysterical and hold his bowel movements. We didn't want to get into issues of fecal retention. So instead we set up a plan. Stan explained to Paul, "I think there's something about going in the toilet that frightens you, but big people do use the toilet. How can we make it better? How can we make it feel more comfortable and safe for you?" Together they decided that Paul would practice dropping tissue paper in the toilet and flushing it because the flushing scared him. His dad also agreed to stay in the bathroom with him while Paul just sat on the toilet. When Paul wanted to get off, he was allowed to do so. His father kept encouraging him, and they made it routine that even though Paul used a diaper, he went into the bathroom for his bowel movement. Finally they looked at a calendar and realized that in six weeks Paul would be five and a half. They chose that date as the day Paul wanted to poop in the toilet. In preparation for the big day, they kept talking and practicing; but when the date came, Paul couldn't do it. His father said, "That's okay, soon it will be better. You're close, we'll keep practicing." It took another ten days, and then he did it. Sometimes it takes a little nudge and a lot of support to help your child feel comfortable doing.

Recognize the Power of "No"

It's important to know that two-year-olds love the word *no*. You can offer a two-year-old candy or juice and he'll say no. That's because two-year-olds are elated to find out what happens when they say no. It's such a powerful word. It can make adults go crazy. So when your two-year-old says no, don't grab the bait; instead, use your sense of humor. If he's really serious, you can acknowledge that he really didn't want to do something, but if he's playing with no, recognize it. Repeat "no, no, no" with him. Scoop him up and giggle with him as you both say, "no, no, no." Sidestep it. Instead of asking a yes or no question such as, "Do you want to wash your hands?" say something that invites him to *do* something, like, "Do you want to turn on the water or get the soap?" Don't let *no* catch you when it's more about the joy of discovery than a meaningful, "I don't really want to do that."

Adjust for Differences

Sometimes when children aren't doing, the real issue is that they're not doing it the same way their parents would. Kids who prefer introversion and are temperamentally cautious in new situations need to observe and think before they're ready to do. If you're an extrovert who also happens to jump right into new situations, it may be difficult for you to understand your child is learning through observing before actively participating. He isn't being obstinate. He's just doing in a different way.

Remember, by your child's very nature, he is driven to do; if he's not, there's a reason. Look for it.

Hold On to the Vision

Teaching your child to stop and supporting him as he learns to do aren't easy. But when you give your child that solid foundation and encourage him to fly, it's a time when heart and mind meet. Dreams become realities, and memories for a lifetime are created, memories like those I hold about my grandmother.

When I was a preschooler my grandmother kept a flock of chickens. Every afternoon she would mix a pail full of chicken mash, fill another metal pail with fresh water, and trudge the four hundred yards from the barn to the chicken coop. If you ask me today, I will swear to you that when I was four I fed the chickens. I'll admit that Grandmother helped a little, but I will adamantly insist that I carried those buckets, and I dumped the feed and water in the troughs.

Now you may realize that it is just about impossible for a thirty-five-pound four-year-old to carry two full, two-gallon pails that weighed over sixteen pounds each. But my grandmother didn't scoff at me when I asked to help. Nor did she leave me struggling with full pails that I would have dumped before I got them a foot down the path. No, Grandmother stayed right there with me. She got me my own pail and after mixing her mash helped me mix mine. It didn't matter to me that it was only about a quart's worth of mash. It was *my* mash! Then she instructed me to grab my mash pail as she grabbed hers. We both took ahold of the water pail's handle. It dangled between us as we crossed the farmyard together talking about what we'd do after feeding the chickens.

My grandmother died in 1984. But whenever I hear children asking to do things that the adults in their lives aren't sure they're capable of, I am reminded of the gifts my grandmother gave me on the way to the chicken coop. Her gift to me had nothing to do with toy stores or athletic departments. It didn't wear out. It has stayed with me, giving me the guts to take on the challenge of writing books, getting degrees, skiing mountains, and having kids. My grandmother was my emotion coach who taught me I could do.

Coaching Tips

Learning to "do" is an essential life skill. You can choose to stop your child *and* teach him what he *can* do.

- Teach your child why you are stopping him so that he can learn to stop himself.
- Support your child as he learns to do.
- Acknowledge your child's frustration when he has to stop.
- Understand that when your child is not doing, he isn't being lazy—there's a reason. Find it.

FIFTEEN

You're Not My Boss!

Learning to Be Assertive Rather Than Aggressive

"I guess when she's sixteen and starts dating the college freshemen, I'll want her to be able to say no, but does she have to practice on me now?"

—*The father of a ten-year-old*

We were sitting at the table drinking an ice-cold glass of lemonade garnished with fresh-cut lemons. "Mom," my daughter began, "is it true that squirting lemon juice in a kid's mouth will stop him from saying bad things?" Before I could inquire where she'd heard this advice, my son plucked a lemon slice from his glass and quipped, "You mean like this," as he stuffed it into his mouth. He grimaced when the lemon juice struck his tongue, then clamped the lemon firmly between his teeth and flashed us a big yellow smile. "Does that stop you from swearing?" I inquired casually. Popping it out of his mouth, he gleefully retorted, "Hell, no!"

Learning how to get and use power is a critical stage of emotional development for all children. The window for this stage opens sometime around your child's fourth birthday and continues for years. You'll know your child has hit it when she turns to you and declares, "You're not the boss of me!" Don't ask me how she learned this sentence structure, I don't know. But I do know that the statement is remarkably common. And once she's sprung this announcement on you, it will probably be followed by the grand slam, "I hate you!" or "You're the meanest parent in the world." Your initial reaction may be one of stunned disbelief and then alarm. If this is how she's talking at four, what will she be like at fourteen?

When your child hits this stage of development, it doesn't have to be a nightmare. Your little angel doesn't have to turn into a bad-mouthed monster. What she's trying to do is figure out how to get and use power. Your job is to teach her the difference between being assertive and being aggressive. The lessons, however, do *not* begin with lemon juice. They begin with these steps:

- Enforce clear standards: Teach your child to be respectful.
- Establish an understanding of the emotions that fuel the words and actions.
- Teach words that allow your child to get and use power respectfully.

Step One: Enforcing Your Standards: Teaching Your Child to Be Respectful

It was Friday, the end of the week, time to unwind. We were eating dinner around the antique oak harvester's table. The conversation was easy and warm. My son had a basketball game later in the evening. Reveling in the mood of the moment, I suggested, "Why don't we all go to the game and then we can stop for ice cream afterward." The words had no more left my mouth when my daughter, then eleven, shoved her chair back from the table, threw her napkin onto her plate, and declared, "I'm not going to his stupid game. You can't make me!"

Blood rushed to my face. I could feel the heat of it and the pulse pounding in my throat. The vehemence of my daughter's response shocked me. We'd just been joking and laughing. Where had this intensity come from? And I felt invaded. This wasn't acceptable behavior to me. I'd made an innocent suggestion, that was all. I took a deep breath. "Try again," I said. My eyes boring into hers, my voice firm.

She shrank back in her chair, knowing she'd blown it. She, too, took a deep breath, sat up straight in her chair, and then calmly said, "Mother, it's been a very stressful week. I haven't had any time to myself. I've proven myself to be very responsible. The neighbors are home tonight. May I please stay home alone?"

While I still may not have been able to consent to my daughter's request, you can bet that I was much more open to listening to her. Most important, we were still talking and working together. We had started practicing the skill of being assertive rather than aggressive when she was four. Seven years later she was able to use it after a firm reminder. It took another two years before she was able consistently to assert herself without being aggressive first. And when she was fifteen and establishing her independence, I was ecstatic that she had this skill. The lessons begin with learning the limits.

The Difference Between Bulldozing and Persuading

When your child steps over the line by using words, phrases, or a tone that is offensive or invasive to you, call him on it. You can tell him, "Stop. That's bulldozing." Most kids know what a bulldozer looks like. It creates for them a mental image of a great beast of a machine pushing dirt and rocks in front of it. The term helps them recognize what they are doing to other people. And it doesn't carry the emotional baggage of "Stop sassing," "Stop being mouthy," or "Stop talking back."

Your goal when you say "stop" is to clarify the limit and to allow you and your child to pause. Don't get pulled into a power struggle trying to force him to stop. If you scream or threaten, "Don't you talk to me like that," or "Stop it, or I'll wash your mouth out with soap," not only will you disconnect, but he'll retort back, "You can't make me," or "Just try it." Remember, he's trying to find out how to get and use power in your family. You *want* him to learn how to be assertive. It's very important that when he's sixteen he knows how to say no to his peers. So rather than directly taking the full force of his attack, redirect that energy. Set your limit and then immediately help him understand what he's feeling and what he *can* say. The challenge, of course, is to keep your cool long enough to do it.

Step Two: Identify the Emotions: Keeping Your Cool

When kids are learning how to get and use power, they push and poke us with their words. Taking a look at those words and understanding the emotions they fuel is essential. I'll let you peek into one of the power struggle classes to hear a few of the emotions other parents experience to let you know you're not alone when that rush of adrenaline hits you.

As the class filed in, I wrote on the board "The things kids say that push your buttons."

"That'll be no problem," Bill quips before he sits down.

Each parent is given a card and asked to write down all the things their kids say that drive them wild. As we go around the table to read the cards, Debbie volunteers to start. "I've got three examples just from this morning when I asked my seven-year-old son to clean his room. His first response to my request was, 'Make me!' But I didn't blow. Instead, I reminded him that everyone in our family has responsibilities. His response to that was 'You're unfair.' When I insisted that he do it, he said, 'I want a new mom.'"

Stephanie hooted as Debbie spoke. "I heard all three of those this morning, too, but my ten-year-old daughter doesn't stop there. When she gets angry, she starts yelling, "'You're stupid!'"

Liz listened attentively. "Maybe mine's not quite so bad," she remarked. She held up her card and read, "You're not my friend." She explained, "Whenever we go to my sister's house, Danielle, my four-year-old, starts fighting with her cousins. It's really embarrassing. They'll be playing fine, but all of a sudden I'll hear her threatening them. 'If you don't do this, I won't be your friend.'"

"We have issues at other people's houses, too," Stephanie agreed.

"Yesterday I wanted my ten-year-old to come home from a friend's house for dinner, but when I said that she needed to come home, she said, 'I'm not coming!' I wanted to scream at her, but I didn't. I stopped and asked, 'Why don't you want to come home?' 'We're playing a game, and I'm winning!' I understand winning. I'm competitive, too, but I still don't want her to talk to me that way."

It was then that Bobbie flipped over her card and read, " 'No, I'm not going to do that!' We're dealing with the refusals, too," she said, "but now my son is fifteen and he's bigger and stronger than me. There's no way I can make him do anything, and he knows it."

Tara flipped over her card and read, " 'I'm telling Dad!' My husband and I divorced last year," she said. "I feel like such a failure every time my eight-year-old says that."

The room seemed to be closing in us. Moods soured as I listed the phrases one after the other on the board. Shoulders sagged and worry lines appeared. It was then that Bill flipped over his card. "I'm not going to invite you to my birthday party," he read. The others roared. "It's the worst thing my four-year-old can muster." He laughed.

When all of the cards had been shared, I read the entire list, slowly and emphatically.

Make me.	You're unfair.
I want a new mom. . . .	You're stupid.
I'm not going to . . .	I'm telling . . .
You're not my friend.	I'm not inviting you to my birthday party.
You're not my boss.	Fine!
I hate you.	I'm not your slave.
You just don't understand.	Everyone else can.
Shut up.	This is dumb.
I have rights.	You're so old-fashioned.
You don't love me.	I don't care.

The phrases jabbed us, each one like a knife point nicking our skin. For some the reaction was immediate, the emotions keen and sharp.

Some responded with:

1. **Anger:** "I would never have spoken to my parents like she talks to me. It's so disrespectful. I might have thought it, but I never would have said it."
2. **Embarrassment:** "It's as though I can constantly feel other people looking over my shoulder, judging me. A good mom wouldn't have a kid who talked like that."
3. **Fear:** "I'm failing. I'm raising a rude, spoiled brat."
4. **Guilt:** "I must be doing something wrong."
5. **Injustice:** "I don't talk to her like that, why would she do it to me?"
6. **Frustration:** "Why does it have to be so difficult to get anything done?"
7. **Loss**: "I'm not his hero anymore. When he was little, he looked up to me. He thought everything I did was wonderful. But I'm not the hero anymore. Now he just thinks I'm stupid. Sometimes I feel less than human."

For others it was as though they'd entered a time machine. Suddenly the phrases weren't so much coming at them, but out of them. They could feel the "child" inside of them and the words not only pushed their buttons but pricked their souls, swamping them with emotions such as these:

1. **Fear:** "My brother would never listen to me, so I would yell and scream at him. My parents hated the fighting, but they'd never insist he listen to me. Instead they'd send us each to our rooms and leave us there. I realize now when I hear those words coming out of my son's mouth I feel that isolation and abandonment all over again."
2. **Resentment:** "I was the youngest. My opinion never seemed to matter. I just wanted someone to listen to me, to understand *me*!"
3. **Frustration:** "Sometimes there was something that was really important to me. I couldn't get my father to understand that."
4. **Powerless:** "I never felt heard as a child, and now when my daughter hits me with those words, I feel powerless to stop her."

No matter whether the rush of emotions hits you in the head or in the gut, you don't have to let it push you over the edge and disconnect you from your child. Take time to reflect on the emotions you experience. Write down your reaction. What feelings strike you? Then look at those emotions and decide what they tell you. Some you'll definitely want to pay attention to and use as a guide that your boundaries are being invaded. No one deserves to be verbally knocked around. You can expect to be treated respectfully. This is anger that, as Julia Cameron, author of *The Artist's Way*, writes, "is meant to be listened to."

Other times you might realize that when your kids "push" your buttons, they've actually tapped into your own struggles learning how to assert yourself. If as a child your attempts to assert yourself were met with shame or anger, your emotions may overwhelm you as you try to work with your child. These are the emotions you'll want to examine carefully.

Catching your emotions and becoming aware of them makes it much easier for you to help your child understand what she's experiencing. It also allows you to be "the bigger person." When you recognize the "hook," you can swim past it. You don't have to grab it and get pulled into a confrontation. Instead, you can choose to find a way to keep your child working with you, even when the two of you disagree.

Step 3: Teaching Your Child What He Can Say

The next time your child hits you with words or actions that "invade" you, tell him, "Stop, that's bulldozing! I think you have something very important to say, but when you say it that way I stop listening. You can say it in a way that persuades me to listen." Then think quickly, What's the emotion that's fueling this behavior? You can even ask your child, "Are you frustrated?" "Do you need some power?" "Did you think I wasn't listening to you?" "Do you need a choice?" Once you've helped your child identify the emotion, or at least given it your best shot, you can help him think of a way to express that emotion that is more suitable to the situation and respectful to the people in it.

Changing Bulldozing to Persuading

Here's a little exercise that might help you. Grab a piece of paper and on the left side of your sheet, write down all the phrases your child uses that "push your buttons." Feel free to include the nastiest, most embarrassing, and infuriating ones. You can even include a few that you've heard other kids use, just to give yourself more practice and to enjoy the relief that your child hasn't tried them—at least not yet!

Now pull out your second-grade picture, the one in which you have no front teeth. Or perhaps one from early adolescence when your body hasn't caught up with your nose or your feet. Place the photo right there on the table in front of you. Try to remember back to the times you shouted, or thought about shouting, "You're not my boss!" or "You can't make me!" What were you feeling? What were you trying to say?

Now use your wisdom and experience as an adult to change those "button-pushing" statements to words that clearly communicate your feelings but at the same time are respectful to your listener and that persuade him to keep listening and working with you. If you can't connect at all with the "child" in the picture, think about your office. If you disagreed with your boss, it is unlikely you would scream, "You can't make me." Instead you're more likely to ask, "Can we talk about this?" The point is to open a disucssion. Your list may look like this:

Bulldozing statements	Statements that persuade others to listen
You're not my boss.	I'd like a choice.
You can't make me.	Can we talk about this?
I'm telling Dad.	Please listen to me.
You're not my friend.	I'd like a turn.
I hate you.	I didn't like what you said.
I'm not your slave.	This doesn't seem fair.
You're mean.	This is important to me, please listen.
Shut up.	I need to take a break.
I'll do what I want.	I need to try.

Bulldozing statements	Statements that persuade others to listen
You're stupid.	There are things I need you to understand.
You don't love me.	I need attention.
Fine!	I'm feeling pushed.
You just don't understand.	Please listen to my point of view.
Everyone else can.	I don't want to be left out.
What are you going to do about it?	I feel like I am capable and responsible.
Mom says . . .	I'm confused.
It's not fair.	I feel left out.
You're being so old-fashioned.	I'm feeling pressured.
This is dumb.	I don't know how.
I can't do it.	Please help me.
I have rights.	Please let me have a choice.
I don't care.	I'm scared.

Practice Makes Better

If your child is young or you've never spent time teaching him to be assertive before, you'll need to give your child the exact words he might use. If he's older and you've been working with him, you can simply say, as I did to my daughter, "Try again." Thanks to your previous instruction and practice with him, he'll be able to do it on his own. It may take a few tries until he gets the tone to match the words, but when you help him to redirect his drive rather than try to suppress it, it works! Brenda found this to be true and shared her story in class.

"My daughter wanted to sleep upstairs in my bedroom this weekend," she told the group. "Her brother and sister were staying with friends. The kids' bedrooms are downstairs; mine is up. But she didn't ask. Instead, with hands on hips and a defiant tone that begged me to challenge her decision, she stated, 'I'm sleeping upstairs tonight, and you can't stop me!' I didn't appreciate being ordered around by a nine-year-old. But I didn't grab the hook. I stopped what I was doing, took a deep breath, and then firmly said to her, 'Becca, that's bulldozing. If you're uncomfortable sleeping downstairs and would like to sleep on the floor by me, you can say, "Mom, Jeff and Katrina are gone. I'm not comfortable sleeping downstairs by myself. May I please sleep next to your bed?" Now try again.'

"She repeated the words, but her tone was still defiant.

" 'It's much easier for me to see your point of view when you use those words,' I told her, 'but the tone has to match. Try again.'

"I was amazed at how calm and in control I felt. I think it helped her, too, because she repeated it, this time very respectfully. It was so pleasant to hear her ask that way. I was much more open to working with her and together we got out her sleeping bag and made her a campsite. That night as we went to bed, she gave me a hug, and said, 'Thanks, Mom, for listening.' "

Sometimes it's difficult when your child starts to assert herself, even if she does so respectfully. When she says, "Can we talk about this," just as you've taught her, you may still want to scream, "No! I don't want to discuss it!" However, at least it's easier to pause, take the deep breath, and then decide if you want to say, "I'm sorry I don't want to right now," or to calmly ask, "What is important to you that I'm not hearing?" The choice is yours. Just because your child asserts herself respectfully doesn't mean that you always say yes, but it does mean you are connected and working together.

Adjust for the Individual and the Situation

As you go along, remember teaching life skills takes time and practice. Every child and situation is unique. The pace at which your child learns may be different from that of another child. Keep the faith. When you run into stumbling blocks, think about making adjustments for your child's temperament, stress level, or medical issues in order to be more successful. You're not alone in the challenge of being an emotion coach and just to prove it, I'll let you peek once again into a class to see what hurdles other parents have faced.

Consider Your Child's Temperament/Type

Nicole shook her head. "My kids are so different. One of them is a magnificent little bulldozer. She's very direct. She tells you what she's thinking and is adamant she's not going to sugarcoat anything just to be nice. Teaching her is a constant challenge. Then there's the younger one. If I tell her to try again, she's likely to burst into tears. Why are they so different? Am I doing something wrong?"

All kids will bulldoze, but extroverted, thinking kids seem to be the most proficient. They tend to be very strong individuals who focus on truth and equality. When you're coaching them, they'll want to understand why it's important to change their wording, and they'll also need help identifying the "true" feeling because they want to be honest. Their natural tendency is to say what comes to mind, so learning to be assertive rather than aggressive may take more time and practice.

Next time Nicole's oldest daughter bulldozes, she might say something like this: "No matter how angry you are, it is not okay for you to call me stupid. Our family treats each other respectfully. Next time you're angry at me, you can say, 'Mom, please listen,' or 'I'm angry.'"

Because factual kids want proof, she may have to add, "This is the rule in our house, and Dad, Grandma, or your teacher will tell you exactly the same thing." Then let go of the topic.

Nicole's younger daughter probably prefers to process her feelings first. If your child is more of the feeling type, learning to assert herself can be more challenging. Kids who need to deal with feelings first dislike conflict and value harmony. Be gentle as you guide them. Stop the bulldozing, but don't crush the drive. Learning to assert oneself is an essential life skill.

Adjust for Stress

Kim had woken late. Exhausted from packing for their move, she'd slept right through the alarm. Now she was rushing, trying to get her two sons ready for school and herself out the door. She couldn't afford to be late for work again. Suddenly Brad insisted that he had to find his library book. "Forget it," Kim tried to tell him. "Everything is in boxes. I can't find it. We'll find it when we get to our new apartment." "No," he screamed back. "I want it now! Get it for me!" The accusations and demands hit Kim so fast and furiously she couldn't even respond to them. There was no coaching to be done here.

When you feel as though every other word out of your child's mouth is a challenge or a demand for power, take a look at the stress level. Something is up. It might be temporary or ongoing, but no matter which, your child is drowning in intensity. You have to deal with that first.

Kim was desperate. She couldn't be late for work again, but she realized she had to bring the intensity down before she could get her son to work with her. Pausing, she bent down and gave him a hug, saying, "I'm sorry, I can't look for your book."

"But my teacher will yell at me," Brad sobbed, pushing away from her. "She already did yesterday."

Kim sighed. Now understanding his vehemence, she promised, "I'll call your teacher and make sure she knows we're moving."

It took Kim two minutes, but that two minutes kept Brad working with her. They got out the door, and she arrived at work on time.

Later, maybe that evening or perhaps after the move, when everyone is calmer, Kim can coach Ben. She might say something like, "What happened today isn't acceptable. Next time you can say, 'Mom, I'm scared. My teacher yelled at me yesterday, and I'm afraid to have her yell at me again,' or 'Mom, please listen, this is very important to me.'"

Consider Medical Factors

Joanne's son was a raving extrovert, who also happened to have attention deficit disorder. "He just doesn't seem to be getting it," she said in class one day. "Keep working," I reassured her. "If your child is an extrovert who thinks by talking and has difficulty managing impulses due to his medical condition, he will have to work harder to learn this skill. His path is longer and more complicated. He will need more concrete practice, and more structure. You may even have to make a chart listing some of the most important statements you want him to use. Adjust your expectations. Be clear and consistent. You'll get there!"

When Consequences Are Needed

If you feel as though you've been working with your child and she's not responding, it may be time for consequences. Remember consequences reinforce the same concept you're trying to teach. If your child is saying hurtful things despite your coaching, you can say to her, "The next time you bulldoze, there will be a consequence. When we say things that are hurtful we are not treating people respectfully. If we're not respectful, we need to make amends. You'll need to do something for that person and/or apologize." Decide together what the consequence will be. Then the next time your child gets angry and starts letting loose, you can say, "Stop, remember what we talked about. Are you choosing to do dishes for me as we decided, or are you choosing to use more suitable words to tell me how angry you are? The choice is yours." Ninety percent of the time you'll never have to enforce the consequence, but if you do, stay cool, be firm. Let your child know she will do the dishes for you. (If necessary, get your backup person to help you enforce it.) Remind her that next time she'll have the opportunity to make a different choice.

"Wait a minute," Paula interjected. "Yesterday my daughter said to me, 'I'm so angry at you I could hit you.' But she didn't hit me, she just said it. Should I punish her for talking to me that way?"

The key to Paula's question is that her daughter didn't hit her. She made a different choice. She used words, honest words that Paula may have not wished to hear, but words. Paula could choose to teach her daughter to say merely, "I'm really angry at you," but she can also celebrate her daughter's ability to stop herself from hitting and instead use words to express her frustration instead. This is progress—not perfection, but progress.

When to Seek Help

Stephanie waited until all of the other parents left before she asked me in a voice that was barely audible, "What do you do if your child says he wants to stab you?"

Preschoolers will often say, "I want to shoot you," or "I want to stab you." This is not unusual behavior. If you clearly set the limit, informing them that such statements are unacceptable, and teach them to say something like, "I'm angry," or "I want a choice," they'll usually respond. If, however, there is a vehemence to your child's words, his threats continue despite firm limits, or your child is older, it is time to contact a professional. You'll want to know if your child's behavior has moved beyond what would be considered the "developmental norm" and to seek treatment if necessary.

This is also true of sex talk. Preschoolers love to see the reaction of adults when they add words like *butt, penis, vagina,* or *poop* to their vocabulary. You can guide your child by teaching him to use these words in private. If, however, his vocabulary includes words unusual for a child of his age or expressed with an intensity that startles or invades you, there is the potential that your child has been molested or exposed to inappropriate sexual materials or behaviors. If you are concerned, seek professional guidance and get the information and support you need to help your child.

Keep the Vision

Teaching your child the difference between being assertive and being aggressive takes time. It isn't an easy skill to learn. It requires years of practice and is typically reviewed and refined as your child moves into new stages of development. In case you are feeling your energy flagging, I'll share with you a story that I hope will keep you going.

One night my friend and I were discussing women's sports. "What sports did you play in high school?" she asked.

"I didn't," I replied.

"But you're very athletic," she countered. "Why didn't you?"

"Because," I explained, "when I went to high school, there weren't any organized teams for girls."

Incredulous, she asked, "Why not?"

"Because," I explained, "Title IX legislation, which mandated equal athletic opportunities for women, wasn't enacted until a year after I graduated from high school. And the Minnesota companion law authored by Representative Phyllis Kahn took another few years."

Shocked, she blurted out, "How old are you?"

I'm not *that* old, but the accepted practice of the time excluded girls from sports. No one questioned it. Thanks to Mrs. Ostergaard, our physical education teacher, however, the girls at my school did get the gym for a week of intramural basketball tournaments after the boys' basketball season ended. Of course, we didn't really play basketball. We played by "Iowa rules." Either you were a guard or a forward. You could dribble the ball only three times, then you had to pass. Guards stayed on the defensive end of the court and never shot. Forwards were on the offensive end and never played defense. Only the ball crossed the center line, not the girls.

Today, as I watch my daughter score on a fast break, I am thrilled that somewhere, someone had the gumption to say, clearly and firmly, "This isn't fair!" And when I watch the Minnesota State Girl's Hockey Tournament and know that there are now six thousand girls on the ice thanks to the voices of five concerned parents, I am reminded that learning to assert oneself is an essential life skill.

If all of this seems a bit too far away from the foot-stomping five-year-old in front of you, remember that sooner than you can imagine she'll be a teenager spending more time with her peers than with you. Do you want her to be able to be assertive and strong, even when everyone else is having a few beers or suggesting a party at Todd's house because his parents are gone? If you want your child to be assertive when she's sixteen, she has to start practicing now—with you! It's an essential life skill.

Coaching Tips

- Learning to be assertive is an essential life skill.
- You can teach your child to stop bulldozing and instead to use words that persuade you to listen.
- Your child can be respectful and say what he needs.
- You don't have to grab the "hook."
- Your child's drive to learn how to get and use power need not be a threat to your authority as a parent.
- Being able to clearly and respectfully communicate one's feelings fosters healthy relationships.

SIXTEEN

Can We Talk About This?

Learning to Get Along with Others

*"Tell me, I may listen. Teach me, I remember. Involve me,
I will do."*

—*Chinese proverb*

I was in the midst of the final edit for the *Spirited Child Workbook*. It was a grueling and arduous task. I love writing, but the task of editing is exhausting to me. So when my son came home one fall day of his senior year, I was not in the best of moods. "Mom," he exclaimed when he came in the door. "My French class is going to France for two weeks next summer. May I go?" At that moment the only thought that sprang to my mind was that the one who needed a vacation was me, not him! My response reflected my mood. "I've never been to France," I replied jealously. "You're not going before me!" There it was, twenty plus years of parent education forgotten in a flash once again! Fortunately my son was much wiser than me. He didn't lose his cool. He didn't try to bulldoze me. He simply said, "Then meet me in Paris."

That was it. With his quick suggestion, my son addressed my needs while at the same time considering his own. He did get to go to France with his class, and we did meet him in Paris. He got a month in France and the embryo of a dream to return for further study and a potential career. The rest of us got the best two-week vacation of our lives and memories to cherish.

Teaching kids to problem solve is an essential life skill. It is the key to cooperatively working with others and balancing one's needs with theirs. And today, in a world that is increasingly interdependent, adversarial, win-lose attitudes don't work anymore.

Negotiation Is One Tool

When Stan walked out the door, his father said, "It's cold out, you'd better put on your mittens." Stan turned, and the look on his face immediately told his mom a battle was brewing. "You need to be careful in really cold weather," she interjected. "Your father and I are worried that you'll get frostbite. If you don't wear your mittens, what else can you do to be sure you're safe?"

"I have them in my pocket," Stan countered. "I'll put them on if I get cold." His mom let him go out the door. Afterward, she and her husband got into a huge fight. He thought Stan shouldn't be allowed to get away with not listening and wanted to force him put on the mittens. She said, "He's ten years old, he knows when his hands are cold. He's not going to freeze at the bus stop, and anyway, he did listen to us; he agreed to take the mittens with him. It was all right to let him think of another solution. He's fine."

Whenever I introduce the concept of emotion coaching, inevitably someone groans and asks, "Does being an emotion coach mean I have to negotiate everything with my child?" Absolutely not! Standards, for example, are never negotiable. No matter how angry your child is, he may still not hit you. But there are many situations that are not defined by a black-and-white rule. It's these situations that may be open to negotiation. Ultimately, it's the ability to problem solve with you that keeps your child listening to you.

Negotiation is only one of many tools, as you've seen in this book. You get to choose when it's implemented. You are the leader. But it's critical that your child develop problem solving and negotiating skills. It's worth your time to teach your child these skills, because it's these skills that teach him to think and allow him to work cooperatively with peers and with you—especially during adolescence.

The Process Is Most Important

The spring ahead to daylight savings time had left everyone in the family exhausted. Kelly had gotten up late and now realized that if she went for her usual morning run, she wouldn't be there to help her eleven-year-old daughter with her hair. Zatana could do her own hair, but it was a morning ritual they enjoyed. "Could you dry your hair now and we'll curl it?" Kelly asked. "Then I can go run." "But I like to eat my breakfast first," Zatana replied. "I know," Kelly said, "but if I wait for you, I'll run out of time. I understand you're tired and want to keep your morning routine the same. How can we work together?" Zatana thought for a moment. "What if I ate peanut butter toast instead of cereal? I can eat that faster." "Hmmmm," Kelly replied thoughtfully. "And while you're eating, I guess I could lay out my clothes and pack the lunches so that those jobs would be done and I wouldn't have to do them when I come back." "Then we can do my hair," Zatana added, "and you can go for your run, and it won't matter if you come back a few minutes later because your other jobs will already be done."

It's the *process* rather than the final solution of negotiation that is most important. When you negotiate or problem solve with your child, you are letting her know that what she thinks and feels matters to you. It validates her basic worth. People often think that to negotiate means to give in or give up. But in truth, negotiation requires that you clearly identify that which is most important to you: your interests, your emotions, and your needs. And in so doing you also seek to understand and respect that which is most important to the others involved. Your final solutions are reciprocal, addressing the emotional needs of all respectfully and creatively.

Negotiation teaches kids to think clearly about what they value. It requires that they be able to present their thoughts effectively, listen to the point of view of others, and consider the repercussions of potential solutions. The end result is kids who can make sound decisions that truly reflect what is most important to them. This is an essential life skill. It is a skill that takes years to learn. It begins when you offer your toddler simple choices that consider his feelings, like, "Oh, you wanted to choose your glass; would you like the red one or the blue one?" It continues as you explore possibilities with your school-age child. "The dishes need to get done, you want me to look at your paper, and your favorite television show is on tonight. How can we work together?" And it is a must for adolescents who need to evaluate all that they've learned from you and decide what they will keep as they move toward independence. "How else can you express your individuality without piercing your tongue?"

Keeping Your Cool

Negotiation requires thinking, and you can't think when the intensity is high. Before you try to solve a problem with your child, you have to bring down the intensity, for both of you. Understanding your own emotions and reactions helps you to keep your cool.

Negotiating with your kids can take you back to your own childhood experiences. When as a child you tried to explain your point of view, you may have encountered that intimidator who was indifferent to your feelings and opinions. You may have not been allowed to work through and test your feelings with others.

Or perhaps you were taught that the "good" thing to do was to keep the peace at all costs—to minimize your feelings, to ignore your needs, and to care exclusively for others.

Think about your experiences. What emotions come to mind when you think about problem solving? Do you get "hooked" when your child wants to negotiate? Let your new knowledge of emotions and emotion coaching allow you to enter into negotiations with your child, trusting that to do so validates what is most important to you. What each of you feels matters! Your child will feel the connection and be more open to working with you.

Helping Your Child Manage the Intensity

Kicking and screaming, Matt was deposited in Lynn's office by a substitute teacher. "I want my momma!" he wailed.

Softly, Lynn said to him, "Sometimes kids say they are missing their mommy, but what they are really feeling is scared. Did something scare you today? Are you scared because your teacher is gone?"

Matt sniffled. "Jennie my favorite teacher is gone," he replied, his bottom lip slipping into a pout. "Oh, you're scared that you'll never see her again?" Lynn asked. He nodded. "Do you have things you want to tell her?" Lynn questioned. "Yes." He nodded once more. "Do you want me to write her?" Lynn offered. "No," he replied, "I want to color her something."

Before Lynn could get Matt to problem solve with her, she had to assist him in bringing down his intensity. In this situation he needed a break from his classroom and help identifying his feelings. Sometimes, if the issue is a big one, you may find yourself negotiating over a period of days. Every time the intensity goes up, you have to take a break and agree to come back to the topic later.

Sunday night when the bell rang, Lindsey rushed to the door to find her neighbor and friend Jenny standing there. "I'm having an overnight birthday party," Jenny announced excitedly, and handed Lindsey an invitation. Lindsey's face lit up, elated that she'd been invited to her first overnight, but when Jenny left, Lindsey's face contorted, and she declared, "I'm not going!" Then she ran to her room.

Her mother knew a strong cautious reaction when she saw it. But she also wanted Lindsey to go to the party. If she tried to make Lindsey go, however, she knew that it would turn into a huge power struggle. So she waited twenty minutes, giving Lindsey time to calm down, then she said, "I think you're a little worried about staying overnight because you've never done that before. Jenny only lives three doors down. I think this might be a great opportunity to practice and have fun, too."

"I'm not worried!" Lindsey shouted. "I don't want to go!"

"This is Sunday; the party isn't until Friday," her mother replied. "You don't have to decide right now. I think you would have fun, and I'm afraid you'd feel badly if the other girls talk about it later and you had missed it. Think about what would make you feel more comfortable, and we can talk about it later."

"I'm not going!" Lindsey grumbled once more.

The next day the kids were talking about the party at school and how much fun it was gong to be. After school Lindsey came to her mother and asked, "What if I went to the party until ten-thirty P.M. Would you and Dad be willing to pick me up then?"

"Of course," her mother responded, delighted that Lindsey was beginning to problem solve. "We'd even come at midnight if you wanted to stay longer," she added.

Lindsey shook her head. "No, ten-thirty is fine. Don't push me!" Once again her mother recognized the intensity was up and stopped talking. The next day the kids were talking about the party again, deciding on the movies they wanted to watch. Lindsey changed her mind. "I'm going to the party and staying until midnight," she announced when she arrived home. Her mother agreed and added, "Maybe by then you'll decide it's only a few hours until morning and choose to stay. You're a good problem solver; I bet you can think of a way to make it feel more comfortable to you." Lindsey wasn't going to talk about this anymore and growled so low in her throat that the dog, who hated intensity, left the room.

It wasn't until Friday after school, when the group's excitement for the party had built to a frenzy, that Lindsey came home and asked, "Mom, could I take your cell phone with me in case I wanted to call you?" "Yes," her mother replied. "And do you think it would be all right to take my favorite teddy bear and keep it in my backpack?" Once again her mother agreed. Then Lindsey proudly announced to her mother, "I've decided I'm staying all night!" And she did.

It took only five days of breaking down the problem into manageable increments, allowing time for reflection, and, most important, knowing when to back off in order to manage the intensity to keep Lindsey and her mom working together. Problem solving does take time, but when you allow that time, not only do you keep your child working with you but you also teach her to think about what's important to her and what are potential solutions.

Bringing down the intensity is necessary whether you're trying to figure out how to help your child take medicine or make after-prom plans. In order to negotiate you've got to be calm and so does she. Let your child know you understand that something is very important to her. You will listen, but at that moment the intensity is too high. It's necessary to take a break. When you frequently problem solve with her, she can trust that, indeed, you will listen and that you will come back to this issue. Her feelings are important to you. You do care about her opinions. As a result she'll be more willing to step away, or allow you to help her calm herself so that later she can come back ready to work with you. Once the intensity is down, your work can begin.

Helping Your Child Problem Solve

Tara was the kind of kid who was very cautious in new situations. She hated to make the phone call, knock on the door, or ask the librarian or salesperson a question. Her parents had spent years encouraging her, letting her know that someday, with practice, she would feel more comfortable. They had always invited her to try and had assisted her when she said she wasn't ready. But they were still surprised and amazed when she came home from school and declared that she was going to sell magazines door to door in the neighborhood.

Her father agreed to walk with her. She went to seven houses, described the school magazine program, and asked if they wanted to buy. The neighbors across the street were takers. She was elated and filled out their order, skipping home in delight at her achievement. It wasn't until later that she realized she'd forgotten to get their check. "I can't believe I forgot to get the check," she muttered, pressing the palm of her hand against her forehead. "I'm not going back," she declared in a near panic. "You do it!"

Fortunately, this father recognized that his daughter was a very responsible child. She rarely forgot anything. This wasn't a kid who needed a lesson in responsibility. This was a kid who had been willing to try. Now there was an opportunity to help her problem solve. It didn't have to turn into a power struggle.

When you're teaching your child how to problem solve, there are five steps you can use:

- Describe the problem—what you see and hear.
- Clarify the feelings—what's important.
- Explore potential solutions.
- Evaluate the potential solutions.
- Select a solution.

And that's what Tara's father did. "Let me make sure I understand the problem," he said, knowing that was the first step. "The problem is you have an order but no check, and in order to get credit for the order, you have to have a check. Is that correct?" Tara nodded. "And right now you're maybe feeling a little scared or embarrassed?" Tara nodded once more, adding, "I want to get credit for the order, and I want the neighbors to get their magazines." "So you want to be responsible?" her dad questioned. She nodded.

"Well, there are lots of ways to solve this problem," he continued. "We could rob a bank," he teased, adding a little humor to help keep the intensity down. Tara gave him a look of disgust, but she smiled. "I could just go tell them I made a mistake," she said. Her father agreed and offered, "You could pay for the subscription with your own money if you didn't want to go back." Tara frowned at that solution, then smiled and slyly said, "Or, you could pay for it so I didn't have to go back." Her father hooted.

"Let's look at what happens with each of these solutions," he continued. "What do you think about robbing a bank?" Tara gave him the "get serious" look. "All right, do you want to pay for them?" Tara shook her head no. "It's twenty-seven dollars, I don't have that much, but you do," she replied hopefully. Dad shook his head. "Sorry," he said, "I'm not willing to do that." Tara sighed. "I guess I have to go back then. Will you come with me?" "Of course," her dad said, and added, "I like your choice. You made an honest mistake. The neighbors will understand, and I'm very proud of you." Tara was still uncomfortable when she went to the door, but her back was straight and her head held high. She knew she could solve this problem, and she did.

Researchers have found that optimists see problems as opportunities for problem solving. They feel capable and are confident that they can find a workable solution. Pessimists, on the other hand, believe that problems reflect their own weaknesses and that they are helpless to overcome them. When you take the time to teach your child how to problem solve, you give him the gift of optimism! It's this gift that allows him to go out from you knowing that whatever comes his way, he can handle it.

Helping Kids to Negotiate with One Another

When I walked into Paidea Child Development Center, three four-year-olds were sitting at the table playing with Play-Doh. Suddenly two of them started to tussle over a rolling pin. The third child sighed deeply, turned to the other two, and stated matter-of-factly, "When two children both want the same toy, there are many things we can do." At four years of age, this child was already a proficient negotiator and problem solver.

Initially, when you see two kids disagreeing, your first response might be to step in and offer solutions. Of course, if one child is hurting another, you will have to stop him. But after you do, rather than telling your child what to do, recognize this situation as an opportunity to teach your child how to think and problem solve by saying things like, "How else could you tell him you wanted a turn?" or "You both want the same toy, what could you do?" or "You both want to do different things, how could you work this out?" Your child may amaze you by coming up with solutions that you never even thought about. In order to get kids to problem solve together, you have to get them to listen to one another, and then you have to help them understand why learning to negotiate is important.

Insist on Listening

The issue was sibling rivalry. Nine-year-old Luke was constantly yelling at and hitting his younger sister, Katarina. When I met the two of them, Luke greeted me politely but clearly stayed back, observing me. Katarina moved in immediately, asking, "What's that?" when she noticed my bag and the puppets I was carrying.

My immediate impression was one extrovert and one introvert, which quickly proved to be true as I watched Katarina jump into her brother's space, talking nonstop. He yelled at her to stop. She didn't. He told her to leave him alone. She didn't and instead moved in closer, still talking. That's when he shoved her.

Their mother sighed. "Luke can't stand Katarina to be close to him. If they are in the backseat and she puts her foot within six inches of his, he's complaining, 'Get her away from me.' Why is he so intolerant?"

Luke's an introvert, I explained. "He's triggered by people moving into his space either physically or verbally. He's actually using words, telling her to stop, but she's ignoring him. I suspect that he may be resorting to hitting because he's not heard until he does."

It's your responsibility as an emotion coach to insist that kids listen to each other and consider each other's point of view. Stopping to listen doesn't mean giving up what's important to them, or even giving up the toy or whatever they're fighting about. But it does mean that the feelings and needs of both individuals matter, and they *must* listen.

Sometimes you have to teach your child to listen. When entering a group, it wasn't uncommon for Alex to immediately disagree with another child by saying something like, "That's not right!" or "You're doing that wrong!" What she didn't know was that by immediately disagreeing with others, attempting to take the lead too quickly, or changing the subject too abruptly, she was setting herself up for failure. Researchers have found that learning to listen and to consider the feelings of others is essential for effective social interactions. In order to help Alex be more successful in groups, her teacher taught her to stop and listen before attempting to join the conversation, explaining that even if she disagreed with what was happening, she wouldn't be listened to if she was too abrupt. Then she taught Alex phrases like, "I wonder if there are other ways to do that?" or "That's an interesting way, I wonder if it would work if you . . ." Sometimes kids need help learning that listening for the interests and needs of others is an essential component of working together.

Helping Your Child Understand the Value of Negotiating and Problem Solving

Jamie and Victoria were riding in the car with their mother. Each of them had an individual headset and CDs. Jamie was listening to one CD, but another of his was lying on the seat next to him. Victoria asked to listen to it. Jamie immediately refused. "But you're not using it right now," she protested. "Why can't I use it? I'll give it back to you." Jamie totally ignored her.

Describing the Problem

Their mother stepped in, but she didn't just take over and insist that Jamie give up his CD or that Victoria stop asking and use her own. She saw this as an opportunity for teaching negotiation skills. She clarified the problem for both of them. "Victoria would like to use a CD that belongs to Jamie, and Jamie is saying no." You'll notice she just stated the facts. She didn't say, "Victoria is asking nicely and Jamie is being mean or a jerk." Nor did she tell Victoria she was being spoiled and that she already had enough CDs. She simply stated the facts. There were no interpretations of them. When you state the facts, you keep both kids working with you. If you add interpretations or judgments, one of them is likely to feel that his or her feelings are being minimized and the intensity will go up.

Clarifying the Feelings

"Jamie," their mother said, "Victoria used really good words. She's telling you she'd like to listen to your CD. Did you hear her?" "Yes," he retorted, "but she might break it. She scratches all of my CDs!"

"I'm not remembering a time when Victoria broke or scratched one of your CDs," their mother responded, and continued. "In our family if you break something, you replace it."

Explore Potential Solutions

"Fine," Jamie declared. "She can use it, but the next time Victoria has candy, she has to give me half of it." Victoria sputtered, "That's not fair!"

Evaluate Potential Solutions

"There's a difference between sharing a CD and candy," their mother explained, wanting them to understand the repercussions of the solutions. "When Victoria uses your CD, she plays it and gives it back to you. You have the whole thing. But if she gave you half of her candy bar, she doesn't get anything back." And then, because she wanted him to consider Victoria's point of view, she asked, "Would you agree to give away half of your candy if you were Victoria?" Jamie shook his head no. "Sometimes," she continued, "the solution you pick may not seem the best at the moment, but in the long term it is. You don't always have to share your possessions, but sometimes you really like it when your sister shares her things with you." Helping your child to see the long range effects of a potential solution is critical.

Select a Solution

Ultimately, Jamie did allow his sister to use his CD. Of course, on the ride home he also wanted to use one of hers. She was willing to give it to him. A simple car ride turned into a wonderful opportunity for learning essential life skills.

When it comes to creatively solving problems, the more options your child can see, the more likely he is to get his needs met. The younger your child, the more you will be responsible for coming up with options. Remember, as you do so, that toddlers are learning the concept of what's mine, which means sharing is extremely difficult if not impossible for them. It's unlikely that a suggestion to share a toy will work. A much more agreeable solution would be to find another toy just like the first one. This is also true when it comes to breaking things in half. A half of a cookie is no longer a cookie as far as a toddler is concerned! Offering the option of splitting something is not going to work with toddlers.

Older kids can begin generating their own possibilities, especially if as toddlers you've been offering them options. Given the opportunity, kids can be very creative problem solvers. When sixteen-year-old Katie drove into the city for the first time, she missed her exit returning home. Lost, she found herself on the way to the international airport. But she didn't panic. Katie knew she was a good problem solver. She could figure this out! She didn't have a cell phone with her to call home and ask for directions. She thought about her options. She could stop and ask for directions, but that was easier said than done at the busy airport. So she drove through the airport until she saw the sign for rental cars. She knew there be would parking spots and people with maps there. Pulling right up to the main office area, she jumped out to ask for help. Inside she got the information and the map she needed to get herself safely home. Taking the time to teach your child to effectively solve problems is an essential life skill!

When Your Child Won't Pick a Solution

If your child refuses to select a solution, it's not just because he's being stubborn. Think again about who this person is. You may have an introvert who needs time to process his feelings before he's ready to commit. Perhaps he's not feeling well, or a medical issue makes it difficult to process all of this information at once. Check the intensity. Has it gone up again and now is too high? If so, agree to take a break. You can say, "We'll put that toy away until you can think of a better solution." Avoid pushing for a commitment or rushing your child.

You can also ask your child, "Are you not making a decision because you're not ready or because you need me to make the decision today?" Sometimes your kids need you to give them the out. They don't have the energy or feel comfortable making the decision, and they need your support. If this had been the case with Jamie, his mother might have said to Victoria, "Jamie isn't ready to decide what he needs and wants right now, so we'll give him space and some time. Play another one of your CDs and then we'll try again."

Following Through

When eight-year-old Steven and his nine-year-old brother were fighting over the new rope swing, their mother helped the two negotiate an agreement in which each got a five-minute turn before they would switch. Steven went first, but when the timer went off, he refused to get off the swing. His mother caught the swing and stopped him, stating, "In our family we keep our word. You agreed to five-minute turns, and you need to follow through. Your brother is not going to be willing to listen to you and work with you if he can't trust you. You need to get off the swing. If you have decided you don't like the solution you chose, you can ask to renegotiate it, but you cannot simply ignore it."

It is critical to insist that your child be trustworthy and follow through on his agreements. That's why he needs to think before he selects a solution. He has to be willing to accept the consequences. If Steven refuses to honor the decision he must come in the house and lose his turn. When you know your child has lied or failed to follow through, avoid backing him into the corner by asking him, "Did you do that?" Since you already know he's guilty, tell him, "I know you didn't follow through. In our family if we are not trustworthy, the consequence is . . . ," then follow through with the consequence you've established. If you don't have one, take him out of the situation and tell him you need to think about a consequence that will teach him to be trustworthy. If he's older he may work with you on what the consequences might be, but make sure it fits the crime and teaches that in your family you keep your word.

Working Together

When you facilitate problem solving between two kids, you get to stand back and watch the process. When you're negotiating with your child, you're in the middle of it. While you're helping your child to figure out what's important to him, you also have to determine what's important to you. And you've got to manage the intensity. Fortunately, the steps are the same.

Describe the Problem

A "to-do" list a mile long ran through Michael's head as he drove home from work. His wife was out of town, but fortunately, his fourteen-year-old daughter, Kim, didn't have school the next day. She could help out. But when he asked her to go grocery shopping with him, she refused. This could have become a major power struggle, but it wasn't.

Michael paused, took a very deep, slow breath, and said, "I hear you saying you don't want to go grocery shopping." Notice he didn't say, "I hear you saying you're not willing to help me." That would be an interpretation, and it wasn't what Kim had said. She had simply said, "I don't want to go."

Clarify What's Important

Kim nodded. "Right, there's a party at Annie's house tonight, and I need to shower and do my hair before I go over there. Buying groceries takes at least an hour, and I don't have that much time."

And then Michael had to think, What was really important to him? What was he feeling and needing? "Your mom is out of town; the refrigerator's empty; we need groceries; the snowplow went through, and the driveway has to be blown out; and there are dishes to do. I need some help, especially if you also need me to take you to the party."

"I do," Kim clarified.

"So what you want is to go to the party and for me to give you a ride." Michael said. "And what I need is some help getting these jobs done."

Explore Possibilities

"Can't we wait until tomorrow?" Kim asked. "That's an idea," her dad responded. Even though he didn't like it and knew it wasn't the solution he'd select, they were brainstorming. "What if you went to the party later?" he offered. Kim didn't like that one, but she'd had lots of practice negotiating with her dad, so she kept going. "What if I blew out the driveway and you went and got the groceries? By the time you got back I'd be ready to go." "The driveway won't take very long," he responded. "What if you did the dishes, too?"

Select a Solution

The ideas were on the table. "I'm not comfortable with waiting until tomorrow to shop," Michael explained. "There's nothing to eat in the house. The drive just gets harder to clear the more it's driven over, and you'll want to sleep late in the morning." Kim sighed, "All right, I'll plow the driveway and do the dishes." Michael took off for the grocery store. When he came home the drive was clear, the dishes done, and Kim was ready to go to the party. Together they put the food away and headed out.

This Isn't Giving In

This really is a true-life scenario. It worked because both Kim and Michael were able to identify what was important to each of them. They also trusted each other and knew that their feelings were important to the other person. They could work together, and they did.

Kelly found it harder to identify her feelings and initially struggled negotiating with her son. One Sunday morning a phone call awoke her. It was her father calling to say that her mother had fallen. He needed her to come. It was a two-hour drive to their home. Kelly woke her fifteen-year-old son to ask if he'd go with her. She thought he'd want to because he'd just gotten his learner's permit, and she offered to let him drive. But it was eight o'clock in the morning, and he declined. Her husband was sick, and the other kids were too little to be much help. She started to get ready to go alone, getting more frustrated and angry as she thought about her son's refusal to accompany her. What if Mom falls again? she thought. I can't get her up by myself and Dad's just had surgery. He won't be able to help. She needed her son. And that's when it hit her. She hadn't told him that she *needed* him or what was important to her. She had simply said, "I'm going to Grandma's. Do you want to come? I'll let you drive." She went back to his room. This time she explained, "I didn't really com-municate to you what I'm feeling. I'm scared. Grandma fell. I'm afraid she might fall again, and if she does I won't be able to get her up by myself. I need your help. I need you to come with me. I understand you're on vacation and you wanted to sleep. You can sleep in the car. I'll drive." Her son rolled out of bed. He didn't exactly rush through his shower, but he did get ready. He slept all the way, but he did go.

When Amy heard this story, she sighed. "Last night my six-year-old wanted tea with milk in it. We eat kosher, so I told him no, and he threw a fit. Now I realize I never told him we were having meat, and I didn't want him to have meat and milk together because it's not kosher. I just told him no."

If your child is whining and refusing to take no for an answer, step back and make sure you've clearly clarified what her real feelings and needs are. Are you considering those feelings or negating them? When you respond by clarifying your child's interest instead of just saying no, you won't trigger her. You'll keep her working with you and open to problem solving, looking at all the possible solutions that feel right to both of you.

And if you are feeling as though your child is disregarding your feelings, make sure you've communicated them clearly. Identifying what's important to you *and* to your child is essential for effective negotiation.

Adjust for Temperament

Katherine had an appointment to meet with her son's teacher right after school. She knew that would not please her ten-year-old daughter, Jessica. So she explained to her, "I need to meet with Tommy's teacher after school. We live too far from school for me to pick you up, take you home, and come back. You'll have to wait for me." "But I want to come home and go sledding!" Jessica retorted. Katherine knew that Jessica was a high-energy kid who found sitting in school all day very exhausting. Waiting for her mother would not be easy. "What if I brought your clothes and the sled, and you could slide down the hill at school?" she asked. "But I don't want to sled alone!" Jessica declared. "It's no fun." Katherine knew that her daughter was an extrovert and that waiting turns all day in school was very taxing to her. "Tommy will be there, too," she explained. "He could sled with you." It wasn't the best answer in the world, but it wasn't too bad. "How long?" Jessica asked. Knowing Jessica loved to barter, Katherine said, "One hour." "Thirty minutes," Jessica countered. "Forty-five," Katherine responded, knowing that was really the length of her appointment. Her major needs met, Jessica agreed. After the meeting Katherine found two cheery kids, relaxed from their exercise, ready to head home. Together they'd found a solution that worked for all of them because it fit who they are.

Introverts need time to think before they're ready to negotiate. Teach the introverts in your family to say, "I heard you, but I need time to think." This way the extroverts won't continue to ask questions, thinking they haven't been heard. If you're an extrovert and the introverts in your family don't tell you that they're thinking, instead of getting angry with them when they don't respond, ask them, "Are you thinking?" It's understanding who we are and what we need that helps us to be most effective.

Adjust for Stress and Medical

Kindergarten threw Casey for a loop. She'd looked forward to starting school, but once she did she wasn't sure she liked the place, nor believed that it was safe. Mornings became a time of tears and pleading, "Don't make me go. I don't want to go." Fortunately, her mother recognized her daughter's anxieties and fears and understood the stress that was driving them. Casey's dad had taken a job in another city and was commuting on weekends. The stress levels in the family were very high. Mom also remembered that new situations were often challenging for her daughter. So she listened and asked, "How can we make it better?"

After consulting with the teacher they all decided that each morning Mom would write the teacher, letting her know what kind of evening Casey had had and how she was feeling that morning. Casey was allowed to tell her mother what she'd like to be written in the note. The teacher agreed to call Mom each day at noon to check in and let her know how things were going in the classroom.

Casey saw her mother and teacher were working together with her. It was worth the teacher's time to place the call and Mom's to write the note because these measures vastly reduced Casey's fears, which ultimately resulted in the end of the morning blues.

One of the most empowering messages we can give our children when they are stressed is that together we can find a way to make this situation better. We can't change it or control it necessarily, but we can find a way to cope. We are problem solvers!

When You Realize You've Made a Mistake

Sarah had waited weeks for the end-of-the-school-year parties. Usually her family celebrated by going out to dinner, but now that she was in eighth grade, Sarah wanted to celebrate with her friends. When she asked her mother if she could go, her mother immediately said, "No, we celebrate as a family." Sarah tried to explain that this year was different. She was older now, but still her mother insisted that they celebrate together. It was only after hearing the sadness in Sarah's voice as she told her friends that she'd miss the parties that Mom realized how important the parties were to Sarah and that she really was growing up. Maybe it was time to problem solve together to find a way to celebrate as a family *and* with friends.

Kids can hit you out of the blue with requests that at the moment seem ridiculous or insignificant to you. Your first response may be to simply say no. If you find yourself in a situation where you've said no but realize later that you didn't consider your child's point of view, nor did you do a good job of communicating your feelings, you can go back to your child and honestly say, "I've been thinking. I know I said no, but now I have more information," or "Now that I've had time to think or I'm more focused, I realize it's more important to you than I thought. Let's talk about it."

You can teach your child phrases like, "Can we talk about this?" or "Think about it, Mom, and we can talk later," or "Do you need more information?" When your child has these phrases in her vocabulary, she doesn't have to blow up to get your attention. She will learn to negotiate respectfully, considering your feelings as well as her own. Teaching her these phrases begins by modeling them. You can tell her, "Right now I can't think about what's important and what's not. We'll have to talk later, but we will."

Savor Your Successes

You are an emotion coach, and as an emotion coach you get to choose when and what you'll negotiate with your child. Remember, it's the process of negotiation that is most important. This process teaches your child to think and creatively solve problems. It also says to your child, "What you feel matters to me." It's a message that connects you and allows you to win *together* for a lifetime.

Coaching Tips

- Teach kids to problem solve; it's an essential life skill.
- Let your child know that you are listening and trying to understand.
- Remind your child that he is a good problem solver.
- Ask your child to think about what else he could do.
- Let your child watch you and other adults problem solve together.
- Bring down the intensity *before* you try to problem solve.
- Help your child to identify what she is feeling and what is most important to her.
- Teach your child to evaluate the consequences of potential solutions.
- Remember that the most effective solutions consider the feelings of all involved.

PART FIVE

Celebrating the Child Who Is *More*: Caring, Competent, and Connected

EPILOGUE

"A dazzling place I never knew, but, now, from way up here it's crystal clear that now I'm in a whole new world with you."

—*Tim Rice*

I am hopeful that this is not an ending but a beginning. I hope I have been able to share with you a new perspective, a whole new point of view. Together we've gone below the surface to the feelings and needs that can fuel power struggles. And it is there in the depths of those emotions that you have discovered your child is not out to get you. Your child is experiencing a feeling or need and doesn't know how to express it respectfully. You can teach him.

It's true that emotion coaching will not eliminate all of the power struggles in your life. I wish I could say that it would. But I do know that when that emotional bond is strong, you and your child will find yourselves in a new place—a place where you can celebrate who your child is and who you are, a place where each new stage takes you to a higher level of understanding, strengthens your skills, and opens you to a dazzling array of emotions. Once you've experienced this connection, you'll never want to go back to where you used to be.

The journey of learning new skills takes us on a twisting path. It winds up hills and down, sometimes gradually, at times sharply. There are points when every stroke is an exertion, and then, just when we think we cannot cover another inch, we get to coast. Our challenge is to enjoy the thrill of the ride.

I thought about all of this one day when I was bicycling to the village near our summer cabin. I was on a mission to get the morning paper.

Out of the corner of my eye I caught sight of a nest. Six feet across and formed of sticks, it was hard to miss, perched on the top of the high-wire pole. Two osprey chicks clung to its edge. I'll have to stop and watch them when I come back, I thought to myself and rode by. Then I heard my mother's words echoing in my head. The proverbial farm woman, her favorite motto was, "Make hay while the sun shines." I haven't made hay in almost thirty years, but her words still caught me. "The birds are there," I told myself. "Stop now." I hesitated. It wasn't in my plans, but then I veered into a U-turn and went back. I watched as the chicks stretched their necks and arched their wings, great wings that flapped in the breeze. Their screeches were shrill and sharp. It was a wondrous experience, one of those moments when you realize you've been given a great gift, if only you slow down enough to grab it. I rode on, more attuned now to the sounds of the insects and birds around me, the colors of the flowers blooming in the ditch, and the sun flirting with the clouds, dappling the road with shadows. I didn't linger in the village; instead I headed back, picking up speed, eager to see the ospreys again. But when I rounded the corner, I saw that they were gone.

Like the ospreys, our children perch on the edge of their nest. They flap their wings, squawk, and arch their necks at us, too. The challenge is to realize that each flap is an opportunity. Every squawk a message. Each arch a gift. It isn't easy to be the emotion coach, taking advantage of those opportunities, because to do so means stopping and grabbing the moment, even when it's not convenient. It requires slowing down, reflecting, and absorbing the sensations and emotions of the moment. The choice is ours whether or not to grab it. We get to make that choice every day as we interact with our children. In fact, it is ours to make at this very moment; for soon, much sooner than you might ever imagine, the nest will be empty.

RECOMMENDED READING

Emotional Intelligence

Goleman, Daniel. *Emotional Intelligence: Why It Can Matter More Than IQ*. New York: Bantam Books, 1995.

Gottman, John. *Raising an Emotionally Intelligent Child: The Heart of Parenting*. New York: Simon & Schuster, 1997.

Hendrix, Harville and Helen Hunt. *Giving the Love that Heals: A Guide for Parents*. New York: Pocket Books, 1997.

Temperament and Type

Aron, Elaine N. *The Highly Sensitive Person: How to Thrive When the World Overwhelms You*. New York: Broadway Books, 1996.

Carey, William B., M.D. *Understanding Your Child's Temperament*. New York: Simon & Schuster, 1997.

Kurcinka, Mary Sheedy. *Raising Your Spirited Child: A Guide for Parents Whose Child Is More Intense, Sensitive, Perceptive, Persistent, Energetic*. New York: HarperCollins, 1991.

Kurcinka, Mary Sheedy. *Raising Your Spirited Child Workbook*. New York: HarperCollins, 1998.

Murphy, Elizabeth. *The Developing Child*. Palo Alto, Calif.: Consulting Psychologists Press, 1992.

Neff, Lavonne. *One of a Kind: Making the Most of Your Child's Uniqueness*. Gainesville, Fla.: Center for Applications of Psychological Type, Inc., 1995.

Tieger, Paul and Barbara Barron-Tieger. *Nurture by Nature: Understand Your Child's Personality Type—And Become a Better Parent*. Boston: Little, Brown and Co., 1997.

General Discipline

Kohn, Alfie. *Punished by Rewards: The Trouble with Gold Stars, Incentive Plans, A's, Praise, and Other Bribes*. Boston: Houghton Mifflin, 1993.

Sears, William, M.D. *Nighttime Parenting: How to Get Your Baby and Child to Sleep*. Franklin Park, Ill.: La Leche League International, 1993.

Stress

Doherty, William, J. *The Intentional Family: How to Build Family Ties in Our Modern World.* Reading, Mass.: Addison-Wesley, 1997.

Sapolsky, Robert M. *Why Zebras Don't Get Ulcers: A Guide to Stress, Stress-Related Diseases and Coping.* New York: W. H. Freeman, 1994.

Witkin, Georgia, Ph.D. *KidStress: Effective Strategies Parents Can Teach Their Kids for School, Family, Peers, the World—and Everything.* New York: Penguin Putnam, 1999.

Medical

Freed, Jeffrey. *Raising a Right Brain Child in a Left Brain World.* New York: Simon & Schuster, 1998.

Garber, Stephen W. and Marianne Daniels Garber. *Beyond Ritalin.* New York: HarperPerennial, 1996.

Kranowitz, Carol Stock. *The Out of Sync Child: Recognizing and Coping with Sensory Integration Dysfunction.* New York: Skylight Press, 1998.

Owens-Stively, Judith, M.D. *Childhood Constipation and Soiling: A Practical Guide for Parents and Children.* Minneapolis: Children's Health Care, 1995.

Development

Davis, Laura and Janis Keyser. *Becoming the Parent You Want to Be: A Sourcebook of Strategies for the First Five Years.* New York: Broadway Books, 1997.

Gerber, Magda. *Your Self-Confident Baby: How to Encourage Your Child's Natural Abilities—from the Very Start.* New York: John Wiley and Sons, 1998.

Giannetti, Charlene and Margaret Sagarese. *The Roller Coaster Years: Raising Your Child Through the Maddening Yet Magical Middle School Years.* New York: Broadway Books, 1997

Greenspan, Stanley, I., M.D. *Playground Politics: Understanding the Emotional Life of Your School-Age Child.* Reading, Mass.: Addison-Wesley, 1993